PROTEST VOTE

HOW MAINSTREAM PARTIES LOST THE PLOT

Tim Newark

GIBSON SQUARE
London

This first edition first published by

Gibson Square

UK   Tel: +44 (0)20 7096 1100
US   Tel: +1 646 216 9813

info@gibsonsquare.com
www.gibsonsquare.com

ISBN 978-1-78334-072-9

The moral right of Tim Newark to be identified as the author of this work has been asserted in accordance with the Copyright, Designs and Patents Act 1988.

Front panel illustration courtesy Roger Penwill

CONTENTS

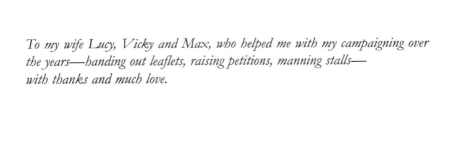

To my wife Lucy, Vicky and Max, who helped me with my campaigning over the years—handing out leaflets, raising petitions, manning stalls— with thanks and much love.

PREFACE

Setting up a political protest party is easy, I discovered. But you've got to get angry—real angry. For me, it all started with a yellow line outside our home. The short, single-yellow line had been painted on the road outside the door of our garage.

A few days later, my wife went to get something out of the car. She came back, looking pale. 'I've got a parking ticket,' she said. She'd never been given a parking ticket before in her entire life.

'That can't be right,' I said. 'You've always parked there.'

Now we couldn't—and we were being punished with a £80 fine if we did on certain days. We lived near Arsenal stadium and new 'match-day' parking restrictions had been imposed on our street by the council even though we'd never had a problem parking before. Suddenly we had to be very aware of whenever there was a home football match. We racked up three more fines over the next couple of weeks—just for parking outside our own garage. I'd urgently phone my wife if I saw the signs—horse dung on the streets from police horses, or the smell of hamburger stalls along Highbury Hill. It was the thin edge of a very fat wedge—a wedge rammed into our lives by the local council. That yellow line had begun the process of protest for me.

I had never been actively involved in politics and am not a member of any party. But, when you hit middle age and have children, you do start thinking about your community. You have to. Suddenly, you're at school meetings and talking to other grown ups about grown up things. Suddenly, your life becomes complex. You have stuff to do, school uniforms to buy, nappies to stock up on, kids' parties to attend, homework to finish. You are exhausted doing seemingly nothing. Then you witness little incidents that reveal that someone in authority is making decisions that aren't necessary to the benefit of your community.

On the morning of 23 July 2004, I was shopping in Highbury, Islington, when I saw a middle-aged man park his car outside our local butcher. There was very little traffic on the road and he was not causing any kind of hindrance. Yet there was a traffic warden outside giving a ticket to his car. His order of food had just cost him £100 more than he was expecting. He returned to the shop looking very sorry for himself. At the same time as the man got ticketed, a woman ahead of me in the butcher's left her order behind on the counter and dashed out to get into her car before the traffic warden ticketed her. I just stood dumbfounded, shaking my head. 'The atmosphere in Highbury has changed,' said the proprietor of another popular shop. 'Our business is down by 15-20% since the start of this parking punishment.'

It was at that point that I decided to do something to help these shopkeepers. I'd do it by rallying local support against the council-imposed Controlled Parking Zone and, because a local by-election election was coming up in the following year, I'd do it by starting my own protest-vote party. There was little alternative. Our Labour councillors were supporting the ruling Lib Dems in their anti-car measures—and so would the Greens—the second largest party in our ward. What about the Tories? No one was ever going to vote for them in Islington. So, with no one standing up to represent concerned locals, we had no choice but to start our own political party.

My family and I sat around our kitchen table, coming up with names. I quite liked the Fed Up party—especially as it could be usefully abbreviated to FU. Lucy liked the Leave Us Alone party—or Get off Our Back party. Vicky, my daughter, being 10, wanted something involving the colour pink.

I've always liked the word Freedom—you can't go wrong with that. But we also wanted it to be about local issues. We wanted to get away from national party politics. I think it's odd to vote on national party political lines when it comes down to voting in someone whose primary job is to look after garbage removal and parking where you live. I don't care what their political stance is on wars in the Middle East. So Local Freedom it was.

I roughed out an A-4 poster asking locals 'ARE YOU FED UP WITH THE COUNCIL?' I put it up in several shops and invited local residents to contact me. The backing of much-loved local traders gave legitimacy to my campaign and gave access to it at the point it mattered most with angry shoppers. Soon I had hundreds of like-minded supporters and that was my voter base.

The local newspapers loved the idea too, and the *Islington Tribune* put me on their front page on 24 September 2004, saying 'A historian has become so disillusioned with his councillors he has formed his own political party in Highbury.' 'I never thought we'd be involved in local politics,' it quoted me as saying, 'we've all got better things to do—but the breathtaking arrogance of councillors has left us no choice—their wrong-minded judgements are affecting our daily lives.'

Political commentator Peter Oborne—and Highbury resident—mentioned us in his column for the *Evening Standard*. 'Islington Council is waging a vicious vendetta against motorists,' he wrote. 'But local residents are hitting back with the Local Freedom Party, which will fight seats in the next council elections promising to put an end to this harassment. This party will get my vote, and other London boroughs, where ordinary motorists are victimised just as disgracefully as in Islington, ought to follow their example.'

Supporters began to donate money to help fund our newsletter and leaflets. One pledged to give us £50 every time he got a parking ticket. 'Because this was my very first political donation,' he told the *Islington Tribune*, 'I wondered how much to give but then I thought it made sense to give a proportionate amount to the amount I have given the council—£250 so far.'

Political journalist and Islington resident Nick Cohen gave us his support, too. Cohen wrote in the *Evening Standard* in February 2005. 'You may find this a little out of proportion or, indeed, mad. But it makes sense to me. Every time you turn on the news, there's a politician or pundit saying that what the English want is US zero-tolerance policing… No we don't,' argued Cohen. 'English policing was as much about order as law.'

Six weeks later, Cllr Mary Creagh (now MP) announced she was stepping down to become a prospective parliamentary candidate for a safe Labour seat in Wakefield, Yorkshire. That meant there would be a council by-election in my Highbury West ward on 5 May 2005, the same day as the general election. No problem! We now had 700 supporters on our lists. We decided to go for it and the *Islington Tribune* claimed I was 'Britain's first anti-parking candidate.'

Lib Dem council leader Steve Hitchins was forced to respond directly to us. 'Of course we want to support local businesses,' he insisted. I personally pounded every street of our ward and put leaflets through every letterbox. In the north was the infamous Finsbury Park mosque—a favourite worshipping place of Muslim extremists, including a couple of Al Qaeda terrorists. I bowled in there and handed them one of my anti-parking posters. Why not?

On the night of the count, I stood on a stage in a Highbury sports hall to hear the results. I got 437 votes. That was way behind the victorious Labour Party candidate, but just behind the Lib Dems. Their candidate had got less than 20% of the votes. 'We feel it was a fairly good result overall,' he said, adding sourly 'And we beat the parking party and showed what a silly campaign that was.' My result also meant I'd pushed the Tories into last place, which came as a shock to their leader. Not bad for a party that had been in existence for just six months. Soon after, parking policy was radically modified in Islington and the local traders were grateful for our intervention

I might not have become Local Freedom's first councillor, but the combined pressure of relentless campaigning, letters and articles in the local press, and the proof that some voters would turn their backs on the Lib Dems and support an anti-parking candidate, had delivered a victory for Highbury residents against inadequate local politicians and civil servants. It had been fun too. Once roused, you cannot easily remove that spirit of defiance.

Out of that, my interest in protest vote politics was born. It is, as I discovered first-hand, a reaction to arrogance—to those who feel they know better than you and do not listen to you. When the Lib Dems broke Britain's cosy two-party rule in 2010 and with UKIP regularly coming third in national polls in 2013, I sat up. Something was stirring in the history of British politics that merited a book as the electoral battlefield became bloodier and outcomes unpredictable. Everything seems possible and I wanted to investigate what had changed in our national politics.

The purpose of this book is to tell the story of the rise of 'protest vote' parties over the last 25 years or so. Principally, the UK Independence Party, but also the Referendum Party, the Green Party and the British National Party, along with some leading campaign groups, such as the Countryside Alliance and the TaxPayers' Alliance. By doing so, it defines the key moments when the two leading political parties, Labour, Conservative, who have been dividing government power between each other for a lifetime, disconnected with many of their grassroots supporters.

It was the election of 2010 that made clear that something fundamental had changed. For the first time in 65 years a party was in government that was not one of the usual two suspects. While it is tempting to think of it as a blip that had more to do with the poor personal appeal of Gordon Brown or David Cameron, it did reflect a growing unease with the political establishment and a punk attitude that neither of the two major parties is listening to the real concerns of the British public. Voters are no longer loyal to the old order and are keener to shop around and shake things up. The 'ugly' provincial voter who doesn't fit in with the urban elite at Westminster appears to be in the driving seat. His or her views might not be politically correct or socially sophisticated, but they count at the ballot box.

Tim Newark
Bath

FOREWORD

When Margaret Thatcher died in April 2013, it reminded many voters of what they were missing in contemporary politics. Where was that voice of conviction, speaking out for what she believed was right for Britain, not what was popular for herself or the party? Putting country before party marked Lady Thatcher out as a maverick, not wholly comfortable among her fellow MPs who preferred to play the game of politics to win power, not to govern. This book is about those individual sometimes abrasive voices that have spoken out over recent decades to object to a consensus in politics that increasingly seems to ignore the views of grassroots supporters in order to further the interests of a patrician class of politicians.

Some of these mavericks were very rich, like Sir James Goldsmith who could afford to fund an entire party devoted to giving British voters a referendum over membership of the European Union. Others are just bloody-minded, awkward so-and-sos, like Professor Alan Sked who founded UKIP because he couldn't stand the corruption, deception and arrogance of the unelected EU's governing class. When Sked stepped away from UKIP, Nigel Farage has shown a similar stubborn dedication to the cause of reversing Britain's absorption into the EU. Then there is the Green Party, a ragbag of bitching, in-fighting idealists who have transformed the language of recent politics by bagging piles of votes in past elections. All of them have stood up against the prevailing current of careerist politics and, ignoring all good sense, have devoted much personal effort to the pursuit of giving voters an alternative voice—all for very little reward.

The appearance of these mavericks is mirrored by the ascendancy of the professional politician—the university graduate who bounds into a career in politics with little experience of the 'real' world outside Westminster. As a result, it is not surprising they have so little patience for the concerns of ordinary people. Even the

Labour Party is now dominated by middle class professionals. In 1979, there were 98 working-class MPs, former manual workers, in Parliament, some 16% of all MPs. By 2010, this had gone down to just 25 MPs, four per cent of the total.

Party membership has collapsed over recent decades as supporters no longer feel their party leadership speaks for them. In the 1950s, the Conservatives could depend on nearly three million members, while the Labour Party had a million. Recently, the House of Commons declared that Labour had approximately 190,000 members and the Conservatives around 150,000, although even those figures appear to be an overestimate and have been challenged. Conservative membership has halved since David Cameron became party leader and pursued a modernising agenda that put his party even more at odds with its traditional supporters. Labour Party membership usually comes automatically with trade union affiliation and some members don't even know they are joined to the Labour Party. This is set to change but will result in even fewer workers joining Labour. The only party attracting new members is UKIP.

Just as political tribal loyalties are waning thanks to the patronising postures of party leaders, so there are new choices for voters who still care about how their country is ruled but just don't want to go along with their party lines. If they object to particular government policies, they can now go online to protest or march alongside influential campaign groups. The Countryside Alliance and TaxPayers' Alliance are just two of these recent groups that offer alternatives to joining political parties.

My original idea for this book was to concentrate solely on Nigel Farage and UKIP, but when my agent pitched this to leading publishers, they all turned it down. One publisher even said, 'it is a sensitive subject, especially when many of our authors are left of centre and might be hostile to the UKIP agenda.' And that's a reason for turning it down! Gibson Square Books, however, took it up, but as we discussed it further, we realised the story was a bigger one about disaffected voters and how they have expressed their discontent with the political establishment—and that has resulted in this book.

1

FUNERAL OF A MAVERICK

The funeral of Baroness Thatcher on 17 April 2013 caught the political establishment—the open-collared cool patrician class that had ruled Britain since 1997— by surprise. They'd been expecting—hoping—for the funeral procession of the 'divisive' leader to be disrupted by noisy protest—as it would help to confirm their characterisation of the 1980s as a dark period of strife and unrest never to be returned to.

The BBC had thoroughly enjoyed the furore caused by the re-release of *The Wizard of Oz* soundtrack song 'Ding Dong! The Witch is Dead' to coincide with the funeral. The 51-second song was launched into the music charts at number two after selling 52,605 copies and posed the Controller of Radio 1 with a quandary. 'On one side there is the understandable anger of large numbers of people who are appalled by this campaign,' agonised Controller Ben Cooper. 'On the other there is the question of whether the chart show – which has run since the birth of Radio 1 in 1967 – can ignore a high new entry which clearly reflects the views of a big enough portion of the record buying public to propel it up the charts.'

'To ban the record from our airwaves completely,' insisted the BBC's Cooper, 'would risk giving the campaign the oxygen of further publicity and might inflame an already delicate situation.'

The day of the funeral dawned cloudy with rain in the air, and you definitely needed a coat to wait in the chilly morning for hours to ensure a good position on the pavements alongside the route of the funeral procession. Some critics feared the claimed £10m cost of the funeral was a terrible waste of taxpayers' money as few people would bother to turn up. In fact the actual cost was £1.2m and thousands of ordinary people surged into central London, determined to pay their respects to the dead Prime Minister. Estimates of the crowd numbers varied from 100,000 to 250,000. These were mostly people who had been touched by Thatcher's time in power and wanted to show their gratitude to her.

'We got up at 4 a.m. to come here to pay our respects,' said a 39-year-old builder who had travelled from Newcastle with his family. 'She did so much for this country.' 'She brought us into the light and out of the dark ages,' said a 58-year-old Londoner who had arrived the day before to secure his place. 'I don't think I will see the likes of her again in my lifetime.' 'I just had to come to pay my respects,' said a retired bookkeeper from Gravesend. 'Everything she did, she did for Britain. She might have upset some people on the way but she was doing the right thing for the country.'

As the quiet, dignified crowds grew and the anticipation of any meaningful protest subsided, even former political foes in the BBC studio commenting on the event began to take up the mood of sombre appreciation. 'Margaret Thatcher saw politics as being extremely serious,' noted Shirley Williams, co-founder of the Social Democratic Party in 1981. 'Unlike male politicians who she regarded as playing games, she never played games with politics— she was always serious.'

At 10.00 a.m., the great clock of the Palace of Westminster signified the hour but the chimes of Big Ben had fallen silent. The coffin of Margaret Thatcher was carried from the MPs' Chapel of St Mary Undercroft, draped in a Union flag, and placed in a black hearse. The car drove beneath the statue of Winston Churchill in Parliament Square and along Whitehall, past Downing Street, where for 11 years she had been the longest serving Prime Minister of the 20th century.

'So far, no signs of the protests that we heard might happen,' intoned the BBC's principal commentator David Dimbleby.

Red-coated soldiers lining the route bowed their heads and reversed their guns, muzzles pointed downwards. At the RAF church of St Clement Danes, the coffin was transferred to a gun carriage pulled by the King's Troop Royal Horse Artillery for the last part of the route along the Strand and Fleet Street towards St Paul's Cathedral. As the road narrowed, the crowd was tightly pressed between shop fronts and barriers, many leant out of office windows, and a few builders stood in cranes to watch the procession.

Barely a hundred anti-Thatcher protestors had arranged to gather at Ludgate Circus to vent their anger but as the gun carriage trundled closer, their half-hearted chants were overwhelmed by a surge of applause that rippled along the street, growing in intensity as the coffin approached the cathedral. That was it! A few banners held aloft for the TV cameras and some protestors turning their back on the coffin, being heckled by the crowd if they dared to raise their voices. So much for the Witch being dead! Suddenly, the 80s were back in fashion and thousands of voters at the funeral and millions of viewers watching it on TV were wondering 'why don't we have a leader like that now?'

Whatever happened to those politicians who did the right thing, not because it was popular, but because it needed to be done? Where was the strength of purpose, the courage? Earlier that month, Thatcher had topped an Ipsos Mori poll of recent PMs as the leader best equipped to get Britain out of an economic crisis. Who could match her?

Inside St Paul's Cathedral, even a representative of what she might have called the 'wishy-washy' Church of England was doing his best to demolish a much-loved fabrication of the Left that Thatcher believed there was no such thing as society.

'Her later remark about there being no such thing as "society" has been misunderstood,' said the Bishop of London, 'and refers in her mind to some impersonal entity to which we are tempted to surrender our independence.'

The funeral service had been selected by Margaret Thatcher. Some of her favourite hymns evoked her Methodist family background and the final hymn 'I Vow to Thee My Country' was sung passionately both inside and outside the cathedral.

It was a beautifully directed event, one of the great establishment events of recent years—one notch below a state funeral—and you could be forgiven for thinking it was also a great three-hour party political broadcast for the Conservatives. Certainly, that is what Prime Minister David Cameron and his colleagues may have hoped for when they embraced the death of their past party leader—their most successful post-war party leader—and yet even on this day Cameron was edging away from her when he spoke to the *Today* BBC radio programme before the funeral.

'In a way, we are all Thatcherites now,' he said, making a measured and significant use of the phrase 'in a way', being careful to maintain that everyone, not just the Tories, had to admit her influence—thus placing her achievements in the past and keeping them at arms distance from his own party. 'One of the things about her legacy is that some of those big arguments that she had everyone now accepts. Nobody wants to go back to trade unions that are undemocratic or one-sided nuclear disarmament or having private sector businesses in the public sector.'

But Cameron's Tory party was not Thatcher's party, he wanted to make clear. 'I have always felt it is important you learn from all of political history.' History again! 'What we have needed to do is take that great inheritance and then add to it. As well as an economic renewal there has been a need for a great social renewal. That side of Conservatism needs to have a big boost and that is what I have tried to do over the last seven years.'

Maybe Cameron would have been less ready to distance himself from the Thatcher legacy if he'd known the size of the crowd lining the route of her funeral carriage a few hours later. But there again Cameron was part of the liberal establishment that had been running the country since 1997 and there was no way he'd wave the flag wholeheartedly for Mrs T.

The awkward fact is that though Margaret Thatcher may have been loved by the thousands on the streets outside St Paul's, she never quite fitted into the establishment that had now done such a good job of presenting her funeral to the world. To be honest, that's largely why they'd done it. As Cameron said, 'I think other countries around the world would think Britain had got it completely wrong if we didn't mark this in a proper way.' Exactly, she was a good part of the UK heritage industry—Americans loved her!

But Thatcher was loathed not just by those politicians on the opposite side of the House of Commons. A good many of her own party disliked her too. She was a maverick—a rebel politician who'd had to fight hard to rise in the ranks of her party against a patrician establishment that didn't like the way she rocked the boat and didn't like the way she appealed to a certain kind of voter—the aspiring working class. They considered her pushy and vulgar and she had embarrassed the older Tory class by being successful. She was, in fact, the recipient of the greatest portion of protest votes in recent political history. People voted for her because they were fed up with the consensus politics of a decade of floundering Labour and Conservative governments in the 1970s that had brought their country to the edge of ruin. Labour voters who would never have considered supporting the Tories voted for her in 1979—the year she came to power. They wanted something different from her—and that's exactly what they got.

To get a good sense of the maverick Margaret on the day of her funeral, you had to walk only a short distance away from St Paul's to a more raucous commemoration of her life, taking place at the Pavilion End pub on Watling Street. The Freedom Association—a libertarian group founded in 1975—had invited its members and friends to attend, but anyone expecting a sedate affair was disappointed as hundreds of Thatcherites funnelled into the basement bar, so many in fact that those already ensconced downstairs began to fear perilous overcrowding and bouncers were stationed at the top of the stairs to regulate the flow of those wanting to get in.

In the low-ceilinged basement, Simon Richards, the jovial director of the Freedom Association, was the MC, swaying with a tumbler of Famous Grouse whisky in one hand— 'in honour of Maggie'—and a microphone in the other, handing it to leading libertarians to give their own eulogy to Thatcher. It was karaoke for right-wingers!

'She left us with a quote which is right at the core of everything we treasure,' recalled Matthew Sinclair, then chief executive of the TaxPayers' Alliance, 'there is no such thing as public money!' Big cheers erupted from the boozed-up audience.

'She remains a beacon for us never accepting that relative decline is Britain's future,' Sinclair continued, 'there is only us now… we need to get out there and fight for Britain's future, fight and maintain the legacy of Baroness Thatcher!' A storm of applause followed.

The broad social appeal of Thatcher was captured by a former member of the far-left Militant group from Liverpool. He remembered protesting at a meeting attended by Thatcher at Cambridge University. He'd taken two eggs to hurl at her. 'I launched them at Mrs T at point blank range. One missed, the other one she ducked,' he said, imitating her weaving movements. 'I thought, "There is something remarkable about this woman!" I thought, "I'm going to follow Margaret Thatcher from now on. This girl from a grocer's shop in Grantham has changed the whole world."'

Then came the elegantly dressed Daniel Hannan MEP, a Conservative maverick in his own right, a prominent Eurosceptic who'd upset his party on several occasions. He reminded the audience of how bad things had been in the 1970s—the three day week, power cuts, shortages, trade union barons as better-known household names than cabinet ministers, inflation at 27%.

'I was there!' shouted one gentleman.

'I can't bear Britain in decline,' Hannan quoted the PM. 'I can't bear it. And by sheer force of will she turned things around. She loosed the natural enterprise of a free people.'

'I want to reach for my revolver every time I hear someone say she was a divisive politician,' said Hannan. 'How many party leaders today have come close to getting the percentages of the popular vote that she did?'

That point got a big cheer from the disgruntled Tories in the subterranean bar.

'Those who can't forgive her find her very success to be the unpardonable offence. She never lost an election to them. She took a country that was ruined, indebted and dishonoured and she left it confident, prosperous and free. And what was the issue that she was brought down over?'

'Europe!' bellowed the audience.

'She didn't think the United Kingdom should joint the euro,' said Hannan. 'Well, knowing what we now know, who called that right?'

Everyone in the beery basement loved that.

But it was Oxford academic and journalist Adrian Hilton—who'd fallen out with his own university colleagues by criticising them for their knee-jerk hatred of her—who best conveyed the rebellious character of the dead PM. He did it by drawing on her Methodist background. 'She was a non-conformist revolutionary because Jesus was a non-conformist revolutionary,' he said. 'She spoke up for the ordinary man against the privileged elites because her Saviour did precisely that.'

'She believed in the British Christian spirit,' he argued. 'Her notion of morality was based on the opportunity of free choice. These values contrast starkly today with the values of the establishment elite, the meddlesome priests who were so troublesome to her in the 80s, the landowners, the university academics—especially at Oxford where I'm now based.'

'Ooh!' commented someone cheekily among the beer-stained tables.

'The Foreign Office,' continued Hilton with his list of Thatcherite targets, 'and the paternalistic, corporatist, Europhile Tories whose Christian faith, as David Cameron once said, faded in and out like Magic FM in the Chilterns.' It was a witty comment and a good summary of many of the vested interests Thatcher had riled, but the reference to Cameron ensured that the erudite speech did not get a barnstorming round of applause. The problem felt by many in that basement was that Cameron was no Thatcher and he was betraying her legacy.

And so it carried on throughout that afternoon, but the speeches of remembrance and acclaim came not just from fed-up Tories and libertarians but from a new wave of political activists, party members and newly-elected councillors of UKIP—the UK Independence Party—who were starting to taste some of the populist success at the polls that Thatcher had once achieved. They turned up at the Pavilion End pub and they too had their recollections of what she meant to them. It was clear, on this day of Margaret Thatcher's funeral, the race was now on for who could genuinely claim the crown as her true maverick heir and win the protest votes that had brought her to power.

*

Just as Prime Minister Cameron had been keen to distance himself from Thatcher's legacy with his nuanced comments for the BBC's *Today* programme, another rising politician was less delicate. On St George's Day, a few days after the funeral, Nigel Farage, the 49-year-old leader of the UK Independence Party, was in an ebullient mood.

'Who is the heir to Thatcher?' he told the *Telegraph*. 'Is it David Cameron? Good God, no. Most certainly not. She was about leadership... And I cannot believe that a young Margaret Thatcher leaving Oxford today would join the Conservative Party led by David Cameron. I think she'd come and get involved in UKIP and no doubt topple me within 12 months or so.'

In an earlier interview with the *Sun*, conducted before the funeral, Farage made clear his debt to Thatcher. Wearing his Shire outfit of waxed jacket, mustard coloured trousers and a tie bearing cranks and gadfly motifs—a reference to a Tory insult of his party—he told the tabloid's political reporter that: 'Coverage of her death has reminded people what a real Conservative leader used to be like, and they contrast it with this current lot. I believe it is likely to drive more people towards UKIP, I really do.'

Like her, he wanted to appeal to the aspiring working class.

'Mrs Thatcher was able to get working-class people voting Conservative — the C2s, as they are famously called. That is UKIP's key target support area. So the kind of people that vote UKIP, many of them, regardless of whether they come to us from Labour or Conservative, were attracted to Thatcher 25 years ago, or are younger people who have had something inside them awakened by what they have witnessed over the past few days.'

This was in stark contrast to the other leaders of British mainstream political parties. In a surprisingly laudatory statement to the House of Commons, Ed Miliband, leader of the Labour Party, had said: 'Whatever your view of her, Margaret Thatcher was a unique and towering figure. I disagreed with much of what she did but I respect what her death means for many, many people who admired her and I honour her personal achievements.' Nicely put and his speech was received in respectful silence. As one commentator put it, 'His Commons tribute was more substantive and heavier than Cameron's and quoted more of Thatcher's own words.'

When Nick Clegg, Deputy Prime Minister of the Coalition government and head of the Liberal Democrats, stood up, he was far more abrasive.

'Like all of us here who are not members of the Conservative party, and as someone who strongly disagreed with a lot of what she did, I've thought long and hard about what to say,' he told the assembled MPs, who hummed with conversation as he spoke. 'I'm also a Sheffield MP – a city where the mere mention of her name even now elicits strong reactions.'

He said he shunned the tenets of Thatcherism. He then made the mistake of repeating the famous misinterpretation of her society speech. 'I remember vividly, aged twenty, reading that Margaret Thatcher had said that there was no such thing as society. I was dismayed,' he said. 'This was not the kind of thing that a wide-eyed, idealistic, social anthropology student wanted to hear.' That was too much for one Tory backbencher, who loudly heckled him.

As far as Clegg and the Lib Dems—past recipients of a good portion of protest votes in their own time—were concerned, there was little value to be had from popular interest in her passing. He wanted none of it. But was Farage right in thinking that the major coverage of the PM's death could bring electoral benefits in 2013?

The death of Thatcher had occurred half way through the UK local election campaign in April 2013, culminating in a vote on May 2nd. Up for grabs were seats in 34 English county councils and one Welsh. UKIP were fielding larger numbers of candidates than ever before—1,745, just 18 fewer than the Lib Dems. Their optimism, however, was fuelled by a sensational by-election result just over a month before in Eastleigh.

*

Jennifer Salisbury-Jones might seem an unlikely footsoldier, but at 3.30 a.m. on 28 February 2013, the 20-year-old physics student set

off from Bristol to Hampshire to wage battle on behalf of the
Conservative Party at a by-election in Eastleigh. She, like most of
the Tory election machine, thought it was a two-horse race between
them and the Lib Dems. With their Coalition partners mired in a sex
scandal, involving allegations against the Lib Dems senior campaign
director Lord Rennard, plus the former Lib Dem constituency MP
Chris Huhn being proved to lie and lie again, they felt they might
even be on to a winner. They had to overturn a 3,684 Lib Dem
majority, but one local poll said they were 3% ahead of their rivals
at the start of the campaign. They certainly threw everything at it.
But Jennifer soon got a different feeling. Arriving on polling day,
knocking on doors, canvassing the locals, she got the same answer.
'We'd thoroughly pissed them off. Not just the Tory party but
everyone.'

What was worse was that Conservative Campaign Headquarters
(CCHQ) was deploying Mosaic, a digital database developed by
Experian that profiles every household in the country. Pooling
together information from censuses, electoral rolls, credit and
purchasing records and house price data, it was originally devised to
classify consumers but was now being used to predict the voting
intentions of residents. Conservative campaigners were now
homing in on those households that they thought they could
depend on, but they were in for a terrible shock.

'It turns out it's really successful,' says Jennifer, 'at predicting
houses covered in UKIP posters. The ones that Mosaic thinks are
going to be Tory, historic Tory, were covered in UKIP posters.'

Jennifer and her colleagues had started early at 7.00 a.m., but
such was the gloomy feeling on the final day of campaigning that by
9.30 a.m. the Eastleigh Tory HQ had got out the vacuum cleaners
and were dismantling their office. 'A friend of mine was running
around with guys from CCHQ, he's a veteran campaigner, but by
2.30 p.m. they were in the pub and saying that'd get the train back at
four and be in London for five. You can't leave six hours before the
polls close. But [the feeling was] we're done here. Nothing to be
done.'

The party machine was in disarray. Despite top Tories bragging
that the gloves were now off and they were looking forward to

bashing their Coalition partners, their party apparatus in Eastleigh was simply not up to the job. The local Tory association had been decimated in 1994 by the Lib Dems and no longer had the ability to campaign. An advance guard of four Tory MPs soon discovered this when they arrived in the Hampshire town.

'The MPs rang the intercom buzzer at campaign HQ to get into the first-floor office,' reported the *Daily Mail*. 'And waited... and waited. There was no one in. So they walked into the town centre and passed the Lib Dem HQ on Eastleigh High Street. The building was festooned with balloons, windows were plastered with posters of their candidate, and a constant procession of people was going in and out.'

At one point there were more Westminster MPs giving out leaflets than local party activists.

'The Lib Dems are like limpets,' noted Tory campaigner Jennifer Salisbury-Jones. 'Removing them from their stronghold on short notice where they have every single council seat and have reduced council tax... why did we throw £100,000 at it? It's just embarrassing.' And embarrassing it was too when the local Tories issued a get-the-vote-out purple and yellow flyer that aped UKIP colours, promised a referendum on UK membership of the EU and claimed support for their candidate from a former UKIP MEP. The leaflet mentioned UKIP more times than the Conservatives. Oh, and by the way, their Merlin computer system kept crashing...

Many Tories were less than impressed by their by-election candidate, but in many ways she was the perfect person to connect with disaffected Conservative voters. Maria Hutchings was a hard-working, straight-talking mother of four closely connected with her community. On the streets, she was liked by locals and shared many of their tougher views on getting out of Europe, cutting immigration and opposing gay marriage. Indeed, Daniel Hannan MEP in his blog for the *Telegraph* went as far to say that she was so much in tune with UKIP supporters that they should vote tactically for her. 'If every Conservative MP had been like her,' he wrote, 'UKIP would never have needed to exist in the first place.' The only problem was that her views clashed with those of Cameron and the Tory liberal elite. So much so that their minders from CCHQ feared she would stray dangerously off message—and embarrass the party with her grassroots views—that they hid her from view for the last days of the campaign. There were even rumours she'd had a nervous breakdown.

In contrast, UKIP's attractive candidate, Diane James, had the complete confidence of her leader Nigel Farage and was helped by a fully functioning party headquarters in the centre of the town, passionate street campaigners, and a simple uncomplicated message—we're the genuine thing. Because, weirdly, the Conservatives had managed to manoeuvre themselves into a situation where—despite having a firm grassroots candidate—their party was perceived not to be solid on its core values. So much so that, at the last moment, it was trying to pitch itself as a version of UKIP. And of course, given the choice between the real thing or the fake, you're always going to go for the genuine article.

On the night of the count, against the green walls of a sports hall, Maria Hutchings was the last leading candidate to step on to the stage as the results were announced, but the first to get the news of how she'd done.

'Hutchings, Maria Josephine,' said the returning officer. '10,559 votes.'

She stared straight ahead at the Elvis Loves Pets Party candidate next to her as he waved the paws of his toy dog at her in a gesture of sympathy.

Next came her main rival.

'James, Diane Martine, UKIP, 11,571 votes.'

Labour was represented by a comedy scriptwriter and political author.

'O'Farrell, John Peter,' said the officer. '4,088 votes.'

The came the Lib Dem candidate, Michael Thornton: '13,342 votes.'

The Lib Dems had retained their seat in Eastleigh and proved they were still a formidable grassroots campaigning machine, but UKIP had come second, knocking the Conservatives into third place. They had increased their share of the vote from 3.6% in 2010 to 27.8%. After the Lib Dem candidate gave his speech of thanks, UKIP's Diane James was handed the microphone to make the most of what had just happened in the hall.

'I also want to applaud the Eastleigh community,' she said. 'I may have come second this evening, but you Eastleigh voters have delivered one humongous political shock.'

The hall erupted in applause.

'And can I say,' she continued, 'no longer will UKIP be excluded from being in the surveys in the polls. We will now always be included in all of the interviews, and gentlemen, no doubt, amongst the media, I will meet you again.'

Finally, stepped up Maria Hutchings. With a faltering voice, she thanked her campaign team and her family, but keeping it short, she stepped off the stage into the arms of stony-faced Tory aides who bundled her through a scrum of journalists asking, 'Why did you do so badly? You came third in a two-horse race. Who do you blame? David Cameron or the coalition government? Why don't you say something?'

With tears in her eyes, she just kept grinning and, bizarrely for a political hopeful, saying absolutely nothing. 'This is unbelievable,' said one bemused journalist.

A beaming Nigel Farage was keen to make it clear how close UKIP had come to winning and gaining their very first MP.

'On the votes cast today we're first,' he told the BBC's political commentator Andrew Neil. 'Where we're not first, of course, is on the postal votes. The Lib Dem strategy of getting this out of the way was entirely right from their perspective.' This would not be the first time that Farage would express his admiration for the campaigning skills of the Lib Dems.

Then came the zinger that would make all the newspapers.

'If the Conservatives hadn't split our vote, we'd have won.'

But there was the nagging question that had Farage himself stood as the candidate rather than Diane James, then he, with all his charisma and wide recognition, could have maybe bridged that 1800 vote gap with the Lib Dems and become UKIP's first MP.

At the start of the campaign, he'd reminded the media that 'I stood in Eastleigh back in 1994, famously beating Screaming Lord Sutch by 169 votes. It was UKIP's first electoral fight, and the idea of standing again has its romance.' In fact, it had been an humiliation, coming second to last and just in front of the Monster Raving Loony Party.

Now, speaking to Andrew Neil, he took a different tact, saying he would rather lead his party into the European elections in 2014 and he couldn't do that as an MP. But still there was the feeling that his nerve had failed him a little, having suffered so many previous by-election defeats, and maybe this dramatic result had even surprised him.

'What are you going to do for an encore?' wondered Andrew Neil. 'What's next, Mr Farage?'

'You'll find out on the night of May 2nd,' he promised, 'that what happened here in Eastleigh was not a freak result. Something is changing. People are sick and tired of having three social democrat parties that are frankly indistinguishable from each other. We're the party prepared to talk about and confront difficult, tough issues that everybody else wants to simply brush under the carpet.'

In the week following Eastleigh, Farage was invited to dinner with media mogul Rupert Murdoch at his Chinese-minimalist styled apartment in Mayfair. It was the first time they had met each other. Would this be as significant as when Tony Blair flew halfway round the world to meet Murdoch in 1995? For New Labour, it had been a vital step towards their landslide victory in 1997.

'Stagnant Europe wracked by discontent and resentment of EU. Glad we contributed to UK resisting the euro over many years,' tweeted Murdoch. 'Farage reflecting opinion.'

'He's a remarkable bloke,' said Farage. 'I enjoyed meeting him enormously but the political content I am going to choose to keep private.'

Some of the dinner party chat, however, was leaked to the *Telegraph*, with Farage telling Murdoch he'd be happy to join forces with the Tories in the 2015 general election so long as they dumped Cameron. Murdoch was no fan of Cameron ever since he felt victimised by the investigation of News Corporation following the phone hacking scandal. The media tycoon was said to be supportive of UKIP's views on Europe and their backing for new grammar schools, but as an Australian immigrant himself, was not so wild about their attack on immigration.

A few days later, Farage flew to North America to meet with former-Australian Prime Minister John Howard and US Tea Party guru Ron Paul to discuss right of centre political strategy. Two weeks after that, a new anti-EU party was formed in Germany— Alternative for Germany (Alternative für Deutschland)—capitalising on a European-wide disillusionment with mainstream parties and a failing EU economy. It looked as though the political current might well be turning his way.

But was it his success or was it the failure of the mainstream parties that had propelled Farage to this point?

The death of Thatcher, five weeks after the Eastleigh by-election, had underlined a national respect for conviction politics rather than spin, and a desire for straight-talking politicians. Even a 20-year-old physics student could see that. When asked if she thought that maybe the Tory leadership was just too posh to connect with the popular vote, Tory campaigner Jennifer Salisbury-Jones retorted smartly: 'People don't have a problem with poshness—no one has a problem with Boris Johnson or Jacob Rees-Mogg—they have a problem with falseness. They believe Cameron is attempting to hide or dupe them, rather than have a problem with him being posh.'

It was a question of authenticity and that next test for all the main parties was fast approaching on 2 May 2013.

2

THE UGLY VOTER

There is something slightly shambolic about a UKIP meeting. No one had bothered to check the sound levels of the speakers' microphones and when the early evening sun shone through a skylight it covered Nigel Farage's face in blocks of shadow making him look a Sioux warrior. But Nigel didn't need a microphone to address the two hundred or so West Sussex residents that packed the hall near the village of Pulborough on the night before St George's Day. His voice was loud and clear and everyone enjoyed his well rehearsed jokes and jibes at the government. This meeting was part of his Common Sense Tour, rousing voters for the county council elections on 2 May 2013 and, since his Eastleigh by-election triumph, everywhere he visited was standing room only.

'Just a couple of dozen people would normally turn up at these meetings in the past,' said Scouser Ray Finch, one of Farage's campaign assistants. 'UKIP membership is up 50%. We're on 30,000, but aiming to take over the Lib Dems with their party membership of 42,000 and falling.' As for the Tories—'A day isn't complete when we haven't annoyed Cameron,' smiled Ray.

This evening had started like others on the election tour with Farage meeting local journalists in a nearby pub. He likes a pint before a meeting.

'I used to drink massively 25 years ago,' says Farage. 'I had a big reputation for it—"Christ, you're having lunch with him. You'll be stretchered out." But a big reputation for coping with it. My relationship with drink now is a grown up one. I probably drink more than most, but by my standards, it's very in control drinking. I rarely wake up with a headache.'

A few minutes before the meeting, with every seat taken and more supporters standing at the side and back of the hall, a tanned Farage bounded in and kicked off a crowd-pleasing routine. Like some stand-up comedian, he got a good laugh with a reference to his German wife, Kirsten—'I know what it's like to be bossed around by Germans!' He declared he must be the only political leader to have had a proper job—not been part of the political elite that proceeds from university to party aide, MP to Cabinet seat. 'You can't put a cigarette paper between them.' It's the unique selling point of the UKIP brand.

Farage is the star act, but this was a meeting of the local UKIP branch and there were others on the stage that wanted to speak. That's when the poor sound level started to matter. Roger Arthur, a local councillor, stood up. A tall, thin old-fashioned man, he was struggling with the microphone. Not only did it not pick up his voice too well, but it was also positioned too low so he had to stoop constantly to be heard in the hall. At one time, he attempted a rhetorical gesture and nearly knocked it over. Could someone please help the gentleman! But Nigel Farage just sat on the stage, eyes glazed, willing him on—because he was on the frontline of the political earthquake in the Home Counties and had something really interesting to say.

'I have been invited to outline the reasons behind my defection from the Tory party to UKIP and I am pleased to do that,' said Cllr Arthur. 'If UKIP was once a one-trick pony, then it is not any more and it offers hope, where the main parties offer none.'

He attacked the lack of democracy in the European Union and its cost. He deplored the way the EU had put its hands in the pockets of Cypriot residents who faced losing a large chunk of their savings thanks to the latest failure in the Eurozone. He then compared the Tory Prime Minister Cameron with the previous New Labour premiere Tony Blair.

'When he became Tory Leader, he could have modelled himself on the great leader of conviction that we mourned last week,' said Cllr Arthur, referring to the funeral of Thatcher. 'Instead, he preferred a smooth master of spin as his lodestone. In his wish to be heir to Blair, he naively associated strong conviction with the "nasty party" label, which he feared being tagged with. In making that choice, he allowed those who coined the label, to put him into a corner, from which he has never emerged.'

Lacking the delivery of Farage, the councillor's speech was failing to fully engage the audience in the hall, but it was a perceptive denunciation of Cameron's leadership style that explained why the Tory party was haemorrhaging members. It had already fallen from 258,239 to 177,000 in the five years since Cameron had become leader in 2005 and that process was now accelerating. It also revealed why this man was leaving the party he once loved.

'Like Blair, the PM has pursued the soft, politically correct, centre ground of politics, portraying anyone who prefers substance to style as extremist or mad, hoping to close down legitimate debate and blur differences of opinion.'

Cameron was failing to make the tough decisions and his Chancellor was soft on reducing the current deficit and the national debt. Then came the stooping man's assault on the Tory politicians he and his grassroots comrades were expected to campaign for.

'Many Tory candidates have been short-listed based on background or politically correct criteria,' he said. 'The CVs of many UKIP candidates on the other hand reveal real substance. For me, it is a relief not to be asked to canvass any more for amateur career politicians.'

It was another dent in the Tory's political machine and another addition to UKIP's.

'Ladies and gentleman,' said Cllr Arthur, with a limp flourish that rattled the microphone base. 'The Blair/Cameron experiment has left little clear water between the three main parties and has diminished respect for politicians and institutions. It has run its course and needs to be brought to an end. There is now just one party and one leader that has not been dumbed down and are not frightened to speak out and that leader is on my left.'

Farage nodded, staring straight ahead at the audience.

'Since the PM has failed and since his colleagues will not change him, we must change them,' concluded Arthur. 'Needless to say, I wish that I had made my move sooner.'

The speech did not receive the rousing applause it deserved, but it did express one man's struggle with his own conscience, with his own sense of party loyalty that he now considered had been abused.

After the speeches, dozens of the audience crowded around Nigel Farage as he signed copies of his autobiography. No one went up to Cllr Arthur, but it was the impact of his political defection and countless others of the formerly-party faithful that would be heard loud and clear in Whitehall.

*

As the days counted down to the May 2nd vote and CCHQ heard the same story repeated across the country, Cameron unleashed his attack dogs on UKIP or, more properly, his attack tortoise. The only minister in Cameron's government to have served under Thatcher was Ken Clarke, an avuncular 72-year-old who Tories like to think had the 'common touch' because he enjoys a smoke and a pint of Real Ale—their version of Nigel Farage in effect. He had recently dug himself further into a hole by recommending that sentences be reduced for serious criminals, including rapists, if they pleaded guilty at trial—confirming the worst fears of many grassroots Tories that the Cameron government had gone soft on crime. Bearing all that in mind, he was precisely the wrong person to attack voters thinking of swinging to UKIP. But presumably CCHQ knows best...

Standing in his back garden, wearing a loose polo neck jumper that drew attention to his scrawny neck, Ken Clarke was asked by Sky News to comment on revelations in national newspapers that weekend that some UKIP council candidates held homophobic and racist views and some had even flirted with the EDL (English Defence League) or BNP (British National Party).

'They of course have not been able to vet their candidates. Fringe right parties do tend to collect a number of waifs and strays,' said Clarke. 'The trouble with UKIP really is it is just a protest party—it is against the political parties, it is against the political classes, it's against foreigners, it's against immigrants. It doesn't have any very positive policies—they don't know what they are for.'

Getting to the heart of the matter, he said 'The temptation to ordinary voters of UKIP is these are very difficult times. The political class are regarded as having got us into a mess.'

Then came the sound bite that would travel across the media.

'It's very tempting to vote for a collection of clowns or indignant, angry people who promise that somehow they will allow you to take your revenge on the people who caused it. You should actually vote for people who you think are going to be sensible county councillors.'

It echoed David Cameron's 2006 comments to LBC radio saying that 'well UKIP, it's, you know, they're a bunch of… They're just trying to make a bit of mischief …'

'They're a bunch of what?' asked the radio reporter.

'Fruitcakes and loonies and closet racists basically.'

Just the sort of thing you'd say privately over a drink, but now announced to a national audience. At that time, the Tories really didn't think they had to care about them. Now, seven years later, on Sky News, Ken Clarke was asked whether he agreed with this assessment

'I have met people who satisfy both those descriptions in UKIP,' said Clarke. 'Indeed, some of the people who have assured me they are going to vote UKIP I would put in that category. I rather suspect they have never voted for me.'

The next day, the *Sun* plastered a photograph of the tortoise-like Clarke in his loose-necked jumper under a headline saying 'Wind your (polo) neck in, Kenneth.'

'It is obvious Mr Clarke holds millions of people in this country in utter contempt,' responded Nigel Farage with glee. 'Instead of slagging them off maybe he should try to wrap his head around the idea that UKIP are appealing to people due to the failure of the bloated self-satisfied political machine of which he is such a typical member.'

Even Lib Dem Business Secretary Vince Cable wondered at the wisdom of Clarke's statement, saying: 'I've never believed it's sensible to deal with UKIP by insulting them.'

Outspoken Tory backbencher MP Nadine Dories went further. 'I suppose Ken Clarke's strategy of being rude to and insulting Tories about to vote UKIP means we don't want them back for general election?' she said on Twitter.

Clarke's tag would now be the media characterisation of UKIP for the rest of the campaign with Farage portrayed by cartoonists in big boots and a red nose as a malevolent clown—more like the Joker really in *Batman*.

*

Two weeks after Thatcher's funeral, British voters went to the polls in county council elections. In Ramsey, a pretty market town in Cambridgeshire, there was particular interest as this was the first UKIP-controlled authority in the country. Since 2011, when UKIP had won nine out of 17 seats on its town council, the UKIP Mayor Lisa Duffy—and Party Director—had worked hard to establish a model of what a UKIP-run authority could look like. It helped that the 44-year-old mother of six had a supportive family, as her husband Peter Reeve was also a councillor—as is his mother—and their children are happy to hand out leaflets too. It's a one family party machine or the 'Duffy Mafia' as the media called it.

Cllr Peter Reeve liked to show what it is like to be a real hands-on community politician, and, by the end of his working day, rolling up his sleeves, he grabbed a mop to clean his local public toilet—having knocked on the cubicles first to make sure no one was in them. If he wasn't doing that, he'd pick up litter or scoop up dog pooh—all to save the town council money and improve the local quality of life. The Tory Prime Minister liked to talk about the Big Society, but UKIP Cllr Reeve was it in person. On May 2nd, he got his reward. In the county election, he got 66.7% of the vote. It was staggering achievement—the highest of any UKIP county council candidate that night.

'For me the most telling result of the night was that of Cllr Pete Reeve,' said Nigel Farage. 'This is in an area where local people have experience of UKIP working on the ground. Where UKIP wins, we put in the work. And that work pays dividends in the ballot box.'

Across the country, the momentum established at Eastleigh continued with UKIP winning an overall 25% of the popular vote and gaining 139 county council seats—their best showing ever. The Lib Dems were knocked into a poor fourth place on 13% of the votes. UKIP gains were strongest in the Eastern Counties and the South East. UKIP finished ahead of the Conservatives in almost 500 seats across the country. The Tories lost 335 councillors in total and the Lib Dems lost 124. It was a shattering result for the political establishment.

'Send in the clowns,' Farage told the BBC, 'we've been abused by everybody, the entire establishment and now they're shocked and stunned that we're getting over 25% of the vote everywhere we stand across the country. This is a real sea change in British politics. Up until today it's always been characterised that we're putting pressure on the Conservative party. What we've seen in many seats overnight is we're taking just as many votes from Labour as well.'

He then revealed that he was looking at how other protest parties managed to turn council success into seats in parliament.

'If winning council seats in concentrations changes the perception of the constituency and makes people think we're in with a chance of winning—just as Caroline Lucas managed to win a seat for the Greens in Brighton by building up a local council base—that is exactly the model we have to follow.'

The day after the results, former Conservative leadership challenger David Davis said his party had to get real. Farage had forced them to rediscover their roots, 'more straight talking and fewer focus groups; more conventional Tory policies, not because they are Tory, but because they work; less pandering to metropolitan interest groups; and please, please, no more Old Etonian advisers.'

In a leader column entitled 'The Rise and Fall of the Political Class', the *Sunday Times* analysed the appeal of Farage. They dismissed the idea that a vote for him was a mere protest vote that could be won back by a change in policies by the main parties. They compared the rise of UKIP to the success of other unconventional parties across Europe such as Beppe Grillo's Five Stars Movement in Italy—in which a real 'clown', a professional comedian was railing against the establishment and had hoovered up 25% of the vote in a recent Italian general election. All against a background of austerity and EU interference.

'In all this [voters] do not just feel badly served by the

mainstream parties,' said the *Sunday Times*, 'they also feel insulted by them.'

And when the political leader that most represents their aspirations and concerns also gets publicly insulted—gets called a 'clown'—then that creates a bond between voter and leader. Both have shared the same experience of being made to feel small and powerless. Which, in turn, makes the establishment look like a bully.

'The man dismissed as an anachronistic golf club bore by the Westminster sophisticates is liked because he is a character,' said the *Sunday Times*. 'The voters rightly or wrongly, think he has principles—and sticks to them.'

The *Sunday Times* concluded that the only other British politician to have a similar appeal to Farage is Boris Johnson, the Conservative Mayor of London. '[He] has overcome the political disadvantages of his Eton education and has the populism, character and instinctive Euroscepticism that appeal to voters.'

In him lies the greatest rival to Farage as even UKIP's most senior supporters warm to his bumbling appeal. On the front page, in the same edition of the *Sunday Times*, Stuart Wheeler, UKIP Treasurer and former Tory party donor, was interviewed. He confirmed Farage's view that UKIP would consider a pact with the Tories at the 2015 election, but Cameron would have to go first, with Johnson being the favoured replacement. 'I like Boris so much,' said Wheeler. 'If Boris Johnson's policies were acceptable, which I think on the whole they would be, I would be happy to do that [an electoral deal].'

That deal would mean UKIP would not field candidates in seats held by Conservatives who pledged their support to UKIP's Eurosceptic agenda. They might even share logos on the ballot paper.

It was all so beautifully stage-managed—one part of the establishment media, owned by Rupert Murdoch, had woken up to the populist appeal represented by Farage's electoral success and was forging a comedy alliance by proposing the working together of the two greatest 'clowns' of British contemporary politics.

The *Sunday Times* political cartoonist, Gerald Scarfe, completed the analogy by portraying Farage as a clown downing a pint of beer containing a drowning Nick Clegg, the Lib Dem leader and Coalition partner of Cameron.

A public insult is a powerful weapon and if Farage's election success in May 2013 was helped in part by being dubbed a 'clown', then the collapse of voter trust in the political mainstream establishment that contributed to his rise in the polls also turned on a particularly notorious insult delivered, this time, by a Labour Prime Minister. It was the subject of the insult that also got to the heart of the resurgent appeal of UKIP.

*

It was a bright spring morning on April 28th 2010 when New Labour Prime Minister Gordon Brown visited the Labour-Lib Dem marginal seat of Rochdale in Greater Manchester, nine days before the General Election. He was there to charm voters with a walkabout and as the crowd surged round him, his eye was caught by the bold red lapels of a jacket worn by 65-year-old Gillian Duffy. A retired council worker who'd devoted 30 years of her working life to looking after children and the disabled, Duffy came from a family of life-long Labour supporters. She recalled her father singing the socialist anthem *The Red Flag* with gusto. As the TV cameras homed in on the famously awkward PM, the stout lady questioned him about the national debt and what he was going to do about it. She then asked him about false benefit claimants.

'There's too many people now who aren't vulnerable but they can claim and people who are vulnerable can't claim, can't get it.'

'But they shouldn't be doing that,' responded Brown. 'There's no life on the dole for people any more. If you're unemployed you've got to go back to work. It's six months...'

Then Duffy interrupted, expressing a real frustration shared by many people.

'You can't say anything about the immigrants because you're saying that you're r...' she held back from saying 'racist'. 'All these Eastern Europeans what are coming in, where are they flocking from?'

'A million people come from Europe but a million people, British people, have gone into Europe,' said Brown, ignoring her core concern. 'You do know that there's a lot of British people staying in Europe as well?'

The conversation continued for a few more minutes with Duffy talking about her grandchildren and then the Prime Minister extricated himself, telling her to 'take care'. He'd been polite and measured, but moments later when he got into his car, he let rip with his true feeling about Mrs Duffy and her comments on immigration. Unfortunately for him, he was still wearing his Sky News microphone and his rant was broadcast to the nation.

'That was a disaster,' he said. 'Should never have put me with that woman... whose idea was that?'

'What did she say,' asked his communications director.

'Ugh, everything,' he sighed. 'She's just a sort of bigoted woman, said she used to be Labour. It's just ridiculous.'

Within three quarters of an hour, Mrs Duffy was besieged by news reporters wanting her reaction to the PM's insult.

'Very upsetting,' she said. 'I'm very upset.'

'Did you expect that from him?', asked a journalist.

'No. He's an educated person,' said Duffy, 'why has he come up with words like that? He's going to lead this country and he's calling an ordinary woman who has just come up and asked him questions—what most people would ask him, they're not doing anything about the national debt, it's going to be tax, tax, tax for another 20 years to get out of this national debt—and he's calling me a bigot.'

Interestingly, she avoided mentioning immigration again—obviously stung by the PM's rebuke of her on the subject. She vowed never again to vote Labour—or for any other party.

Shortly afterwards, Brown got his opportunity to apologise to her on national radio. 'Is she not allowed to express her view to you?' asked the interviewer.

'Of course she's allowed to express her view,' said a bumbling Brown, 'and I was saying that. The problem was that I was dealing with a question that she raised about immigration and I wasn't given a chance to answer it because we had a whole melee of press around us. But of course I apologise if I said anything that has been offensive and I would never put myself in a position where I would want to say anything like that about a woman I met. It was a question about immigration that really I think was annoying.'

Not exactly articulate—but on the button. It was the question about immigration that had rattled him. It put a finger on the New Labour weak spot that ten years of open-door mass immigration had not gone down well with working-class voters—his core supporters. But the topic of immigration had been so highly sensitised over the previous decades by the establishment that even the mildest of references to it could elicit the rebuke of being 'racist' or a 'bigot'.

That afternoon in an attempt at rapid crisis management, Brown visited Mrs Duffy at her home to apologise further. But his odd comments only served to highlight his disconnection with ordinary voters.

'So I wanted to come here and say to Gillian I was sorry,' he told the crowd of reporters. 'To say that I'd made a mistake, but to also say I understood the concerns that she was bringing to me and I had simply misunderstood some of the words that she used.'

What was there to misunderstand? She directly expressed her concern about the impact on her community of thousands of Eastern European immigrants. What Brown was really sorry about was that his knee-jerk prejudice against the views held by people like Mrs Duffy had been broadcast to the world. It was these people that Nigel Farage and UKIP seek to represent—talking about the supposedly unspeakable. Mrs Duffy, and all those who identified with her, had been very publicly humiliated by the establishment elite and that pushed them even further away from their previous political loyalties.

Nine days after the insult passed at Rochdale, Brown and New Labour were out of power. Without doubt, it had been concerns over mass immigration and the inability of the Labour government to do anything about—as highlighted by Gillian Duffy—that had cost their party many votes from previously loyal supporters. How a very successful political machine should help bring about its own destruction by embracing mass immigration and alienating its own supporters will be described later in this book, but it is now time to look at the origins of UKIP and other Eurosceptic parties.

3

NIGEL FARAGE

The broad, pebble strewn Charmouth beach in Dorset on the south coast of England is famous for its crumbling cliff faces that can deliver up fossils from the ancient seas of the Jurassic period. In the mid-70s, while most children might be at home listening to David Bowie or the Bee Gees, one schoolboy was ambling across Charmouth beach picking over stones in the hope of finding an ammonite.

Born in Kent in 1964, Nigel Farage spent his early years in the village of Downe, where his garden backed on to the grounds of Down House. This was the home of Charles Darwin and was where he wrote *On the Origin of the Species*. Farage's mother was bewitched by the association and developed a love for natural history, which she passed on to her son, and would go on to give lectures about the great man.

Farage liked to 'rummage', as he called it, across the local landscape and his love of collecting inspired a fellow pupil at Dulwich College. Philip Hollobone, now known as one of the most rebellious MPs in the Conservative party, remembers him as a very distinct character at school. 'He liked fossils,' he recalls, 'and he rather inspired me to go off searching for fossils too.'

It's part of his life he misses now.

'I've been an avid collector of things over the years,' says Farage. 'Victorian bottles and pot lids, drawers full of fossils I've collected on Charmouth beach, First World War recruitment posters, lots of passions and interests, but there's not much time for that sort of thing now.'

His father was a dandy, the best-dressed man at the Stock

Exchange in Savile Row suits, hand-made shoes, a bowler hat and a tightly furled umbrella. He worked long hours in the City, was barely at home and drank too much. Despite his father's poor record as a father and husband—his parents divorced when Farage was five—Farage was keen to follow his path—in all ways.

At Dulwich College, he enjoyed the broad social range of pupils. 'I went to the greatest grammar school in the country,' he recalls. 'It was called a public school but it wasn't, because we had so many free-place working-class pupils from south London in the days when that opportunity was afforded to ordinary people—all gone of course, all gone. I grew up mixing with a massive cross section of people. Of all the boys in the school, I was the friendliest with the porters and the grounds-men and would go to their lodge for a cup of tea. I've always enjoyed a mix of people.'

His first political moment occurred at school when Sir Keith Joseph gave a talk to Dulwich pupils in 1978—the year before Thatcher came to power. Joseph was never a comfortable public speaker and sweated profusely when he stood up before rows of schoolboys, but was determined to put over the message of the new Conservatism and its struggle with the socialist state.

'He argued vehemently against public ownership of industry,' remembers Farage. 'He envisaged a Britain—and Britons—free to deal as they would with one another and with the world… Ultimately the people and the market will regulate themselves.' The next day, the schoolboy joined the Conservative Party. He was not especially active within the party, however, focusing all his attention on getting a job in the City. Impatient to make his way in the world, he left school at 18 with no desire to proceed to university.

Farage's father took him to lunch at Gow's, a hundred-year-old seafood restaurant in the heart of the City next to Liverpool Street station. Over a menu that included dressed crab, cold poached lobster and Colchester oysters, enlivened with glasses of champagne, the young man heard stirring tales of gambling and derring-do in the exchange. He wanted to join these ranks of garrulous blokes, but didn't want to get a job through his father's contacts. Instead, he made his own connection with the managing director of a metal exchange dealing company while playing a round of golf at a club near his home.

'I strode into Maclaine Watson,' he remembers, 'shed my suit jacket and deposited a gold pen, a lighter and two packets of Rothmans on my desk.' It was his first day at work in September 1982.

'Hmm,' said a colleague. 'Good start!'

He loved the atmosphere of hunting million pound deals on the metal exchange, schmoozing clients, hanging out with working-class boys on the make and public school dropouts in City winebars and pubs. 'A third of the room was disinherited members of the aristocracy and the rest all came from the Essex marshes,' he chuckles. His company was owned by the buccaneering New York firm Drexel Burnham Lambert, the inspiration behind the movie that captured the exuberance of the period—*Wall Street*. He drank almost continuously: drinking to make contacts, drinking to celebrate trades, drinking to relax.

One night, coming home late from a day of boozing, the 21-year-old high flier stepped out of Orpington train station into the path of a Volkswagen Beetle. He was flung over the bonnet of the car and landed badly. He avoided serious damage to any of his internal organs, but had many broken bones and was in hospital for three months. He wore plaster for many more months after that and, just as soon as it was removed, he had a stabbing pain in his groin and was back in hospital again. This time, it was testicular cancer and he had to have one of his testicles removed.

The experience could have unnerved him, but it gave him an even greater appetite for life—friends brought round bottles of wine rather than bunches of grapes—and as soon as he could he resumed his place in the City.

'If people have been through very bad times, they have a much greater sense of perspective,' says Farage. 'Getting myself smashed to pieces. All the things I've had go wrong. If I hadn't have been through all those difficult things, I wouldn't have done all this. I'd have stayed on a set path to being rich and fat.'

It was while in hospital recovering from his car accident that Farage fell for one of his nurses and his enforced time out of the Square Mile's bars meant he had the opportunity to get to know her.

They were married in 1988, with their first son born shortly afterwards.

Throughout the 1980s, Farage had been happy to have Prime Minister Margaret Thatcher in the background of his life, overseeing the revival of the British economy while he made his own pile of money. Although a Tory voter, he was not an activist and he barely mentions her in his autobiography. It would only be in retrospect, as a politician, that he would claim to be a Thatcherite. Like most young people, he was too busy living his life to get involved in politics. This changed in October 1990, when Britain joined the European Exchange Rate Mechanism (ERM), a process for regulating European Union members' currencies in preparation for them joining a single currency—the euro.

Thatcher had been profoundly against the ERM and had already suffered the political blow of losing her long-serving Chancellor, Nigel Lawson, to their disagreement over this. As all her senior colleagues were set on joining the ERM, there was little she could do about it and would soon after lose her premiership over this in a titanic row at the head of the Conservative Party. She was not the only one put out by it, so was Nigel Farage.

'I was incandescent,' he recalls, standing with his trading friends at a Corney and Barrow bar. 'What sort of stupid, asinine moron is this Major [Thatcher's new Chancellor]? This cannot work! This will not work!'

It spurred him on to explore further the ways in which the European Union was imposing its regulations on Britain and the free-flowing capitalism he loved. He realised that, like himself, most Britons had gone along with the whole enterprise without ever having been given the opportunity to comment on or reject its impositions through a ballot—since first joining what was then known as the European Economic Community (EEC) in 1973. He believed the founders of the EU had lied about their true intentions, hiding their determination to eradicate European nationhood behind a Common Market. As a keen sea angler, he also mourned the decline of the British fishing industry thanks to EU directives.

Above all, he was furious at the way the Conservative Party—the party he supported—had colluded in this process, from Edward

Heath onwards. With Labour and the Liberal Democrats wholly committed to the European project, he felt it should be the Tories who stood up for British national sovereignty against the EU but again and again they failed to do so, bringing down Thatcher with it.

'The Tories will strike anti-EU poses, make anti-EU noises and promise referendums whilst remaining committed to the cause of integration and signing the bulk of the articles of surrender,' he says. 'Euroscepticism thus becomes a feature of Conservative old fartery and Europhilia an espousal of modernity and egalitarianism.'

Not one of the main political parties was offering him an alternative to EU membership. Interestingly, his despair with them had already been expressed the year before when he lodged a protest vote in the European Elections of 1989—he voted for the Green Party. At the time, they were strongly Eurosceptic.

He remembered telling the head of his local Tory branch about his change of voting pattern—and the gentleman nearly had a heart attack.

Soon after, he established a lunch club at Simpson's Tavern, a wood panelled restaurant with cosy booths established in 1757 down a narrow passageway near the Royal Exchange. There, friends and colleagues met to share their passion for all things British and a mistrust of the EU with glasses of claret over shepherd's pie and roast beef. He was following in a long tradition that stemmed back to the 17th century, when City taverns and coffee houses were the favoured abode of those dissatisfied with the rulers of the day, where they could speak freely and excitedly—so much so that King Charles II tried to ban them as dens of 'scandalous reports' that threatened the peace of his realm.

Farage stepped up his political involvement by attending a meeting of the Campaign for an Independent Britain (CIB). This was a cross party coalition established in 1969 to oppose entry into the EEC in 1973. Its aim still is to 'campaign for the restoration of full national sovereignty to the UK by its withdrawal from the obligations of the Treaties of European Union and the repeal of the European Communities Act 1972.' It has links with like-minded groups, including The Freedom Association and the Bruges Group, and its members include MPs from both Labour and Conservative parties.

Following his anger at ERM membership, Farage attended a meeting of the CIB in November 1991 at Westminster Central Hall. There, he was most impressed by Labour MP Peter Shore who warned of the perils of signing the Maastricht Treaty in 1992, which would pave the way for closer integration within the EU and the creation of a common currency. All the speakers urged the audience to vote for their parties in order to do something about it, but one 44-year-old wild-haired academic from the London School of Economics (LSE), sitting among the audience, doubted whether the mainstream parties would deliver on their promises. Fed up with all the party political prattle, he jumped to his feet, believing a more radical solution was needed.

'I intend to start a party which will lead Britain out of this mess,' he declared. 'If you professional politicians won't take the responsibility, we will.'

It was a call to arms and Farage strode up to the man at the end of the meeting. His name was Dr Alan Sked and his academic specialisation was the decline and collapse of another European multinational confederation—the Habsburg Empire. Farage volunteered his help to Sked, alongside others at the meeting, but although enthusiastic about his aims, Farage found Sked too academic in style to connect with the general public, and expressed his initial support by just sending him a cheque for £50. It was the beginning of a fraught relationship between the two garrulous Eurosceptics, which would eventually evolve into an ugly, public vendetta.

*

Alan Sked was born in a council house in Glasgow and lived there for much of his early life until he eventually moved to London for his post at the LSE. His father was a foreman in an engineering company. He went to his local state primary school and got a scholarship to Allan Glen's, a selective local authority secondary school set up in the mid 19th century to give a 'good practical education' to the 'sons of tradesmen or persons in the industrial classes of society.' It had a strong emphasis on science and technology and for some time, Sked wondered if he'd like to be a scientist but his love of history proved stronger. He left school at 16 and went to Glasgow University where he studied for four years.

From there, Sked applied for post-graduate studies at Oxford and Cambridge and got invitations to both, eventually settling on Merton College, Oxford. By then, he was determined to research the history of the Habsburg Empire, but at first they could not find anyone to supervise him. Then one day they asked him whether he would mind being taught by AJP Taylor.

'No,' he said, 'he'll do.'

Sked was delighted, having grown up watching Taylor deliver lectures on television. The most famous historian in Britain, he was noted for his impish style. Taylor welcomed Sked by sending him a letter saying 'Haven't studied the Habsburgs for 30 years. Look forward to learning all about them again from you.'

When Sked met him for the first time, he looked exactly like he looked on TV, wearing his trademark round spectacles and a bowtie. He asked the Glaswegian student how good his German was. Sked replied he was planning to learn it in Vienna when he went to explore their archives.

'That won't do at all,' tutted Taylor. 'You must learn it at once.'

He pulled a thick 19th-century history off the shelf of his study printed in Gothic German.

'There you are,' said Taylor, 'come back when you've read that.'

Sked bought a German dictionary and grammar and for the next four weeks, he poured over it, finally feeling he was ready to go back to Taylor.

'Look,' he told the venerable historian, 'I have translated the introduction and the conclusion but quite frankly, if the middle pages are as boring as they are, I'm not doing it any more.'

Taylor was impressed and took him on.

'He was great fun and a fund of stories,' remembers Sked. 'I miss him still.'

But several years later there was a sting in this tale when Sked read Taylor's autobiography. In it, the historian revealed that when he first went to Vienna he didn't know any German either and had taken private lessons in the city.

'"You bloody hypocrite", I thought!' chuckled Sked.

It was while carrying out research in Vienna that Sked met Norman Stone, a rising academic at Cambridge, and it was Stone who later introduced him to Patrick Robertson, a precocious young student who set up the Bruges Group. Norman Stone became Professor of Modern History at Oxford in 1984 and began to challenge the pervasive leftist views of the university with his stridently expressed support for Thatcher's brand of conservatism. He became her foreign policy advisor and wrote speeches for her. In September 1988, Thatcher gave her celebrated Bruges speech in which she said 'We have not successfully rolled back the frontiers of the state in Britain, only to see them re-imposed at a European level.'

Taking this as his inspiration, the 20-year-old second-year modern-history student Patrick Robertson founded the Bruges Group the next year while still at Keble College, Oxford. In his undergraduate study piled with books and a poster of Lenin— revealing a previous interest in Marxism—he ran the group from rooms overlooking a quadrangle, with even a secretary to answer the phone.

'If the EEC remains true to its original intentions—economic deregulation and the creation of a single European market—it will be a power for good that no one could reasonably quarrel with,' he told *The Times*. 'But today there is increasing talk of political integration, with all effective decisions being taken in Brussels and Strasbourg. We would have to conform to common foreign and economic policies. That is ludicrous… Few people are aware of the dangers.'

Robertson admitted he couldn't carry on studying and running the group from his student rooms and so agreed to move out at the end of the term, to return later to finish his degree. He said a future in politics had its 'definite appeal, though not necessarily as an MP. I am more interested in helping to shape public opinion.' And that's exactly what he would do, forming his own political PR company shortly afterwards.

In the meantime, he gathered together like-minded academics including Stone and Professors Patrick Minford, Kenneth Minogue,

Stephen Haseler, Roger Scruton, and Adam Zamoyski. Lord Harris of High Cross, also chairman of the Institute of Economic Affairs, headed the Bruges Group and launched what was called 'The Campaign for a Europe of Sovereign States' on 8 February 1989. It demanded a national debate on the subject of political union in Europe and declared that the decision was too important for government to take alone—a referendum should be called to test public opinion.

Sked went along to one of their first meetings and Stone and Robertson invited him to join their academic council.

'I more or less took it over,' says Sked, 'wrote all their main pamphlets and became their main speaker.'

Previous to this, Sked's main political involvement had been with the Liberal Party. He joined it at the age of 14 in Glasgow when it was led and revived by Jo Grimond and he still considers himself a liberal with liberal values. He voted to join the EEC in 1975, but it was during his period as head of European Studies at LSE from 1980 to 1990 that his views on the European Common Market radically changed.

'Gradually, meeting all these Eurocrats, European politicians and academics, I became convinced it was all mad, anti-democratic, and expensive.'

It was at Bruges Group meetings that Sked developed his provocative style and became one of its leading spokesmen. He'd learned a little from AJP Taylor about to how to stir things up and catch the attention of the media, but his fierce passion for the Eurosceptic cause came from another root.

'It's a Presbyterian Scottish thing in me. If something's wrong you must do something about it. It's your moral duty. It's like Luther "I must take my stand. I can do no other".'

At first, Sked got on well with Patrick Robertson and loved the political badinage, but he was fundamentally out of kilter with the mainly Conservative Party membership of the group. Following British military intervention in the first Gulf War in 1990-91, he'd already caused irritation by using the group as a platform to inform the German Embassy that their constitution *did not* prevent them from sending troops to join the Coalition forces. But worse was to come.

In April 1991, both Robertson and Sked issued a paper calling the Conservative Prime Minister John Major a 'wimp' for going 'wobbly' over his post-war support for Kurdish refugees. This managed to upset their honorary president Margaret Thatcher, who declared 'I had no knowledge of the statement issued by the Bruges Group and I thoroughly disagree with it. I loyally support President Bush and Prime Minister Major in their difficult task.' Other Tory MPs piled in saying Robertson was a zealot 'still in nappies' and the group was never meant to be a 'vehicle for silly little men to use as a Margaret Thatcher Memorial Society and to comment on every issue under the sun.'

Chairman Lord Harris was deeply unimpressed and hinted that Robertson's offending press statement had the whiff of alcohol about it, coming out of a raucous evening celebrating his return from a trip abroad. 'He created the Bruges Group, and now,' he warned, 'if he's not careful, he will destroy it.' Pro-European Tories were delighted by the scandal and so was Labour, believing it revealed internecine warfare at the heart of the Conservative Party. Robertson offered to resign but Sked was having too much fun to go voluntarily.

'All this led to the government putting pressure on the Bruges Group,' he recalls. 'I was told I was becoming an embarrassment to John Major and I got kicked out without being told.' He appeared at a Bruges Group meeting at the Reform Club where Kenneth Minogue praised one of his leaflets and said it was such a pity that Sked had decided to retire from the group.

'I was at the back and the room and said what? Are you sacking me?' Minogue declined to answer and introduced the guest speaker.

In the end it was Lord Harris who resigned, not Robertson or Sked, although Robertson offered to emigrate to America if that would stop Harris going. Thatcher stayed on as honorary president, privately calling the founder a 'very brave young man.' But Sked was already dissatisfied. 'The Bruges Group was a pressure group and I became convinced that pressure groups weren't working and this one had been infiltrated by too many Tories.'

He wanted to set up his own Eurosceptic political party.

'I got to a position where I had a certain amount of publicity and credibility and therefore I could start a party. I wrote a letter to *The Times*, as simple as that, no press conference, saying I was thinking of setting up a Eurosceptic party and would those interested get in touch with me.'

The letter was published on 12 October 1991.

'I am now convinced that the only way to influence government policy is to threaten it with defeat at the next general election,' he wrote, inviting potential supporters to contact him at his flat in Highbury, Islington.

Sked called it the Anti-Federalist League (AFL). It was a 19th century reference to the Anti-Corn Law League because that had converted the Conservative Party Prime Minister Robert Peel to free trade. The AFL was supposed to convert Major to Euroscepticism. He claims this was another reason Patrick Robertson wanted him to go. 'He and I fell out. I was thrown out of the Bruges Group for setting up the Anti-Federalist League. [The Bruges Group] was supposed to be non-partisan but it was all pro-Tory.'

It was the idea of the AFL that Sked took to the Eurosceptic meeting at Westminster Central Hall in November of that year that first attracted Nigel Farage to join him.

*

Another significant figure in these early days was Gerard Batten. A 37-year-old British Telecom salesman, he came from a working-class background on the Isle of Dogs. His father laboured in Millwall Docks, his mother was a housewife. 'I left school when I was quite young. I didn't like school. Started work as a bookbinder because I loved books.' He was unimpressed with conventional politics, having only voted twice in previous elections, once Labour, once Conservative, but he was no Thatcherite.

'I'm not a big fan of Mrs Thatcher but I can remember my mum saying to my dad that'd she vote for Mrs Thatcher because she wants to do something for us, the others don't.'

Batten had always been opposed to Britain's membership of the EEC, having voted 'no' in 1975 in the referendum on joining the

Common Market. For him, the Maastricht Treaty was also the final straw. When Alan Sked appeared on Radio 4's 'Any Questions' promoting the AFL, he'd given out his telephone number, which resulted in him being banned from the programme, but Batten rang him and offered him help.

'There weren't that many people in the Anti-Federalist League. I think Alan said he had about 200 people up and down the country. In London he had a dozen, so I was elevated to the top and stayed there ever since.'

As Sked's right-hand man from 1992 to 1997, it was demanding for Batten with his day job at BT. 'I used to work days there, then I'd do this at night, be up to 2 a.m. in the morning.' Batten was impressed by Sked and his detailed knowledge of the European Union.

'He was quite egocentric,' he recalls, 'but then most people in that position tend to be. I got on very well with Dr Sked. His political instincts seemed okay to me. He had a good grasp of what we needed to do and how to do it. But, of course, we were all amateurs starting from nothing. None of us knew how to organise an election campaign.'

Batten remembers Nigel Farage attending the early meetings.

'I liked him. I didn't have a problem with him. I didn't think he'd end up where he is today as leader.'

Most of these early supporters were not from the right wing of politics.

'We wanted a new alternative political party that we could vote for,' says Batten. 'I wasn't a Tory. Most of the people who set it up weren't Tories. Sked wasn't a Tory. Unfortunately, too many of the people now involved come from a Tory background. Even if many of our policies aren't that way, it makes us appear that way.'

'I'm a revolutionary,' he argues. 'I'm not an old Tory that wants things to go back the way it was when Mrs Thatcher ran it. I appreciate some of the things she did but regarding the European Union she sold us down the river the same as everybody else. I promote unconditional withdrawal.'

The first test for the AFL came in the general election of April 1992 when they decided to field 19 candidates. Sked chose to stand in Bath because he would be opposing Chris Patten, then Chairman of the Conservative Party and a key pro-EU figure, touting himself as a possible leader of the party after Major.

'It was all rather embarrassing. I'd never been to Bath in my life,' remembers Sked. It was foggy and he got lost on the way to the Guildhall for a meeting of candidates. Fortunately, he was helped by Dan Hannan, who would later become an outspoken Eurosceptic MEP, but at the time he was a student at Oxford and brought along fellow members of the Oxford Campaign for an Independent Britain.

Dan Hannan's mother, who lived in Bath, signed Sked's nomination papers. Interestingly, Hannan would be back in Bath a few months later with his Eurosceptic student friends to protest outside an emergency meeting of the EU's finance ministers. A few days later, Britain crashed out of the ERM and Hannan jokingly claims some responsibility for it.

'Exactly 20 years ago today, I was standing outside the Royal Crescent Hotel in Bath brandishing a placard with the words "ERM: Extending Recession Misery",' wrote Hannan. 'The assembled cameramen were delighted to find something other than a line of men in grey suits on which to train their lenses.'

For his campaign, Sked toured Bath with a loud hailer but his message failed to connect with the electorate. He did, however, know how to exploit the considerable media interest in Patten and his fate in this constituency.

'The key moment,' says Sked, 'was at a big meeting where an old lady stood up and said "Mr Patten, will you apologise for the poll tax?" Chris spent half an hour talking about the rates, how iniquitous they were and didn't mention the poll tax. I sprang to my feet and said "Chris, in one word 'yes' or 'no' will you apologise for it?" He had to say no, so the headlines in Bath and round the country were "Patten refuses to apologise for poll tax." That was the end of Patten.'

At the count when Sked saw Patten and his wife crying, he asked them why they were weeping and Patten gloomily replied it was because he was out. 'By how much?' said Sked. 'By two thousand,' said Patten. 'Oh I heard it was twice that,' said Sked with glee.

Apparently he wasn't the only one to enjoy the Europhile's shock defeat. At the Dorchester, Thatcher and Norman Tebbit were also applauding his departure.

Aside from this *Schadenfreude*, Sked had little to celebrate himself. He won only 117 votes, just 0.2% of the total. Undeterred by his poor performance, however, Sked decided to contend two by-elections in 1993 and needed more help. This time Farage was persuaded to get more involved. 'He seemed very plausible,' says Sked of his first impressions of him, 'a good laugh, a good chap.'

In May of that year, Farage drove Enoch Powell to an AFL meeting in Newbury. Stiffening himself with a glass of wine before the gathering and utterly fearless of the demonstrators that surged around the car rocking it, Powell gave a magnificent speech in support of Sked—one of his last public appearances before he died. Farage was inspired. He liked the process of canvassing too. Unlike many politicians, he genuinely enjoys chatting to people.

'He likes people,' says UKIP colleague Gawain Towler. 'He's interested in them. You'd be horrified by the number of people in electoral politics who actually don't like people much. You'd have thought it was a requirement of the job.'

Sked came fourth in the Newbury by-election, but by some way after the main parties—he got 601 votes, 1% of the poll. It was encouraging enough for him to want to carry on.

On 2 September 1993, the Anti-Federalist League met to formally establish itself as a political party in Sked's messy office on the fifth floor at the London School of Economics. Amid piles of books on tables and shelves crammed with academic research, its National Executive Committee pushed for a change of name. They dallied with the idea of calling it The British Independence Party or British Democracy, but it was too close to the racist British National Party, so they veered away from that and considered The Reform Party or Resurgence Party, but that sounded too historical. The Freedom Party was too libertarian and shifted them away from their core issues. Finally, they came back to a national title, United Kingdom, but sufficiently removed from BNP, and then linking it with their desire for Independence from the EU, resulted in UKIP.

With the name settled, they decided to contest the 1994

European Elections and put forward 87 candidates. For help with money, Gerard Batten approached Sir James Goldsmith, a billionaire businessman known for his strongly Eurosceptic views who was funding the European Foundation, a think-tank that advocated 'Yes to European trade, no to European government.' Batten still has the letter of reply from Goldsmith, saying 'I am grateful for your suggestions. However, I will continue to fight for the cause, but on a non party political basis.' In fact, Goldsmith had his own political strategies in mind, which he did not want to reveal to Batten.

While Farage found himself suddenly on the ruling body of a new national party, he was following the fate of his father and neglecting his marriage. Between earning money and spending it in City bars, he was rarely home to enjoy his growing family. He was also setting himself up for a major rift at work. After one soggy lunch in the City, he made the error of taking a similarly inebriated friend on to the trading-floor of the London Metal Exchange. The friend ran amok, picking up telephones and shouting abuse at clients. It was a grave misjudgement and Farage was sacked. It was a severe punishment but he turned it to his own advantage by becoming his own boss and setting up Farage Futures. His failing marriage could not be so easily rectified and it ended in divorce.

With greater freedom in his work and home life, Farage embraced UKIP and became their first candidate in a parliamentary by-election in Eastleigh in June 1994. It had been caused by the bizarre death of the Tory MP Stephen Milligan. Found in his flat naked except for a pair of suspenders and stockings, he had a noose around his neck, a black bin liner over his head and a segment of orange in his mouth. It was an incident of autoerotic asphyxiation that had gone wrong, but was yet another embarrassment for the government of John Major with its 'Back to Basics' policy. The media had misinterpreted this as a morale crusade and the government was beset with allegations of 'sleaze'.

At the by-election, the Conservatives were knocked into third place by the Lib Dems and Labour. The electorate, who had so keenly voted for Margaret Thatcher in the 1980s, were fed up with the Major government and were looking for a change in direction for the country, but concerns over closer integration with the EU were not high on their agenda. Nigel Farage came a far fourth, just a few dozen votes above the Monster Raving Loony party, represented by pop musician Screaming Lord Sutch. Farage and Sutch got friendly over a few beers and staggered back on to the stage for the electoral results—it was hardly high politics.

The results for the European elections were announced three days later and only a little more encouraging. Across the board, UKIP won 150,251 votes, just 1% of the total. Farage was pleased with his personal polling of 12,423 votes, just over 5%. They won no seats. Batten noted where their voters were coming from.

'We got marginally more votes in the Labour seats than we did in the Tory ones. I've always thought our natural constituency was more what I would call the patriotic working class.'

The primary protest vote party at this election was the Greens, with almost half a million votes—3% of the total—but that was a poor performance for them compared to their previous European polling, when Farage had voted for their Eurosceptic stand. Then, they had beaten the Lib Dems to come a remarkable third with 15% of the vote.

Farage blamed in part an amateurish party political broadcast by their leader Alan Sked and his crazy hair. 'The Muppet-like storm cloud atop his head was a major distraction from the good sense that he spoke,' recalled Farage. It was not just campaign strategy, there was a distinct sartorial rift growing between the scruffy Sked and the dapper Farage.

In those early days, the party survived on volunteers and many of these were elderly—those with time to devote to a cause they believed in. 'The sort of people you find working in Age Concern, for charity shops,' says Gawain Towler, 'mostly retired, but wanting to put something back. Decent people.'

Everyone helped in whatever they could. A supporter's horse-box was turned into a mobile information centre. Sometimes they'd announce a meeting at a village hall and no one at all would turn up, but Farage and his colleagues would still rehearse their speeches in front of empty seats. An audience of a dozen was more likely.

Sked wasn't finding it easy either to balance his academic career with campaigning. 'I did all my teaching and research and they couldn't do anything, but LSE weren't all that happy,' he recalls. 'They turned me down for a chair around 1994 and the then director said to me that if I wanted a chair, I would have to tone down my views on Europe. I didn't quite tell him to f**k off but from the look on my face he must have realised that was my response.'

The next test for UKIP came in 1997 with the general election, but this would see a great shift in political tectonic plates with UKIP barely registering on the Richter scale of public opinion. Crucially for UKIP, it would also herald the entrance of another Eurosceptic party and this one would be led by the flamboyant billionaire that had side-stepped their requests for money and would blast Sked, Farage and their colleagues out of the water. The UKIP project looked as though it might be coming to an end before it had even really started to get going.

4

A GOLDEN TOUCH

In 1949, a 16-year-old boy impatient to get on with life skipped school and went to the races instead. He turned up at Lewes race course in East Sussex, infamous for being the location of a razor gang fight later immortalised in the novel *Brighton Rock*. He bet £10 on three horses in an accumulator, where the winnings from the first race are rolled up into the second and then the third. The schoolboy couldn't believe his luck when all three horses won. It was incredible odds and netted him nearly £8,000—enough money then to buy a large house. The boy was James 'Jimmy' Goldsmith.

'A man of my means should not remain a schoolboy,' he supposedly told his fellow pupils at Eton and promptly left to pursue gambling and a career in business.

An older John Aspinall met him soon after his big win at a private gambling party. He remembered the 6-foot-4-inches-tall, confident teenager smoking a cigar. Goldsmith watched the other gamblers playing *chemin de fer*, placing their wagers on the table. Just as the game was reaching its climax, Jimmy made his bid.

'The bank reached £150 and Jimmy just called *banco*. All or nothing,' recalled Aspinall. 'I said with all the condescension I could muster, "Young man, this is a cash game." He gave me a penetrating look and took out a wallet stuffed with white fivers, the money he had made from his Lewes coup. It was more than all of us in the room had together. As I recall, he won. I've never underestimated him since, and it will be a foolish man who does.'

Money-making and politics flowed through his blood. He was born in Paris in 1933. His father came from a very wealthy Jewish family and became a London County Councillor and then a

Conservative MP, but anti-German sentiment in the First World War ended this and he left Britain to develop an extensive hotel empire in France. He changed the family name from Goldschmidt to Goldsmith.

Jimmy Goldsmith brought some discipline back into his life when he did his National Service with the Royal Artillery. From there, he decided to make his fortune in business. He used a small pharmaceutical company set up by his brother to acquire licenses to sell medicines, like Alka-Seltzer. It expanded rapidly but a problem with cash flow brought it to the brink of bankruptcy in 1957. A bank strike, however, gave him the opportunity to sell the business in the nick of time. His next big venture was buying up food brands such as Slimcea bread and Hollands toffees, which he developed into a conglomerate that spanned the UK and French markets. He called it Cavenham Foods, after his father's Suffolk estate. By the early 1970s, he had taken over Bovril and Allied Suppliers and moved into the US market with his purchase of the Grand Union supermarket chain. His business methods attracted criticism from journalists, most notably the satirical magazine *Private Eye*, which ridiculed him as 'Sir Jams' and 'Goldenballs.'

Goldsmith's enormous wealth bought him political contacts and on one occasion, he entertained both party leaders, Edward Heath and Harold Wilson, for dinner. He was given a knighthood by Wilson in 1976 for 'services to export and ecology', a reference not only to his food empire but also to supporting his older brother's environmental interests. He entered the 1980s as a Wall Street corporate raider and the character of Sir Larry Wildman in the movie *Wall Street* is based on him. He targeted American timberland companies, which because of a quirk in accounting listed their forests at a near zero valuation. When he broke up the timber firm Diamond International, he turned a profit of $500 million. He also acquired an oil field in Guatemala. Anticipating a financial crash in 1987, he sold many of his global assets to make himself a dollar billionaire and retired to a vast jungle estate in Mexico where he spent much of his time working with his brother's ecological projects.

In his private life, Goldsmith married three times and had

numerous mistresses. The saying 'If you marry your mistress, you create a job vacancy', often ascribed to him, was actually originated by a French writer Sacha Guitry, but he certainly enjoyed an unconventional family life, moving back and forth between different homes and women. The children from his third marriage to Lady Annabel Birley include Jemima, who married Pakistani political leader and sportsman Imran Khan, and Zac, who continues his uncle's concerns with environmental issues and is a Conservative MP, like his grandfather.

With money to spend and a passionate interest in politics, it is little wonder that Goldsmith should choose to get more involved with this in the 1990s. With his gambling friends, John Aspinall and Lord Lucan, they had long complained about the poor state of Britain in the 1970s. Lucan was the more extreme of them, being part of a small band that liked talking about raising a private army and launching a coup against Wilson's socialist government. Goldsmith never subscribed to this lunacy, but by the early 1990s, he did believe Britain, along with other European nations, was on the wrong track with its membership of the European Union. He outlined these beliefs in a book, *The Trap*, which took the form of a series of interviews with him by a French journalist. It was first published in France in 1993 and then a year later in Britain.

'[The treaty of] Maastricht seeks to create a supranational, centralized, bureaucratic state—a homogenized union,' he said in the book. 'It would destroy the pillars on which Europe was built— its nations. It would convert Europe into one multicultural space, in which national identities would be fused and sovereignty abandoned. It would coerce ancient European nations to merge into the ultimate artificial state.'

Goldsmith believed this process had taken place in secret—'not through carelessness or casualness, but in a deliberately planned and skilfully executed way.' He then quoted Claude Cheysson, a former French Minister of Foreign Affairs and member of the European Commission, who had said in an interview in *Le Figaro* that the EU could only have been constructed in the absence of democracy and that its present problems were the result of having allowed a public debate on Maastricht.

'This belief that the *nomenklatura* knows best and that the public is no more than a hindrance explains why there now exists a profound and dangerous divorce between European societies and their governing elites.'

Margaret Thatcher was a fan of Sir Jimmy, admiring his entrepreneurial spirit, but she was less enamoured with some of his economic and protectionist views expressed in *The Trap*, especially his recommendation of EU tariffs to protect European workers against global competition.

'Welcoming as I do Sir James Goldsmith's intervention in the debate about the future of Europe and agreeing with his support for sovereign nation states,' she wrote in 1995, 'I also find it ironic that he should be prepared to allow central European Union institutions so much power over trade and industrial policy.'

Having outlined his beliefs in *The Trap*, Goldsmith decided to take it further by putting himself forward as a political candidate. At the time, he claimed he did this because his wife was fed up with him complaining about things and she told him he should either do something about it or shut up. In reality it was also because he was seriously ill.

'Part of it was driven by terminal cancer,' says his stepson Robin Birley. 'You don't survive pancreatic cancer. He had it in 93/94. It was his last hurrah. There was an element of let's go out fighting'

With little time to waste, his political career began immediately in France where he stood as an MEP in 1994 for the *Majorité pour l'autre Europe*—a political group he established along with entrepreneur and politician Philippe de Villiers and judge Thierry Jean-Pierre. Villiers had already displayed his nationalist credentials as a young man by building Puy du Fou, a theme park that recreates aspects of ancient and medieval France, including a full size Romano-Gallic amphitheatre that hosts chariot races. Battle re-enactments have plucky Frenchmen beating off marauding Vikings. It is the fourth most popular attraction in France after Disneyland Paris.

A member of the right-of-centre Republican Party, Villiers shared Goldsmith's unhappiness with an increasingly integrated Europe Union. He had spoken out against the Maastricht Treaty in 1992 and his countrymen only narrowly ratified it with a referendum in November with 51% of voters for it. Villiers stood with Goldsmith in the 1994 European Elections. Their group gained 12% of the popular vote, coming third behind the two main parties and both Villiers and Goldsmith were elected as MEPs, along with 11 other like-minded candidates, who were officially recorded as Union for Free Democracy dissidents.

Taking his seat within the European parliament, the 61-year-old Goldsmith chaired the 'Europe of Nations' group of 19 allied Eurosceptic MEPs for two years until 1996. In the meantime, Villiers left the Republican Party and started his own *Mouvement pour la France* party. In 1995, he stood as a presidential candidate and won just under 5% of the vote. He continues to be one of France's leading Eurosceptic maverick politicians.

Energised by his experience in France and yet still seriously ill, Goldsmith decided to establish a political party in Britain calling for a referendum on membership of the European Union. The idea was said to have come from Patrick Robertson, the young man who had founded the Bruges Group in 1989 while still a history student at Oxford. At around the same time, Robertson had been having supper at the home of Christopher Monckton, a former member of Thatcher's policy unit, when they discussed the need for a referendum.

Four years later, Robertson pitched the proposal to Goldsmith and he went for it, making the 27-year-old Robertson his personal PR assistant for the campaign. Alan Sked, founder of UKIP and a former friend of Robertson at the Bruges Group, believes it was intended as a weapon against him.

'The Referendum Party was set up to destroy UKIP,' claims Sked. 'Patrick got Jimmy Goldsmith to front the Referendum Party, which was really his way of getting back at me. It was very personal. Goldsmith liked Patrick because he was tri-lingual, fluent in English, French and Italian. Patrick was useful to Goldsmith as a gofer.'

As UKIP was creating very few waves at the time, this seems highly unlikely. It was precisely because UKIP was achieving so little that Goldsmith decided to do it his way. Goldsmith devoted a war chest of £10 million to the project and the Referendum Party was founded in November 1994. Its aim was simple.

'The sovereignty of this nation belongs to its people and not to a group of career politicians,' said Goldsmith. 'It is the people and they alone who must decide, after a full debate and public vote, whether Britain should remain an independent nation or whether her future will be better served as part of a new country—the single European super-state, also known as a federal Europe.'

Goldsmith's plan was to put forward a candidate in every seat in the 1997 general election campaign where the sitting MP did not support their notion of a referendum on EU membership. His party would not oppose any MPs—especially Conservative Eurosceptic MPs—who supported their demand. In September 1995, his team started to recruit some 400 candidates. Christopher Monckton provided a data base of suitable Eurosceptics. Goldsmith didn't care if the Referendum Party badly dented the Conservatives.

'It could make the Conservative Party unelectable for a generation,' he said. 'It could destroy the party forever. Those who have no concern with retaining our democracy, the Heseltines and Clarkes who have always been corporatists, will go one way and the vast majority of the Tory faithful will go the other—which of the two factions ends up calling itself the Conservative Party time will tell.'

Among the first candidates was Goldsmith's 37-year-old stepson Robin Birley. 'It was wonderful to be in a party of agitators and outsiders,' remembers Birley. 'Jimmy wasn't an insider at all. He always felt like an outsider. He was a colourful, incredibly articulate, charismatic man. And John Major's ludicrous government—a risible man—I was contemptuous of him then as I am now. It was a peasants' revolt with a lot of money behind it.'

Originally, Birley was to stand in Kensington and Chelsea, but their MP was Alan Clark, an old friend of Goldsmith from university, and 'he had strong words with Jimmy, so I stood down. I then stood in a mid Kent seat.'

Goldsmith recruited other candidates over dinners at his home in Wilton Place, Belgravia, attended by several celebrities, including the actor Edward Fox. Academic and journalist Adrian Hilton was one of these guests and remembers the pleasurable plotting. 'I recall once asking him rather impertinently: "What gives a grocer the right to intervene in a British general election?" And back came the swift riposte: "Because I can."

'It was the stirring of revolution—the "Rabble Army", he called us,' says Hilton. 'Jimmy Goldsmith and his Referendum Party were marching for freedom and singing "Let The People Decide" while John Major and Tony Blair and their respective parties were still umming and ahhing over whether or not the people should get a referendum on the Euro, let alone on the whole supranational, anti-democratic project.'

Goldsmith was furious at the deceit perpetuated by the EU's ruling elite. In an article for *The Times* in January 1995, he said Maastricht was a step too far and had awakened public opinion. 'I very much hope that the politicians will realise that they do not have the right to impose their will without public debate and a free vote, and that they will agree, quite naturally, to hold a referendum.'

Goldsmith's rallying cry made many Tory MPs sitting in marginal seats feel distinctly nervous. He had sent out over a thousand letters to MPs and candidates asking them where they stood on his referendum. 'A number of MPs and their associations are anxiously awaiting guidance,' said one backbencher. 'If it is not coming soon, I feel that I will have to go my own way.'

But John Major's government was sitting on the fence, not ruling it out or in, and so was Tony Blair, leader of New Labour. Some Tories, however, had nothing to worry about, happy to applaud the billionaire's intervention.

'Sir James, through his tenacity and hard work,' said Sir Teddy Taylor, MP for Southend East, 'is slowly driving the party towards the only possible solution to our European worries and divisions— namely letting the people decide themselves.'

Among Goldsmith's high-powered supporters was free-market economics guru Sir Alan Walters, whose advice to Margaret Thatcher had so infuriated her Chancellor Nigel Lawson that he had resigned. Walters was now happy to stand as a Referendum Party candidate against Major's current Chancellor, the determinedly pro-EU Kenneth Clarke. Clarke batted away the threat by telling David Frost in a TV interview that he thought it was bizarre that a millionaire who lived in Paris and Mexico should be interfering in

British politics.

Goldsmith's deep pockets meant he could keep in touch with his supporters by taking out full-page adverts in leading newspapers. This way, he published the party's manifesto in the form of a question and answer interview.

'Is there anything else on the Referendum Party's political agenda?' said the advert. 'No,' came the firm reply. 'Once the referendum has been held, the Party will dissolve itself. This is explicitly written into the Party's constitution. The Referendum Party has no other agenda or purpose.'

The party would not fight by-elections and did not need to have professional politicians among its candidates as its purpose was simply to obtain a referendum. They would not stand against MPs who 'formally committed' to voting for a referendum. As for his personal political ambitions, it stated 'He seeks no wider role on the political stage.' And as to why he should want to spend a large chunk of his personal fortune on the pursuit of this project—'There can be no better reason.'

In April 1996, Goldsmith put further pressure on the Tories by saying that he was doubling the amount of money he was spending on the campaign to £20 million and would field 600 candidates at the next general election.

'We cannot underestimate that he is a very serious man,' said the former party deputy chairman and best-selling author, Lord Archer. 'He has the power to lose the election for the Government.' Former cabinet minister John Redwood agreed. 'If he did damage in 25 seats that could be very worrying indeed. There are lots of votes for anyone who says they want a better deal out of Europe.'

A by-election result in Staffordshire South East on 11 April underlined the problem they faced. Labour won the seat from the Conservatives with a 22% swing and worse still UKIP had grabbed 1,272 votes from the fed-up electorate, coming a not too distant fourth after the Lib Dems. Worried Tories believed that if this was repeated across the country, they could lose over 20 seats to Eurosceptics. Lord Archer, the party's public conduit for expressing fear—as its MPs had been instructed not to discuss the party for fear of raising its profile—said that his party should enter into a dialogue with Sir James.

'James Goldsmith has £20 million to spend and is a charismatic figure. What he is going to achieve is letting in a Labour government that will eventually sign up to a social chapter and a federalist Europe,' Archer warned. 'We should be talking to him and asking him if he understands what he is doing.'

Archer compared Goldsmith to the entry of Ross Perot, the billionaire populist independent, into the American elections in 1992 and how his share of votes helped remove George Bush Snr from the White House. But Goldsmith had already made his stance clear when responding to Redwood's pleas to reconsider his actions. 'I will listen to his point of view and reject it,' he said firmly. With further attacks on Major's lack of clarity on Europe, there was little appetite on either side for negotiations and Brian Mawhinney, the Conservative party chairman, publicly ruled out any sort of formal discussion or pact with Goldsmith.

Alan Clark, Tory MP and friend of Sir James, recorded the sense of panic in his diary.

'Anyway for the fourth, or is it the fifth, time in this Parliament the Party is in turmoil—this time over Jimmy,' he wrote on 26 April. 'It starts with the feeling that seats are threatened—threatened more than is usual that is—then a feeling spreads—why not? There is talk of major figures (*passim* Redwood and Lamont) insisting on a referendum now, declaring a splinter Conservative Party and forcing an early election with all the Goldsmith money and campaigning zeal getting behind them. It could be Valhalla of course.'

By the summer of 1996, 78 Conservative MPs defied their leader by backing William Cash's bill calling for a referendum on Britain's relationship with the EU. The vote in the House of Commons also won the support of 14 Labour MPs, two Lib Dems and five Ulster Unionists. Cash, named the most Eurosceptic MP by Kenneth Clarke, had earlier led like-minded MPs in a significant—although ultimately fruitless—rebellion against the implementation of the Maastricht Treaty. He was the founder of the European Foundation think-tank to which Goldsmith had made a donation. This prompted one pro-EU MP to wonder how Cash could reconcile being a loyal Tory MP and yet receive funding from the head of a rival party. Cash's Ten Minute Rule Bill was merely a gesture as it had low priority and so would not have sufficient debating time for it to become law. Its primary purpose was publicity for the cause.

Goldsmith's constant appearance in the news riled Alan Sked, head of UKIP, who was very pleased with his party's surprisingly good result in Staffordshire. He seized the opportunity to gain some publicity off the Goldsmith bandwagon by saying UKIP would run 650 candidates in the next general election—50 more than the Referendum Party.

'We are not a one-man band,' said Sked. 'We do not favour chequebook politics. Britain cannot find leadership from a billionaire MEP. We believe in immediate withdrawal from the EU and to replace membership with a free trade agreement.'

UKIP's Gerard Batten wasn't impressed with Goldsmith either.

'I always thought that it was a con trick. I bought his book *The Trap* and then read he wasn't opposed to the European Union. He wanted a fortress Europe. He wasn't a withdrawal-ist.'

Nigel Farage claims that Goldsmith made overtures to Sked in the run-up to the 1997 election campaign, offering to fund those UKIP candidates who stood on a joint UKIP/Referendum Party ticket, but Sked turned down the proposed alliance as he disliked Goldsmith. Sked denies any knowledge of this.

'This is all a lie put about by Farage and my enemies,' he insists. 'I'd never met Goldsmith in my life. I wrote to him several times and said we should meet. But Patrick [Robertson] was running the show and made sure the letters never got to Goldsmith.'

When Sked was asked during a BBC radio interview why he didn't link up with Goldsmith, he claimed the billionaire didn't want to leave the EU.

'He wants to stay in,' Sked insisted. 'He's an MEP and he wants to keep European institutions. We want to be a normal self-governing Parliamentary democracy, with a British Government accountable to the British people alone.'

Goldsmith augmented the talented team around him by hiring as his chief press officer a former Downing Street aide to Margaret Thatcher, Ian Beaumont. He would soon be busy as the media began to turn its attention to his followers. In the West Midlands, his campaign manager was revealed as having stood for the National Front in previous elections and claimed that the party was crawling with NF members. Another senior party worker was said to have gone on jungle patrols with right-wing Contras in Nicaragua. 'He came highly recommended by respectable third parties' said Beaumont hastily.

John Aspinall, his old gambling pal, announced he would stand as candidate against Home Secretary Michael Howard, but controversy clung to him not least because of his alleged associations with the rogue Lord Lucan and gangster Billy Hill. Peter de Savary, a businessman and America's Cup challenger, said he would stand against Olympic gold medallist Sebastian Coe, who was defending a slim majority of 3,000. But an internal memo was leaked to the press claiming that many of their candidates were 'too old and too few' to fight a campaign.

A major break came when Goldsmith won the right to have a party political broadcast during the general election campaign. The Committee on Party Political Broadcasting had initially opposed his request because they felt he did not have proven electoral support, but they changed this on legal advice, after it was argued that any party fielding more than 50 candidates should be allowed to have at least one broadcast. As he was putting forward so many candidates, Goldsmith insisted on having at least half the broadcasts of the main parties.

By October 1996, the party claimed 50,000 members and announced their first national conference at Brighton. Lord McAlpine, a Tory peer and former party treasurer, came out in support of Goldsmith and said he would chair the conference.

'I am still a Conservative, but on Europe the Referendum Party has got it right,' he said. 'If the party wishes to remove the whip it is entirely a matter for them. I have no intention of getting into a slanging match with Conservative Central Office over whether I should or should not give it up.' Adding cheekily: 'But I am surprised they think they can afford to lose any more supporters. They need every vote they can get.'

Former Labour Speaker of the Commons, Viscount Tonypandy, was about to go into hospital but was determined to lend his support to Goldsmith too and pre-recorded a speech for the conference. With such heavy-hitters on board, the Tory party was wary of coming down too hard and declined to expel any members of their party dallying with Goldsmith.

'I think the party should be inclusive,' said chairman Mawhinney, 'and we would seek to help them understand there was not a successful future for Britain in behaving in that way.' But others saw it as treachery.

*

It might have been raining and windy outside, but the gilded Italianate Victorian interiors of the Grand Hotel, Brighton, never looked more glamorous than on the eve of the Referendum Party's Conference on 19 October 1996.

Paparazzi photographers crowded around the high society friends of Goldsmith. Lady Comisa Somerset, blonde and fabulously thin, clutching a glass of white wine, hugged the gossip columnist Taki as Robin Birley and historian Andrew Roberts stood nearby enjoying the company. Lady Cosima was the niece of Lady Annabel Goldsmith and was having an affair with Sir James, her husband, despite his grave illness. His daughter, Jemima Khan, looking beautiful and pregnant, was a favourite of the snappers.

'It was marvellous seeing Edward Fox, Alistair McAlpine, Robin Page, so wonderful to see all these slightly oddball figures,' remembers Birley. 'It was an insurrection of the mavericks.'

Others were far less impressed by Goldsmith's stardust and sought to undermine his great moment. Alan Sked was holding a rival rally at the more modest Old Ship Hotel in Brighton, where he claimed that four candidates were on the verge of defecting to UKIP after being treated shoddily.

'They are not allowed to express their own views and anyone who is not famous is treated like dirt,' he said. 'They definitely felt they didn't belong to the right social class to be accepted by them.' More irritating was the defection of former Tory MP Tim Brinton who declared he'd changed his mind and thought he was better off helping Major keep Blair out of power, but these were mere pin pricks that would not disturb Sir James' party.

Between 4,200 and 5,000 supporters from all round the country crowded into the conference hall. Left-leaning journalists were on the prowl for fascist nutters, but were disappointed.

'This was not a Mosleyite audience,' wrote Ian Buruma in *Prospect*. 'I saw none of the *poujadist* thugs, in their ill-fitting pin-striped suits and razor haircuts, that add their bit of nastiness to Tory party conferences. Ordinary Mr and Mrs Ref were mostly middle class, mild-mannered, upstanding, bewildered, good-humoured English subjects of Her Majesty the Queen.'

'The rise of the Referendum party is a symptom of a universal modern malaise in democratic states,' he concluded. 'More and more people feel that they have lost their voice, that professional political elites are ruling over their heads.'

He was right. The audience was fed up with decisions on the future of their country being taken away from them and Goldsmith opened the conference with a powerfully delivered speech aimed squarely at them

'We are here today for only one reason,' he said. 'We want the people of this land to be able to make the most important decision a country can face—whether or not it should continue as an independent nation.

'We seek no power for ourselves. We are not politicians and do not want to become politicians. We are people drawn from every walk of life... The sovereignty of this nation belongs to its people and not to a group of career politicians.

'Our purpose is to fight to obtain that right to decide. And when the decision has been made, the Referendum Party will dissolve.'

Although this was meant to be purely the point of the Referendum Party, Goldsmith and his colleagues were also very much against the EU project itself and further integration. The audience loved every hammer blow he delivered against European bureaucracy.

'Already laws passed in Westminster are no longer supreme,' he said. 'As British judges have confirmed, the supreme law of this land is now European law.'

'Shame!' shouted a supporter.

'And the governing European political caste has put forward proposals to transfer to Brussels control over our foreign political policy, our national security and our frontiers.'

'No!' bellowed another.

It was a long speech and towards the end Goldsmith castigated Blair and Major for not being straight on their progress towards further integration. Finally, he quoted the Chancellor of Germany.

'Chancellor Kohl has said that within two years, he will make European integration irreversible. He stated, and I quote: "This is a really big battle but it is worth the fight."

'Let me make just one promise, just one vow. We, the rabble army, we in the Referendum Party, we will strive with all our strength to obtain for the people of these islands the right to decide whether or not Britain should remain a nation.

'Let us borrow Chancellor Kohl's words and accept his challenge. Yes, indeed, this is a really big battle but it is worth the fight.'

The audience stood, shouted and clapped. It was an impressive performance—doubly so from a man with only a few months to live. North London businessman and future senior UKIP member Mick McGough was there. He'd never been that interested in politics until he started reading about the Maastricht Treaty.

'My hands were sore, my throat was sore from cheering and clapping,' he remembered. 'I suddenly found I was surrounded by people who felt like I did, had similar views. I was no longer alone.'

Goldsmith was followed immediately by Lord Tonypandy who spoke in defence of the British Parliament against unaccountable European institutions.

'For me to remain silent now would be an act of treason,' said the 86-year-old, 'for such cowardice would betray the noble heritage handed on to me by former Speakers in the House of Commons. God bless your efforts as you battle for Britain, I wish you well.'

Lord McAlpine spoke next, calling for more honesty in the debate about Europe. Actor Edward Fox put the case for referendums being used throughout Britain's political history for the really big decisions and wondered why Major and his government was failing to deliver one for Europe.

'Because deep within they fear the result,' he said. 'The most important issue of the day, the future of this nation as a nation is not to be submitted to the people because the politicians fear the free vote of free people.'

Other speakers analysed the legal and economic dimensions of the EU and their impact on British institutions and business. They included Sir Alan Walters, City businessman Terry Smith, fund manager Mark Slater, and restaurant entrepreneur Luke Johnson. All of them were also standing as prospective parliamentary candidates for Goldsmith's party. Journalist and farmer Robin Page spoke out against the EU using taxpayers' money to fund its own propaganda.

'That is £220 million paid by the EU out of our money to win our bodies and souls—a propaganda effort to match the best of the Third Reich and of the old Evil Soviet Empire.'

That went down well. Amongst the sober facts and figures, a bit of tub thumping was much appreciated by the audience. Journalist Christopher Booker, long-time critic of the EU, spoke out passionately about the betrayal of the British fishing industry. It was an impressive array of immensely talented and intelligent people. This party could not be dismissed as one man leading an army of loons without substance.

The only odd note was struck by John Aspinall, whose contribution was entitled a 'Personal View', in order to protect the rest of the party presumably. He spoke of a thousand years of war and soldiers' lives lost in defence of the English nation. He saw that spirit in the serried ranks of football hooligans.

'If those who follow, cheer and even fight for Manchester United can be given the opportunity to harness the energy and enthusiasm for more worthwhile and rewarding enterprises they could lift the nation from the lower rungs of power, to which our leaders have allowed it to sink—and make us great again.'

The audience wasn't quite sure about this and gave him a muted response. A series of 'ordinary people' then gave their reasons for standing as candidates. A 16-year-old schoolboy said it wasn't just the older generation that wanted an opportunity to vote on their future. The final words of the conference were given to European politicians. Goldsmith's French colleague, Philippe de Villiers MEP, explained that he had established his own party in order to fight for greater democracy for France.

'We, in the *Mouvement pour la France*, feel closely allied to you in the Referendum Party. We wish you every success.'

Then came the final speaker Charles de Gaulle MEP, grandson of the former president. He wasn't afraid to bring up the 'unmentionable' old enmities.

'By seeking more and more integration,' he said, 'our current government is achieving precisely the desire of Germany: an imperialist hegemony over western and eastern Europe. That is why the battle that Jimmy Goldsmith has engaged here is so important.'

It was a surprisingly martial ending to what had been an elegantly organised conference, but there was one element missing—the seal of approval from the great Eurosceptic leader herself. A video recording of Lady Thatcher was screened. Referring to the Danish referendum on Maastricht, she said: 'At least they had a referendum. I look forward to us having one.' The Thatcherites in the audience, which included most of them, cheered her loudly—she had given her blessing to Goldsmith's campaign.

Shortly after the Brighton conference, the exact wording of Sir James' referendum question was announced on 28 November 1996: 'Do you want the United Kingdom to be part of a federal Europe or do you want the United Kingdom to return to an association of sovereign nations that are part of a common trading market?'

The battle was on.

5

THE RABBLE ARMY

Nineteen-ninety-seven started badly for the Referendum Party. Regional campaign organiser and former Tory party agent, John Bostock, resigned from Sir Jimmy's Rabble Army and told the media it was poorly organised and run by amateurs—and then defected to UKIP!

'The whole thing is a nonsense. It is just a complete and utter fallacy,' he said, then derided its small number of active supporters. 'Fifteen thousand people is a drop in the ocean. It is a nothing party—and if it had been members, it would have been a lot less. They say they will be in a position to put a candidate in every seat at the next election. That is absolute rubbish.'

This came out bang on 1 January 1997 and UKIP was delighted to welcome Bostock, saying he would be standing as their candidate in Preston. Referendum Party spokesperson Priti Patel replied that Bostock was 'clearly slightly bitter' and they had already replaced him, with 48 candidates ready to run in the North West.

Future Tory MP and Minister Michael Gove, then a 30-year-old *Times* columnist, was also happy to put the boot in on Goldsmith's apparent lack of support for his party. 'After a giddy month when 2 per cent of the population pledged him their votes,' he wrote, 'Sir James is marooned in the polls with only 1 per cent support. The party has decided once again to duck a by-election challenge by refusing to contest Wirral South.'

Gove applauded the Brighton conference for attracting an enthusiastic audience more impressive than the Tories could muster, but felt that was Goldsmith's high point and he should now give it up. The billionaire had compelled both the Conservatives and

Labour to adopt a more Eurosceptic stance and pledge a referendum on membership of a single currency.

'The party has been an unhappy hybrid of business and crusade, and applying business methods to crusades doesn't work,' argued Gove. He also criticised Goldsmith for standing candidates against noted Eurosceptic MPs, such as Sir Michael Spicer, merely to pursue a personal vendetta—as Sir Michael had once critised Sir Jimmy's protectionist views. 'It would be more dignified for Sir James to claim an intellectual victory now than to endure an electoral massacre this spring.'

But there was no dissuading Goldsmith. His party organisation had grown from a small office in Hammersmith with two people to a glitzy office block in Westminster with over 100 staff and ten regional offices. He now claimed 100,000 members. In January he launched an eight-page tabloid style newspaper—*News*—run by a former *News of the World* editor. It was distributed free to 24 million homes and its lead article damned former Prime Minister Sir Edward Heath, among others, saying 'They lied through their teeth.'

In March, Sir James had five million copies of a 12-minute video tape sent out to households across the country. Opening with spooky music, former popular consumer BBC TV show *That's Life!* presenter Gavin Campbell told the viewer he was going to reveal 'the true story about Europe—it's the story politicians don't want you to hear—because it shows how they deceived us and betrayed our nation.' Campbell described how the Germans were planning to create a federal European superstate that would merge 25 ancient nations under one parliament and one flag. Those politicians in favour of this superstate had conspired to keep the truth of this project away from people who would not willingly give up their freedoms. He cited how the British were told they were signing up to a Common Market with no erosion of sovereignty, but Britain's laws and economic policy in 1997 were being made in Brussels by unelected bureaucrats. 'Without these fundamental rights we are not a nation but merely a province.'

The most effective part of the video had ordinary supporters—no celebrities—telling viewers why they thought the Referendum Party was so important. 'Some might ask why support a single issue party?' said one systems analyst and campaigner. 'But when you think about it, this is the only issue that counts.' 'The total number of votes cast for us will send a message to the politicians,' said another supporter, 'we want a referendum on Europe and you the politicians do not have the right to surrender the nation's independence. Only the people can make such a decision. That is why every single vote is vital to our future as a nation.'

The final part of the video had Sir James reprising his Brighton conference points, but close up on the small screen, he now seemed tired and his voice thinner. Despite his tan, he looked an exhausted man. He had only months to live.

The same month, the Referendum Party bagged its first sitting MP when the loyal Thatcherite Conservative Sir George Gardiner was de-selected by his local party. He had angered them by comparing John Major to a ventriloquist's dummy sitting on the knee of pro-EU Chancellor Kenneth Clarke in an article for the *Sunday Express*. For his last two weeks before the election campaign, Gardiner threw in his lot with Goldsmith to stand as a Referendum Party candidate in his constituency of Reigate. He told the media that Major was heading for certain defeat and his party would 'go down the pan'.

Gardiner recalled visiting Goldsmith at his house in Wilton Place in Knightsbridge, London. '[It] was certainly opulent, with marble pillars and busts in recesses, very much Second Empire, and a comfortable library. Goldsmith welcomed me to the drawing room and sat me in a deep easy chair.'

Initially, Gardiner wanted to stand as a joint Conservative/Referendum Party candidate, but Goldsmith wasn't having any of that.

'He thought the inclusion of the word "Conservative " would narrow my appeal too much; the Referendum Party's appeal was pitched across the entire political spectrum, targeting former supporters of all parties and supporters of none.'

Gardiner insisted on being able to talk about other topics of interest to his constituency, even though Referendum candidates were only supposed to talk about the one issue. Goldsmith gave in on that and they toasted their deal with some fine claret.

'That conversation pointed up what I later came to believe was a Referendum Party weakness,' reflected Gardiner, 'many of its candidates would have been more successful had they pressed not only the basic message, but also other issues of importance to their local community.'

Despite his illness, Goldsmith hit the campaign trail hard in April and travelled across the country. He began in Cornwall, telling fishermen in Newlyn about the impact on their livelihood of the EU. He received a good welcome and they cheered him when he raised the Referendum Party's flag on a trawler owned by their St Ives candidate. In Cambridge, a vicar and candidate got too excited about his campaigning for the Referendum Party and devoted the front page of his parish magazine to it with a headline above a photograph of the German Chancellor Kohl asking 'Is God Warning Us?' His strident denunciation of a Fourth Reich was criticised by his superiors in the diocese of Ely and he was forced to pulp the magazine.

Goldsmith flew around the UK to minimise the impact of canvassing on his health, but there was no disguising the great pain he was in from his closest friends. After a visit to Folkestone, he collapsed in agony in his helicopter.

'He was campaigning but going to Paris for treatment every week,' says his stepson Robin Birley. 'Two or three days a week he'd have treatment, then come back. He knew he was dying.' He kept going 'by will power and what medicine was then good.' Contingency plans were made to whisk him off to hospital if his health failed him completely during the campaign.

In a poll conducted at the beginning of April, it was clear that Tony Blair's New Labour had a commanding lead of 55% over the Tories on 28%. Tory 'sleaze' was mainly blamed for this and one of the high profile figures of the government who exemplified this was David Mellor, MP for Putney and member of cabinet until 1992, when he was forced to resign. He had been caught having an extra-marital affair with an actress and was supposedly prone to romping in a Chelsea football shirt while enjoying toe sucking, although these more lurid tabloid details were later revealed to be untrue. As a wounded figure of the Major government, Goldsmith decided to make this the constituency he would personally stand in. It was also considered that if the Putney campaign deteriorated into a slanging match, Mellor could hardly take a moral stand and mention the billionaire's busy sex life.

Mellor was dismissive of the Referendum Party, saying 'a vote for Goldsmith is a wasted vote. He's just a bird of passage. I don't think he's even been here.' He challenged Goldsmith's daughter Jemima to campaign in one of Putney's housing estates. In fact, Jemima Khan was happy to canvass for her father, bringing her newborn baby along with her to chat to other mums in the area.

Dr Alan Sked launched his party's manifesto with a dig at all Eurosceptic Tory MPs saying that UKIP was the only party that genuinely wanted to pull out of the EU. He repeated his disdain for the Referendum Party, saying 'We have a democracy inside our party—it isn't about one chief with his chequebook.'

Optimistically, he thought UKIP might win three or four seats, but admitted he was in it for the long haul. '[UKIP] is not a here today, gone tomorrow party. We'll be around for as long as it takes to win the UK's freedom from the European Union. We believe that within ten years, Britain will be out of Europe.' He expected the Conservative Party to descend into civil war over Europe and that both Tory and Labour MPs would join his party.

Instead, Sked was rocked by a scandal within his own party. He introduced to UKIP his protégé, a talented young post-graduate student called Mark Deavin. 'He was a brilliant historian,' remembers Sked. 'He did a brilliant PhD under me—he'd sorted me out deliberately—it was about [Harold] Macmillan and the first bid of Britain to enter the EEC.'

Sked thought Deavin might become director of research in UKIP, but then he received a phone call from the investigative programme The Cook Report revealing that Deavin was a member of the British National Party (BNP). Sked was invited to the studio to see the evidence and then denounced him on camera, but the damage was done, confirming the idea that UKIP was infiltrated by BNP members. 'This caused absolute chaos,' remembers Gerard Batten. Nigel Farage asserts that he'd already heard rumours of Deavin's BNP involvement but Sked just brushed it aside.

Goldsmith got his five- minute party political broadcast on TV, but only the one. Two High Court judges rejected his accusations that his party was being hampered unfairly and unlawfully by not being given more. As the election campaign progressed, the voices of the Establishment came out against him. William Rees-Mogg wrote that it was a party of protest not government and was drawing votes away from Eurosceptic MPs.

A *Times* leader advised its readers not to vote for the Referendum Party, except in Putney, where Mellor was an 'influential supporter of his leadership's hesitant line', and in Reigate. It recognised Blair's achievement in transforming the Labour party and wished him well, but it would not endorse New Labour. It did consider Europe to be at the heart of the political debate and that there was no easy choice for the voter in the coming election, but said that those opposed to further integration in Europe should continue to support the Conservatives or those members of other parties, including Labour, who had bravely revealed their Eurosceptic credentials.

A major rally at Alexandra Palace in north London on 13 April attracted thousands of supporters. Goldsmith was bullish in his first and last press conference of the campaign on 29 April. He claimed the Referendum Party had 230,000 members and was the 'greatest protest movement since the war.' But perhaps recognising that this support might not be translated into votes, he said 'we need to continue as a movement. We will be a conduit for mobilisation. Those who are with us are very committed and will fight for the right to determine whether we remain a nation or become a province of Europe.' He had no comfort for his rivals. 'The Tories have committed suicide. There is no point voting for the Tories. They're gone.'

He wasn't wrong there. Past midnight on the day of the election on 1 May, it became increasingly clear that New Labour had won a landslide. The British people had finally had enough of 18 years of Conservative rule, with Major being a poor successor to Thatcher, and they were delivering their protest votes not to any fringe party but to the main opposition. Tony Blair would be the youngest Prime Minster for two centuries and demonstrated this by sauntering into Downing Street wearing chinos and an open necked shirt. He represented their aspirations perfectly. In total, Labour would win 418 seats, its largest ever number of MPs.

The Tories were slaughtered. Seven cabinet ministers lost their seats, including leading right-wing favourite Michael Portillo. It was their worst defeat since 1906. They lost all representation in Scotland and Wales and the defeat heralded their longest period in opposition.

Goldsmith had chosen his seat well and joined in with the national dismemberment of the Tories. David Mellor had realised he was going down, but when he stood on the stage at Wandsworth Town Hall to hear the results, even he was shocked how bad it was. In this affluent part of West London, support for him had collapsed, giving the Labour candidate a majority of almost 3,000. As he tried to muster a dignified exit, his eyes caught the grinning sun-tanned face of Goldsmith and he turned on him. Goldsmith had only got 1,158 votes, but he was beaming nevertheless.

'The Referendum Party is dead in the water,' barked Mellor. 'Sir James, you can go back to Mexico. Your attempt to buy the British political system has failed.'

Goldsmith didn't care. He clapped his hands and joined in the chant in the hall of 'Out! Out! Out!'

'Every single party has had to adopt a Eurosceptic position,' he told a journalist. 'Every party has ended up calling itself a referendum party. Even the Labour Party.' He was referring to their commitments to a referendum on joining the Euro. 'I think we'll get a million votes. If we do we'll have a movement that will be able to show its anger if Mr Blair doesn't honour his commitment.'

Goldsmith didn't reach his million votes, but his party did get 811, 849 votes, 2.6% of the total, putting it in fourth place. They won no seats and only a handful of their 547 candidates kept their deposits. Rebel Tory turned Referendum Party MP George Gardiner came fourth in Reigate, winning 3,352 votes, 7% of the total. As to how many marginal seats the Referendum Party cost the Tories, claims vary between four and 14 seats, with academic research favouring the smaller number. Many votes went to the Lib Dems who had their best result since 1929, winning 46 seats and 18.8% of the vote. *The Times* reckoned the campaign had cost Sir

James almost £25 per voter.

'The timing was against it,' concludes then Referendum Party candidate Robin Birley. 'Everyone was tired of Major, wanted Blair in. It wasn't a year for outsider parties. Now it would be much more effective.' He agreed with his stepfather, however, that they did shift political opinion towards their cause.

'The result was one thing and one thing only, to nix it. Major offered a referendum on the euro and Blair matched it. That is his achievement. And Blair—so euro enthusiastic—the question is in government would he have gone ahead and tried to line us up for the euro. And knowing it was marginal whether he could win a referendum. That's Jimmy's achievement out of that campaign.'

Just one month later, Goldsmith's family gathered at his hospital bedside. His daughter Jemima had flown in from Pakistan. His battle against pancreatic cancer, first diagnosed in 1993, was coming to an end. By sheer willpower, he had kept going through the general election campaign, keeping up a demanding schedule of visits and speeches across the UK, combined with weekly visits for medical treatment in Paris. But now the campaign was over, he appeared to have let go and the cancer was finally killing him. He lingered on for another month and died on 19 July at the age of 64.

The Times obituary described Goldsmith as a 'tycoon and founder of the Referendum Party'. He would have been pleased with that epitaph, as his final years had achieved something worthwhile. His party was never going to put MPs into parliament, but it did enable British voters to register their disgust at the European project and their lack of say in it. By showing there were nearly a million votes in this concern, both main parties knew that any further steps towards integration that triggered a referendum would be bitter, closely fought battles that would cost them electoral support. It kept them wary of offering EU referendums to British voters for the next 20 years.

Shortly before her husband died, Lady Annabel Goldsmith asked him what she should do about his political movement.

'Give Tony Blair a chance,' he said, but if the new Prime Minister embarked on any major new step towards taking the UK into a European superstate, he urged her to 'fight him with everything you've got.' She later said: 'I feel I owe it to Jimmy to carry on where he was forced to leave off. If he had lived, he would never have let it go... He really didn't give a damn what anybody thought of him. If he thought he was right, he would go on.'

With his death, the Referendum Party came to an end, but his family and closest supporters kept its spirit going in the form of the Referendum Movement. This merged with the Euro Information campaign in 1999, funded by the millionaire businessman Paul Sykes, and was devoted to keeping Britain out of the euro currency zone. Sykes had left the Conservative party in 1991 over the Maastricht Treaty and devoted his considerable fortune to funding Eurosceptic campaigns. The new cross-party pressure group was called the Democracy Movement and was chaired by Robin Birley. Sir James' third wife, Lady Annabel Goldsmith, was its first president. In 2001, they distributed two million pamphlets exposing the pro-EU voting records of 120 candidates in the general election campaign.

'I'm not anti-European,' Lady Annabel told the press. 'My husband was half European and my children are a quarter French. I just don't want to be governed by Brussels, and I don't think people want to give up their sovereignty. Jimmy used to describe it as sitting at the top of the mountain watching a train crash—that was like us heading for the European superstate.'

Goldsmith did not leave a fortune to fund these Eurosceptic movements, but his family funded it alongside Paul Sykes and with donations from 7,000 grassroot supporters. Birley gave up his chairmanship of the Democracy Movement in 2004 to devote more time to his businesses, but he is still fervently Eurosceptic and is now a supporter of UKIP. 'Farage is more effective than Jimmy,' he says, sitting in his elegant new club at 5 Hertford Street in Mayfair, sipping a glass of red wine. 'He's more English. He's like a Ken Clarke on the right. He's a genuinely very popular figure. Jimmy was too exotic and rich.'

But he fears that UKIP could flounder through lack of funds—the sort of money his stepfather could have brought to the party.

'They have very little money,' he says. 'People are worried about giving them money, they think they'll be blackballed. They're nervous of being cold-shouldered by the establishment. UKIP is seen as being controversial. In business, play it safe. Jimmy was always wonderful, he didn't care what the CBI said. Always a contrarian. You have to be quite ballsy to support UKIP.'

*

If Sir Jimmy's death brought an end to the Referendum Party, it almost brought an end to UKIP too. It opened up a massive rift between its leader and senior party members. In fact, it happened while the billionaire was still lying in his hospital bed. In comparison to Goldsmith's party, UKIP had done poorly, attracting only 105,722 votes, just 0.3% of the electorate, and now its leading supporters wanted to take that failure out on Dr Alan Sked.

'They thought they were going to win the election. They were all convinced we were going to become MPs,' says Sked. 'Immediately after the 1997 election, three of them [Farage, Michael Holmes, a retired free newspaper publisher, and David Lott, a RAF retired pilot] announced that they were holding a special public enquiry in Basingstoke. They'd invited the press and they'd invited people from the Referendum Party and others to take part in this public enquiry as to why Dr Sked had failed to win the 1997 general election.'

Sked was invited to attend but thought 'I won't be there chum, don't worry. Why would anybody be so stupid?'

Farage saw it differently. He hadn't expected UKIP to do that well as it was a clear race between the Tories and Labour with few votes going elsewhere. Personally, he'd done well where he stood in Salisbury, reaping the highest UKIP vote with 3,332 and 5.7% of the poll, but most of all he was very impressed with Goldsmith's campaign, believing it had succeeded in drawing attention to the threat from Brussels.

Post the election, he thought it made sense to join forces with those candidates and supporters in the Referendum Party. This would never happen under Sked's leadership, he reasoned, because the LSE academic had made clear his dislike of Goldsmith and his party.

On the weekend of 7/8 June, Farage, Holmes and Lott

organised a summit of 70 leading Eurosceptic figures at a hotel near Basingstoke in Hampshire, which included the most successful candidates from UKIP and the Referendum Party.

'We simply made a lot of new friends,' said Farage, but Sked was furious. He feared his own party would become subsumed into Goldsmith's party. He organised a rival meeting at the LSE where he denounced the three ringleaders of what was being termed a breakaway faction.

'I expelled them for bringing the party into disrepute,' says Sked. 'It was obviously a revolt against my leadership.'

Gerard Batten was party secretary at the time and was irritated at being told about this in a telephone call after the event. 'I said you can't do that. All that will happen is that Holmes is a wealthy man and you will get legal action because you should have made a complaint, suspended them and allowed the NEC to decide the matter.'

Batten was right. Holmes added a libel suit to his action and it cost Sked £15,000 to get legal advice, which he took from the party's meagre funds. It was bad judgement and added to the grievous mistake he'd made when he introduced Mark Deavin into UKIP. It was during this in-fighting that Deavin re-surfaced to offer help to Farage. He said he had useful information on Sked and they met in a pub in St Katharine Docks. This turned out to be untrue but while they were standing outside the pub, Farage was photographed with Deavin and another BNP member Tony 'The Bomber' Lecomber, who had been to prison for trying to blow up the HQ of the Workers Revolutionary Party. 'I had been right royally stitched up,' says Farage, but again it confirmed the perception of UKIP and BNP being entwined.

Despite this error by his rival, Sked felt it was time for him to go. 'I was exhausted,' he said. 'I'd being doing it all for 10 years. I had my full-time job at the LSE. I said I can't take this any longer. I left. I wasn't under pressure.'

Batten saw it differently, saying that Sked was forced out of the party he had founded. 'He had to resign, which is why he hates Nigel's guts now. The initiative was being taken away from him because Nigel and David Lott were recruiting all these Referendum people. He was treated very badly. He put in an enormous amount of effort.' Batten resigned too in protest at the manner of his going. 'He was stabbed in the back.' But then Batten was equally appalled when Sked started pouring vitriol on the party, saying supporters should vote Tory instead.

That Sked only finally realised the importance of Goldsmith's achievement, just before his own departure, is revealed by his account of trying to contact Goldsmith after the election.

'I had lunch with Taki [Goldsmith's gossip columnist friend] and handed him a private letter for Goldsmith, saying we should meet up in the light of the results. I got a nice letter from Jimmy Goldsmith saying that I should come to his flat in London, have lunch, be lovely to see you. It was all very friendly. I'm going on a short holiday, he said, we'll meet up when I return. But he died, so there wasn't a meeting.'

Twenty years on from founding UKIP, is Sked now proud of his achievement? 'I've got mixed feelings,' he says. 'I'm proud that I've been able to found a political party which has got somewhere for whatever reason. It's now doing what it was supposed to be doing, put pressure on the Tories. In that sense, yes. On the other hand, I feel a bit like Dr Frankenstein. I have created a monster.'

As for Nigel Farage?

'I think he's a dim, alcoholic ****** shit basically. Backstabbing and everything else.'

Sked's bile would continue to flow for the next two decades...

6

GREEN TROUBLE

It is little wonder that Nigel Farage voted Green in 1989. They were the only party that expressed some Eurosceptic concern about the Treaty of Maastricht. 'We see "1992" simply as a charter for more growth. It's not about people, it's about profits,' said a Green Party manifesto published in *The Times*. 'As it stands the European Parliament is little more than a rubber stamp for the policies and ideas of the European Commission. You can't vote for European Commissioners, they're appointed by government. This is obviously wrong—not to mention undemocratic.'

If there was going to be a European parliament, argued the Greens, it should have real teeth or otherwise they would rather see a confederation of regions working across national boundaries. 'Our guiding principle is that no authority be held at a higher level than is absolutely necessary.' It was not exactly get out of the EU—and their actual manifesto *Don't let your world turn grey* was not as openly Eurosceptic as their newspaper statements—but those adverts did enough to please Farage. He was firmly against supra-nationalism and 'besides, I am a green at heart.' His thoughts coincided with many others too and in 1989 the Greens were poised for their greatest electoral success.

The roots of the British Green Party went back to 1973 when a group of professionals in Coventry—one of them a former Conservative councillor—came together to form People, a political party devoted to encouraging a sustainable society. They feared that the modern world was out of control and faced imminent catastrophe. This apocalyptic vision was very much the mood of the time and one of its greatest champions was Edward 'Teddy'

Goldsmith, the older brother of Sir James Goldsmith.

At Magdalen College, Oxford, Teddy Goldsmith studied PPE, but he would rather spend time gambling with his friends, including John Aspinall. After National Service in the Intelligence Corps in Germany, he dabbled in business, but was unsuccessful and handed his companies over to his more entrepreneurial younger brother. Preferring to travel the world, frequently accompanied by Aspinall, he searched for animals for his friend's private zoo. It was on these adventures that he developed his own passion for traditional cultures.

'I began to realise that the survival of primitive peoples and of the environment were inseparable,' he said. 'Primitive people were disappearing; so was wildlife, as my friend Aspinall told me. I realised that the root problem was economic development. So I decided to start a paper to explore these issues.'

In 1970, with money from his wealthy brother, the 42-year-old Teddy Goldsmith launched *The Ecologist* and its first front cover featured a man drowning under a pile of rubbish. Inside, articles drew attention to the plight of Eskimos, toxic animal feed and the human population explosion. His radical views sometimes raised eyebrows, as when he told a friend he thought the perfect population for the world was 50,000 people and it is little wonder that he then expressed some sympathy for the Khmer Rouge, at that time enacting a genocide on their own people.

In 1972, Goldsmith published an issue of his magazine entitled *Blueprint for Survival*. It advocated a movement towards a de-industrialised society based around local communities—and the clock was ticking fast on this agenda.

'If current trends are allowed to persist,' he warned, 'the breakdown of society and the irreversible disruption of the life-support systems on this planet, possibly by the end of the century, certainly within the lifetimes of our children, are inevitable.'

His was not a utopian vision embraced by Marxists, but took its inspiration from primitive tribes, who managed to exist for thousands of years with their low-impact technologies and natural population controls—that is, presumably, disease and premature death at the hands of other tribesmen or wild animals. It was all early 1970s hippydom wrapped up in quasi-scientific catastrophizing, but was enormously popular, selling 750,000 copies. It served as a manifesto for the embryonic Green political movement and Goldsmith joined the People Party, becoming one its leading members.

'Governments, and ours is no exception,' said Goldsmith in his *Blueprint for Survival*, 'are either refusing to face the relevant facts, or are briefing their scientists in such a way that their seriousness is played down. Whatever the reasons, no corrective measures of any consequence are being undertaken.'

Against a backdrop of a Middle Eastern oil crisis and British industrial unrest, Teddy Goldsmith stood as an MP for the town of Eye in Suffolk in February 1974—his father's old constituency. His campaign hinged on the fear that intensive farming would turn this part of the country into a desert. Aspinall lent him a camel and his supporters dressed as Arabs to underline this danger. The campaign attracted little support and Goldsmith lost his deposit.

Overall, the People Party stood seven candidates in the general election and attracted only 4,576 votes, but media attention did bring the party to a wider audience and, unfortunately for many of the founders, these new members were mainly left-wingers and took it in a more conventional left-wing direction. Goldsmith did not approve. Like many early members, his views were a mix of traditional conservatism and more radical environmentalism. This split among its members meant it was not well prepared for the second general election later in the same year and it attracted only 0.7% of voters where it stood. Teddy Goldsmith retreated with his *Ecologist* team to Cornwall where, for the next 15 years, they created the farming-based, self-sustaining small community he had described in his writing.

In 1975, the slowly growing membership of People decided that its name did not accurately represent its environmental concerns and they changed it to the Ecology Party. It gained a couple of council seats in 1976 but the next step up occurred at the general election in 1979. Under the guidance of former teacher Jonathon Porritt, a prominent member of the party and an engaging media figure, they fielded 53 candidates and this entitled them to their first

TV election broadcasts. The result was a leap in membership from 500 to 5,000 and 39,918 votes. It was still not a breakthrough performance, however. And the early years of Margaret Thatcher's government, marked by her titanic struggle against the unions, made them look increasingly like a loony left fringe group of only limited appeal to the middle classes. This seemed especially so when they supported the feminist anti-nuclear protest at the Greenham Common Peace Camp.

By 1985, it was time for another name change and this time, inspired by the success of the German *Die Grünen* party, they took up the title of the Green Party. Some might have wondered at the wisdom of this as the German Greens were not without problems of their own. Although far removed from the Nazi party, a couple of prominent members of the Greens in Germany in the 1980s had volunteered for service in the German armed forces during the war, while others had Marxist and Communist backgrounds. There was even a faction in favour of paedophilia that campaigned to repeal the German law against child sex—which unsurprisingly lost the party votes. Despite this controversy, in Britain the Hackney Local Ecology Party registered the Green Party name with a green circle as its logo. This was then accepted by the Ecology Party at its autumn conference.

Riven by internal disputes, the Green Party got its act together for the 1987 General Election and, helped by fears over environmental disasters, like the Chernobyl nuclear reactor disaster in the previous year, improved their performance. Their 133 candidates gained 89,753 votes. This would seem small beer in comparison to their performance in the 1989 European Parliamentary elections. Prime Minister Margaret Thatcher's knack for populism was waning and the European elections provided a 'safe' opportunity for voters to register their discontent. But it was not only the fact that voters were disillusioned with all the main political parties that meant the Greens were on course to ride a tremendous wave of protest votes. The Green agenda was also striking a chord with voters.

A Mori poll in April 1989 reported that 71% of the electorate thought a party's environmental policies would be an important factor in deciding who they would vote for in the European elections. In another poll, the environment had moved from eighth to third in their ranking of concerns. The Greens also had two very effective activists and spokespeople in the form of Sara Parkin and former TV sports presenter David Icke. The sports commentator had a particular facility for a good quote. 'To call this Government or any other Western-style government "green",' he said, 'is like calling Attilla the Hun a pacifist.'

Sara Parkin had trained to be a nurse in Edinburgh, where she met her husband, but she became immersed in politics and made connections with many Green parties in Europe, eventually writing a book about them. Seeing the rise of Green concerns across Europe meant it came as no surprise to her when the same trend happened in the UK. The fact that she knew so much about European Green policies meant that she was much in demand with the press for comments, something that would later breed jealousy among the less media savvy members of the party.

All environmental groups were enjoying a surge in support with 20,000 people a month joining pressure groups such as *Greenpeace* and *Friends of the Earth*. *Greenpeace* led the pack with 192,000 paying members, but the Green Party noted a rise in their membership to 9,600. The Greens claimed 150 people were signing up every week with £100,000 of donations flowing into their coffers in recent months. Their target was to surpass the Social and Liberal Democrats—recently formed out of an alliance of the Liberal Party and the Social Democratic Party (to be known as the Liberal Democrats from October of that year)—and thus make them the third largest party in the country.

The money mattered too as the Greens planned to spend £250,000 on their European election campaign, which included £79,000 in deposits for a full slate of 78 candidates across the UK, with one in Ulster. They also wanted to spend a considerable amount of money on advertising, including their first TV party political broadcast.

In April, Jonathon Porritt, who was now director of *Friends of the Earth*, addressed their annual conference in London and pleaded with them to change their opposition to the European Union. He believed the EEC's legislation would counteract the harmful effects of Thatcher's privatisation of water. 'It is now down to the influence of Europe on this Government,' he told the Greens, 'if we are going to get any significant and rapid clean-up of our drinking water and rivers in this country over the next four to five years.' It was Brussels bureaucrats who could oppose the industrial development of Europe's wild habitats, he argued, with the EEC's Habitats Directive.

'While we may express objections to the way the EEC is,' said Porritt, 'it is critically important that we realize the extent to which it is working to the benefit of the ideals which we hold.'

The Green Party politely paid attention and then ignored him in many of their public announcements. Politicians of all main parties sought to play down the importance of the Greens, although in county council elections earlier that year they had pushed up their average vote to over 8%. Many blamed Margaret Thatcher for raising the profile of environmental issues. She was interested in the scientific analysis of global warming, was keen on James Lovelock's Gaia hypothesis, and preferred nuclear power to coal. She had given a major speech on the subject of the environment at the Royal Society just months earlier and followed that up with another important statement at her party conference.

'It's we Conservatives who are not merely friends of the earth,' she told her party members, 'we are its guardians and trustees for generations to come... no generation has a freehold on this earth. All we have is a life tenancy with a full repairing lease.'

But, trained as a scientist, it was research facts that compelled her. 'There had always to be a sound scientific base on which to build,' she wrote in her memoirs, 'if one was not going to be thrust into the kind of "green socialism" which the Left were eager to promote.' She realised they would never be able to support nuclear power. 'This did not attract the environmental lobby towards it,' she noted, 'instead, they used the concern about global warming to attack capitalism, growth and industry.'

British voters went to the polls on 15 June 1989 and there was mounting excitement as the results came in the Green Party's little office in Balham High Road, South London, on a second floor above an estate agent. Each surge in support was greeted with cheers and then noted down on sheets of green paper. It had been a tremendous gamble to hazard a quarter of a million pounds on the campaign, but it more than paid off in the support the party attracted across the country. In total, they won 2,292,705 votes, a 15% share. In 17 constituencies they got more than 20% of the vote. They knocked the Social and Liberal Democrats (SLD) into a poor fourth place with only 6% of the vote.

At the time, the European elections were run on a first past the post basis, but if it had been proportional representation it was reckoned the Greens would have got 11 MEPs. 'British politics will never be the same again,' said an ecstatic Icke. 'The British political system has suffered the shocking discovery that the Green vision has taken on a political reality,' concurred *The Times*.

Despite falling out with them over the EU, the Greens' tremendous performance did not stop Jonathon Porritt from jumping on their bandwagon and expecting the main parties to now incorporate Green measures in their policies.

'There is simply no future for the [Social] Democrats in continuing to split the difference between Tory and Labour,' he wrote, 'and their only escape route is to go genuinely green, as the original Liberals so nearly did back in the early 1980s.'

'Many Labour spokesmen still sound rather embarrassed when waxing lyrical about the environment,' he continued, 'as if it constituted some fundamental betrayal of the working class.' His greatest hope was that Thatcher would now deliver on her environmental crusade by getting shot of her pro-development Environment Secretary Nicholas Ridley and incorporating stronger green measures in forthcoming Water Privatization, Electricity and Green Bills.

Paddy Ashdown, leader of the SLD, was in no mood for lectures from the Greens so soon after his party's failure. He believed their success was mainly a protest vote—'the fashionable depository for the disenchanted.'

'We must not be intimidated by the temporary Green Party vote into believing that theirs is the true faith,' he told an audience at a meeting held with Jonathon Porritt. 'Nothing could do more damage than a submission on our part to the alleged moral superiority of the Green Party.' But he did want to see a new approach in which most of his party's policies incorporated environmental concerns. Members within the party also blamed their failure on not taking the election seriously enough and not spending enough money on contesting it properly.

Labour leader Neil Kinnock also thought the Green vote was a protest, mainly directed at the Tories. He believed many of their policies were unacceptable to the electorate and left it to the government to highlight their deficiencies. His party launched an enquiry into the Green triumph, but Kinnock did not seem to warm to the topic. While officially not wanting to 'rubbish' the Greens, their general secretary said their policies were 'eminently rubbishable'.

'The Green vote amounts to mood music rather than a challenge to power,' was how Tory Home Secretary Douglas Hurd elegantly put it. Seeing his job on the line, Environment Secretary Ridley was far more robust in his response. At an environmental conference in Newcastle, he said the Green manifesto was 'unscientific rubbish, based on myths, prejudices and ignorance.' On top of that, they were disseminating misinformation about the achievements of the government. It was his department that was setting the pace for environmental protection with a succession of anti-pollution policies, and he feared the anti-growth ideas of the Greens would make the country poorer.

'We could guarantee that that would happen in a very big way if they ever did get their hands on the levers of power,' he said. 'The tragedy would be that the environment would suffer worst of all.'

'We are writing to Mr Ridley asking him to provide details of this "misinformation",' replied Green spokesman Icke. 'The accusations come from a man who not 12 months ago did not know where the ozone layer was.'

Such mud-slinging was not helpful to the Tories as polls revealed that Green support was strongest in their heartlands and not areas of traditional Labour support. Thus, it was a protest vote against the Tories but one underlined by a genuine concern for the environment. To combat this, Tory Central Office thought it was essential to expose the strong 'red' dimension of the Greens and their links with left-wing causes. They viewed it as a matter of cost and only a richer country could afford to reduce pollution, in contrast to the anti-growth policies of the hard-line Greens.

Paddy Ashdown took a similar line for the SLD, saying: 'Just as we will never persuade people to protect the environment by asking them to sacrifice their liberties, so we will not persuade them to be "green" by first requiring them to be poor.'

But by September of that year, Ashdown was also keen to show how serious he was about learning the lessons of the European election by launching a shadow Green Bill. It was sent to the government's new Environment Secretary Chris Patten, who had replaced the more contentious Ridley. In it, the SLD called for an environmental protection agency, a ban on toxic waste trade, further research on renewable energy, tougher standards of vehicle emissions and compliance with the EEC's standards on drinking water.

This was followed the next day with a strident denial of any future electoral pact with the Green Party. At a meeting of Green Democrats, Ashdown unloaded two barrels at the Green Party, calling them narrow-minded, authoritarian and anti-internationalist for wanting to withdraw from the EEC. He said they were the 'new Calvinists' and condemned them as no-growth extremists who 'tend to treat human beings as just another pollutant—an evil, a curse, inevitably sinful in their actions and therefore, if beyond redemption, then of course a proper subject for control.'

Reeling from this assault, the Green Party's David Icke said: 'I find it truly stunning that the leader of a political party that wishes to be taken seriously can have so little idea of what the Green Party stands for.'

*

The media needed a star to represent the Green Party's success and that person—for a party that hated the very notion of a leader—appeared to be one of their most effective spokespeople, the 43-year-old Sara Parkin. A major newspaper profile dubbed her 'protector of planet Earth' and gushed that 'Parkin has emerged as the most coherent, driven visionary of the new apocalypse.'

A child of the 60s, Parkin had been inspired by some lectures by Professor C.H. Waddington, founder of the School of the Man-Made Future who declared the rich would destroy themselves and the poor would inherit the world.

'I had been going around,' she said, 'thinking the world was my oyster, that all was well, then gradually I came to see that all wasn't fine, that there were limits to growth.'

Parkin joined the Ecology Party in 1977 and stood against Sir Keith Joseph in Leeds. When her husband moved to Lyons, she contacted other Green parties and became the international liaison secretary for the UK Green Party. This international experience had revealed the tremendous political potential of the Green movement to her, but she also had a strong strain of political reality within her that would soon clash with her Green colleagues. One of six Principal Speakers in the party—the nearest they came to naming leaders—she found it a struggle to push them towards capitalising on their triumph.

At the 1989 Green Party autumn conference, which should have been one of celebration, the mood was tense. Parkin began to set out a more reasonable array of policies that could help broaden their appeal to the electorate, such as moderating their commitment to immediate nuclear disarmament.

'Ok,' she told a fringe meeting on defence, 'we are not going to build Trident. We are going to get rid of *some* of our nuclear weapons.' She understood that you had to hang on to some nukes in order to negotiate. 'If you are a unilateralist you can be a bilateralist and a multilateralist as well.'

Bigger cheers came, however, when Parkin reiterated her opposition to the Greens electing a single leader instead of their usual collectivist approach. 'Who wants to belong to an organisation which depends on only one person?' David Icke, seen to be a front runner for this position, also declared his lack of interest in a single leader—which was lucky for the Greens, considering his later character transformation.

But nothing seemed to satisfy the Greens at the conference. Even attempts by supermarkets to 'go green' by selling more environmentally friendly products were howled down as just another way of exploiting the customer to make greater profits. Sara Parkin derided the other parties for adopting green measures, doubting their true intentions, saying they were only copying them because 'We are right and they know it.'

Now they had won 15% of the popular vote, Parkin had to warn the Greens that they would be prey to 'parasites' who might invade from the outside and seek to hijack the party, while others, from inside, would try to move the party to the radical left. 'They are usually easy to identify,' she said of these extremists. 'The same old names pop up time and again, in local party meetings, on conference agendas. They will be the ones who always plot and destroy.'

Among the more openly radical at the conference was Marxist academic Derek Wall, editor of the newsletter of the Association of Socialist Greens and freshly elected to the Green Party Council, who went on to write a history of the movement. 'The Green Party,' said Wall, 'although never socialist has always been anti-capitalist.'

Parkin tabled an emergency resolution urging the Labour Party to join with the Greens in a pact to demand a shift to proportional representation, but this was rejected by the party. It was the beginning of a growing rift between Parkin and those like her—who believed that the Green Party stood a realistic chance of getting some form of parliamentary power, but needed to make significant changes to how the party ran itself—and those purists who preferred to strike a radical pose.

'The Green Party, which saw its membership rise up to about 18,000 at that time, was really in a position where it could have cashed in on all this,' recalls Parkin. 'But a lot of people, especially those who had been in the Green Party for a bit, were of a mentality where they actually preferred to be in a small pond. And so there were some people who were really excited and ready to go, and some people who actually did everything they could to prevent that.'

Those opposed to Parkin rejoiced in making the party less efficient.

'There were three speakers for the European election,' says Parkin. 'During the year that followed the European election, they chose 32 speakers. I got two media requests passed on and they were for silly programmes.'

In her attempt to turn the Green Party into a more effective political machine, Parkin joined with the Green 2000 group within the party that aimed to get a Green government by 2005. Jonathon Porritt stepped down from being director of Friends of the Earth in 1990 to support Parkin in her efforts to reform the party. They were also joined by a 30-year-old English Literature post-graduate and CND activist Dr Caroline Lucas, who had worked her way up within the party from being its National Press Officer to Co-Chair in four years.

In 1991, Green 2000 succeeded at their conference in getting the Green Party decision-making process slimmed down: the Green Party Council of 25 was cut down to an Executive of 12 members; Official Principal Speakers were reduced from six to two; a single party Chair replaced the three Co-Chairs. Green 2000 members took over the Executive and Sara Parkin became the Chair. Even though the majority of the party had voted for this, many other prominent characters were outraged by it.

'The right [wing] around the Green 2000 faction wanted to make us into a mainstream party with mass appeal, ditch the radicalism, re-engineer the Party constitution and centralise power,' remembers Derek Wall. 'We fought them. I remember Sara Parkin talking to the *Independent* about "socialist parasites", that is, myself and Penny Kemp who had been members nearly as long as her.'

It initiated a 'period of intense internal political bloodshed that would compare well with anything in the Labour Party or far left groups,' says Wall. Some claim that it was the arguments behind this process that were, in part, responsible for the split in 1990 when the Scots and Northern Irish wings of the Green Party formed their own independent parties, which meant that the main movement was now renamed the Green Party of England and Wales.

Parkin and her colleagues were constantly frustrated in their attempts to improve the electoral chances of the Green Party. Their adversaries in the party were insistent that its electoral strategy should be to increase the overall percentage of its vote. It would do this by standing in safe seats because voters there would feel it was easier to vote for the Greens without rocking any boats. They were adamantly opposed to standing in marginal seats, where a Green candidate intervention could make a difference, where the media coverage was greater. Parkin wanted to put candidates in just those marginal seats.

'[But] the Green Party turned that down because they said we might let the Tories in,' says Parkin. 'My argument was so bloody what. If you are worried about the left-right spectrum on this you should join the Labour Party. That didn't go down well.'

Any attempts to broker deals with other parties were rejected too.

'I'd had a conversation with Robin Cook [a leading figure in the Labour Party at the time], whom I knew quite well because we were both in Edinburgh at the same time,' says Parkin. 'About the potential of Labour giving us a couple of safe seats that we would get in exchange for us laying off some of their marginals. I put that as a motion to the conference and it was defeated.'

The cause of the reformers was dealt a further blow by the poor performance of the Green Party in the 1992 General Election. As many predicted it was a catastrophe for them. The electorate was focused on the great slug-out between the post-Thatcher Tories and Kinnock's Labour Party. They put up 253 candidates, spent a lot of their funds on the campaign, but won only 170,047 votes, a paltry 0.5% of the total. In contrast, Paddy Ashdown's Liberal Democrats had reinvented themselves and got nearly six million votes and 20 MPs elected. It was an embarrassing defeat that shattered the pretensions of Green 2000.

'The 1989 euro result was exciting but the success was illusory,' commented the editor of *The Way Ahead*, a journal of the Green Socialists. 'The Party unwisely based its campaign on soft-focus environmentalism, concealing its more radical social and economic policies... But new supporters and recruits found the Party was not what they had been led to believe. When the bubble burst, all that remained were recriminations and the grounds for internal conflict.'

Derek Wall was more derisory. 'They won and then imploded,' he said of Green 2000. 'When the "realists" believe in achieving a Westminster Parliamentary government by 2000, give me fundamentalism.'

The party turned on Green 2000 and the Socialist Greens harassed and humiliated them at their autumn conference, forcing most of them to resign. Sara Parkin declined to stand for re-election as Chair and, with Jonathon Porritt, left the party and active politics.

'I resigned first of all,' she says, 'because some of the most unpleasant and nasty things that have ever been said or done to me in my entire life were at the hands of members of the Green Party. [In response] the party said collectively that we're a broad church, go and have pint of beer, they would not act on this. And a lot of those people are still in the party.'

The second reason she resigned was that 'the strategy of the party was inimical to breaking through in a country with our electoral system... This was an ideological daftness. Instead of cashing in on it, the Green Party indulged in collective madness. By the time I gave up, we'd gone from 18,000 [members] down to 6,000. I wasn't the first out the door.'

'Sara's exit was followed by that of many of her supporters,' noted Wall without remorse. 'In retrospect, far from being the end of the Party, always under threat in a system without proportional representation, the episode can be seen as a cathartic and bloody end to a long and hard-fought struggle for the organisational soul of the Party.'

Many of those who thronged to the Greens of Parkin and Porritt would strongly disagree. 'The Green Party was not ready to succeed,' concludes Parkin. 'Nothing I was able to do could get them into the psychology of succeeding. I'm not quite sure they've got it yet.'

In 1996, Parkin and Porritt founded the Forum for the Future, a think tank aimed at solving future global problems with practical and attainable solutions. With an annual revenue of some £4m, it continues to run a 'Masters in Leadership for Sustainable Development' course and has offices in London and New York. Parkin maintains her involvement with it. In 2000, Porritt was appointed Chair of New Labour's Sustainable Development Commission, which was subsequently closed down by the Coalition in 2011 as part of its 'bonfire of the quangos'. A friend of the great and the good, including Prince Charles, he received a life peerage.

In 2013, Parkin was invited back to speak at the Green Party's 40th anniversary conference. Her speech was well attended and many Greens asked her to come back to the party but she gave them a resounding 'no'.

'They're homespun and chaotic,' she says, 'which it is possible to feel affectionate about, but is actually a mask for ineffectualness.'

She was delighted when her friend Caroline Lucas became a Green MP in Brighton in 2010—the UK Green's one and only MP—but even this masked a later failure within the party.

'When Caroline stepped down as leader of the party,' says Parkin, 'she did that because she thought it was really important to get more than her, because the Green Party was her. Her hope was that Peter Cranie would become leader, get the profile as leader, which she used to help her get elected, plus piling all the effort in to get somebody else elected. But what did the party do? They elected Natalie Bennett—an Australian. Somebody nobody knows anything about.'

Once again, as Parkin sees it, the Green Party had stepped away from a winning strategy. 'Whether it was not thinking or on purpose,' she sighs. 'I don't know. It's just so depressing.'

David Icke was one of the Green Party's other leading spokespeople in 1989 and a newspaper dubbed him the 'Greens' Tony Blair', but he would have a spectacular fall from grace. At ease with the media, he was one of the party's greatest assets in the European election campaign, but at the same time he was flirting with New-Age healing to relieve the pain of his arthritis. A vision in a newsagent's shop directed him towards a psychic healer in Brighton. She told him Icke had been sent to heal the Earth. Further visions followed and he resigned from the Green Party in 1991. He then declared himself a son of God and predicted the end of the world would come in 1997—for the Tories this would indeed come true.

A notorious TV interview on Wogan confirmed the widespread belief that Icke was now a fruitcake and his family became an object of ridicule. He weathered the humiliation and is now a best-selling author and popular lecturer, promoting his eccentric beliefs around the world. He returned to politics in 2008, standing as a 'Big Brother—The Big Picture' candidate at a by-election triggered by

David Davis MP stepping down over a civil liberties issue. Gaining 110 of the votes, he was still left with something to aim for in the future.

With the departure of Parkin, Porritt and Icke, the Green Party lost the interest of the media and support sunk too. Protest votes were going to New Labour in the mid-1990s and there seemed little future for the Green Party at the polls. The radicals had a firm control of the party. 'The rise of the anti-capitalist movement and the direct action environmental movement in the 1990s helped a lot,' said Derek Wall, who continued to be a prominent figure in the Green Party, realigning it with the Left. 'Out of the 6,000 members,' he claimed, 'many, many of them are ex-Labour.'

*

Their greatest electoral success was behind them, but though they had failed to turn this into parliamentary power, the Green Party's tremendous achievement in gathering millions of votes to their cause had converted all the mainstream parties to a green agenda. As a pressure group, they had been brilliantly successful and green policies would influence government and opposition party decisions over the next two decades. Indeed, they wrote two parliamentary bills in the mid 1990s, one devoted to energy saving and another concerned with road-traffic reduction, which were introduced as Private Member Bills by the Lib Dems and, after much modification, became Acts of Parliament.

However, by the time the General Election came round in 1997, things were looking pretty bleak. They could only afford to field 89 candidates. Their manifesto was still strongly Eurosceptic, opposed to the single currency, and if the EU didn't make its government more accountable and decentralised, 'we will argue for withdrawal.' In the event, they gained only 61,731 votes, just over half of those won by UKIP and less than a tenth of those won by the Referendum Party.

But, just as the Green Party might have thought the game was completely over for them, New Labour came to their rescue. Tony Blair's government established new layers of government with the

London Assembly and the Welsh Assembly, both of which were determined by proportional representation. Most importantly, they changed the form of the European Elections so that they would also function on a proportional representation basis.

The European Parliamentary Elections Act was introduced by Home Secretary Jack Straw. He had advocated the d'Hondt formula as being the truest form of PR, but then had to apologise to the House of Commons for misleading them when it was pointed out the Sainte-Lague formula championed by the Lib Dems was more representational. Despite the bill being turned down six times by the House of Lords, the Act was finally given Royal Assent in January 1999. This meant that protest voters could now register their concerns nationwide and have that discontent turned into elected representatives in the European Parliament. A new layer had been added to the British political system: one that would not produce the usual winner-takes-all outcomes that favoured Labour and the Tories. That would be very good news for the Greens and for UKIP. From now on protest movements would have a genuine political platform, even if European Union politics were so soporific that they were rarely covered by the media.

7

WHEN LABOUR FELL FOR EUROPE

The exact moment when the Left stopped hating the EU and started loving it was on 8 September 1988. Jacques Delors, the 63-year-old President of the European Commission and former member of the French Socialist Party, stood up before the annual conference of Trades Union Congress (TUC) in Bournemouth and told the assembled trade unionists that he was their best chance of getting Labour friendly policies adopted by government.

After nine years of Tory rule and with Margaret Thatcher solidly in place as Prime Minister, their movement stood no chance of influencing policy in Westminster. Instead, Delors offered them a new vision of socialism—one that came via Brussels. His code phrases were 'social dimension' and the 'uniquely European model of society'.

'It was with great pleasure that I accepted the invitation to address congress today,' began his speech. 'Europe is again on the move.' He was there to argue the case for the move towards greater integration as embodied in the Maastricht Treaty of 1992.

'The potential benefits of completing the internal market by 1992 are very large. But we must,' he said, reassuring the trade-union delegates before him, 'maximize these benefits while minimizing the costs, we must also preserve and enhance the uniquely European model of society.' Of this, 'the *social dimension* is a vital element.'

He praised the British trade union movement for being the pioneer and model for other trade-union movements across Europe. They helped 'forge in Europe a new model for society, a model based on a skilful balance between society and the individual.' This included 'collective bargaining' and that model had been successful for three decades after the Second World War, but in recent years it had been threatened by 'adverse economical developments'—he was referring to the resurgent global free market capitalism of Thatcher and US President Ronald Reagan.

'Europe has grown increasingly vulnerable,' said Delors. 'We must now rely on our own forces.' He said the EU was rejecting a drastic reduction in wages and levels of social protection. He wanted to see the creation of a large internal market but that should 'not diminish the level of social protection' and Brussels would continue to 'improve workers' living and working conditions, and to provide better protection for their health and safety at work' which would include the 'area of collective bargaining and legislation'. He also offered a series of sweeteners to the British Labour movement. These included the 'establishment of a platform of guaranteed social rights', the 'creation of a Statute for European Companies, which would include the participation of workers or their representatives', and the 'extension to all workers of the right to lifelong education'. All funded by the European taxpayer.

'In my opinion,' he concluded, 'social dialogue and collective bargaining are essential pillars of our democratic society and social progress.'

It is little wonder that when Delors finished his speech, the trade-union delegates leapt to their feet, cheered, applauded and broke out in a chorus of '*Frère* Jacques.' It was largely choreographed says John Edmonds, then General Secretary of the GMB—the General, Municipal, Boilermakers and Allied Trade Union.

'I remember going round the bars and cafes of the conference centre getting the GMB delegation out so they were in the seats so we could give Delors a standing ovation,' recalls Edmonds. 'He then made a speech which I'm told was very good. Unfortunately, whatever Bournemouth conference centre had, it wasn't a bloody good public address system and we were sitting right in the front. So the people at the back probably heard what he said, so we gave him another standing ovation based on faith.'

But even if they couldn't hear all of his speech, they understood its content and thoroughly approved.

'What he was saying made a lot of sense to trade unionists,' says

Edmonds, 'that is, if you are going to have a single market, there will be winners and losers and you've got to have a social dimension to ensure that the winners share the benefits and the losers are protected.'

The message was also clear that if Thatcher was against them, then Delors was for them. This was immediately acknowledged by Ron Todd, General Secretary of the Transport & General Workers' Union, who had for a long time been a leading trade-union Eurosceptic, calling the EEC a 'bosses' club'. But it was he who had seen the French socialist give a similar speech in Stockholm earlier that year to the European Trades Union Congress (ETUC) and invited Delors to address the TUC. Now he told his supporters that there was not a 'cat in Hell's chance' of getting their issues heard in Westminster and that the 'only card game in town is in a town called Brussels'.

When Margaret Thatcher heard about the speech she went ballistic. She was furious at Delors for trying to outflank her union reforms by promising Europe-wide socialism from Brussels. His declaration led directly to her Bruges speech less than two weeks later, in which she famously declared 'We have not successfully rolled back the frontiers of the state in Britain only to see them re-imposed at a European level.' She later railed against Delors' increasingly political role. 'By the summer of 1988,' she said of the un-elected commissioner, 'he had slipped his leash as *fonctionnaire* and become a fully fledged political spokesman for federalism.'

But Labour's conversion to the EU did not happen in a day. It had, in fact, happened over the previous year and was born out of electoral despair. The Labour Party had gone down to a third defeat against Thatcher in the 1987 General Election and the trade unions that bankrolled it wondered if they'd ever get back in and dismantle the Tory's union curbing legislation. Trades-union membership had slumped from a peak of 13 million in the 1970s to just over seven million.

The TUC's anti-EU attitude had been based on its resolution in 1981 when it joined with the Labour Party under Michael Foot in seeking withdrawal from the EEC. Back then, a young Tony Blair, standing in Sedgefield, had gone into the 1983 general election promising his voters 'We'll negotiate a withdrawal from the EEC which has drained our natural resources and destroyed jobs.' But now, with the realisation of knowing that Labour was going to be out of power for at least a decade, they were in the mood for seeking a new pro-union patron. Over that year, the TUC produced a report entitled '1992: Maximizing the Benefits—Minimizing the Costs'. In his Bournemouth speech, Delors made frequent reference to it. 'Your report rightly points out that there will be far-reaching consequences for industry and the economy,' he said. 'The potential benefits are enormous. Realizing that potential depends on all of us.' Many of the measures he promised would be delivered by Brussels were based on the TUC's proposals mentioned in their report.

Ron Todd's influential championing of the EU was echoed by other previously Eurosceptic trade-union leaders. David Williams, a National Secretary of the GMB, said the single European market would 'happen despite the reservations, the misgivings and policies of many unions represented in this hall' and he was joined by many other left-wingers. A similar process happened within the Labour Party. Despite the continued objections of major figures such as Tony Benn, Dennis Skinner and Ken Livingstone, Labour's National Executive Committee issued a statement accepting membership of the EEC in 1988 and then subsequently endorsed the single market and the TUC's pro-'social dimension' Europe stance at their Labour Party conference in 1989.

John Edmonds, General Secretary of the GMB at the time, was amazed at the speed of the transformation. He recalled that in August 1988, the TUC was against EC membership and calling for withdrawal, but by October, both the TUC and the Labour Party were in favour of membership. He has been quoted as describing this as a 'coup', but he feels it came as a welcome relief to Neil Kinnock, then leader of the Labour Party.

'Antagonism against the EU was out of date,' is how Kinnock viewed it, says Edmonds and was 'losing more votes than gaining them. He was very keen on change in Europe. It was the unions who said we think we ought to do this and Kinnock said "oh good". It was not a matter of convincing anybody very much. The only way to beat Thatcher was in Brussels, you couldn't do it London.'

Edmonds had been a Eurosceptic like Ron Todd of the TMG.

'The TMG who had made much more of the Eurosceptical decision had to be carried along almost on a sedan chair,' chuckles Edmonds. 'In the end, by careful drafting… I remember Ron Todd's speech after Delors, saying "I'm sure you've got a great deal to learn from us and we've got a great deal to learn from you" [with the emphasis on "You've"].'

But, by the end of this process, Edmonds was convinced it was a positive move for the trade unions.

'Part of it was an attempt to realign with reality,' says the former GMB leader. 'The trade unions had spent the Thatcher period getting a good kicking, and of course it was made a million times worse by the miners' strike. On the other hand you go across to Brussels and the discussion is about social partnership. Trade unions are totally involved in the process of employment law and some social law. Not only that but the law that was being produced in Maastricht and so on was very much about employment rights, the sort of things we subsequently wanted Blair to implement in full. In London you get your feelings hurt, in Brussels they listen to the arguments. An awful lot of trade unionists were involved in discussions in Brussels because it was the only way we would get any social progress at all. So that bitterness against the EEC, the Common Market, as a rich men's club, had dissipated.'

John Monks, Deputy General Secretary of the TUC at the time, agrees.

'When Jacques Delors promised a strong social dimension to the single market,' he says, 'after the miners' strike and a whole succession of strikes had been lost, this was a new departure, this was an encouraging development.'

Further TUC involvement with the ETUC followed, at one time headed by TUC General Secretary Norman Willis. This resulted in a raft of pan-European Union agreements on social and employment issues that became known as the Social Chapter and were incorporated in the Maastricht Treaty in 1992. EU directives could now demand maximum protection for workers on their terms. Although John Major's government secured an opt out from the Social Chapter, because this was a legally binding agreement in all other member countries the TUC devoted their efforts over the next five years to pursuing a number of legal actions in Britain in the public and private sectors seeking to enforce Social Chapter directives.

When New Labour came to power in 1997 it signed up to the Social Chapter, but was reluctant to pursue many of its employment regulations as it had acquired a new business friendly character. When the Confederation of British Industry (CBI) reacted furiously to this, Blair reassured them that the Social Chapter was only a set of principles and he would not allow a reassertion of union power. His government proceeded to drag their feet over implementing certain directives until lawyers expert in European Union legislation, such as Cherie Booth QC—that is, Mrs Blair—pulled them up over it. It became a feeding frenzy for lawyers and Islington households grew fat on the proceeds.

The overall effect of this was that the Left in general, either through the Labour Party or the unions, was no longer opposed to EU membership and no longer provided an effective outlet for those left-of-centre Eurosceptic voters in the 1990s or subsequent decades. This was a particular problem for more traditional working class voters who though they could see the political purpose of this about-face by the unions, were not exactly happy with the betrayal of British interests. Characterised as the 'patriotic working class', these people had loved Margaret Thatcher's strident defence of their national interests and were now cast adrift as all the mainstream parties were now committed to the European project. This meant that if anyone was especially opposed to it they would have to vote for one of the smaller 'protest vote' parties, either the middle class Green Party or UKIP or the Referendum Party. It was the beginning of their dislocation from national politics and a feeling that the mainstream parties were run by a metropolitan elite with its own agenda.

If the European Union was the background against which the Left now choreographed its future, it would also be the stage on which the smaller protest parties would have the opportunity to re-enter for a second act.

*

With its founder, Dr Alan Sked, gone by the end of 1997, the new leader of UKIP was Michael Holmes. The 59-year-old had worked in newspaper advertising before starting his own successful free newspaper. He had sold out for millions and had plenty of time on his hands when he attended a UKIP conference and volunteered to match the money raised in a whip-round. Nigel Farage noted the cheque was a long time coming but was entranced by the possibility of him passing on much-needed funds to the party. Gerard Batten was less than impressed by Holmes and refused to serve in a party led by him.

'Holmes was an imbecile,' says Batten. 'The only virtue he had, so he told us, was that he had £7m and everybody thought he might give some to the party and he never did anything. He was tight as a fish's arse.'

Holmes' management style was somewhat abrasive and offended many of the volunteers working in the party office at 189 Regent Street. This was in contrast to the team-building skills of former RAF Squadron Leader David Lott. Farage has made frequent reference to the retired pilot's quiet talents in helping run the party in its early years and he has called him an 'anchor' during its extended periods of in-fighting. It was Lott who took care of the party's national administration, allowing Farage, now party chairman, to concentrate on the campaign for the European elections in 1999. Thanks to New Labour changing the rules, it was being fought on a proportional representational basis.

For Sked the thought of campaigning to get representation in an institution UKIP opposed remains an anathema, a position at first shared by others like Gerard Batten. 'My position up to that time was that we shouldn't take seats in the European parliament,' remembers Batten. 'It was first past the post and we didn't have much chance of winning anyway. In 1999 they changed that and I changed my mind because I thought we can win, provided we keep to the straight and narrow in the European parliament, then we can use the position and the resources to actually promote getting out.'

UKIP's European election campaign got off to a good start when a MORI poll in March noted that support for UKIP was running at 25% and that could bag them 20 of the 87 UK regional seats. The Tories complained the poll was rigged because the question asked 'if the UKIP is the only party to retain the pound and leave the EU, how would you vote in the elections?' In response, Farage wrote a letter to *The Times* saying the Tory accusation was 'complacent and ludicrous.' 'The truth is that the UKIP says what many politicians secretly think' he said, 'and what a huge section of the British public wants—withdrawal from the EU.'

When *The Times* came to publish the main parties' manifestos in May, they included UKIP alongside the Green Party and the Pro-Euro Conservative Party. The UKIP logo now featured their initials superimposed over a pound sterling sign and this was to be the leading issue of the election. 'UKIP will retain the pound sterling as Britain's currency and will never adopt the European single currency,' they declared. 'Keep the £. Vote UKIP' was their slogan.

Labour and the Lib Dems favoured joining the euro, while the Conservatives under William Hague opposed it. This riled two Conservative MEPS, John Stevens and Brendan Donnelly, who resigned from their party because of its anti-euro stance and set up the Pro-Euro Conservative Party. They hoped to gain enough popular support to encourage the replacement of Hague with Kenneth Clarke as party leader.

'Greens believe that the UK Government should be free to set its own levels of taxation, public spending, and public borrowing,' said the Green Party. 'We do not support the single currency. The UK must not join.' Echoing their Eurosceptic tone of the 1989 campaign, they said Green MEPS would 'highlight fraud and challenge incompetence and waste in the activities of the European Commission.'

All parties favoured the enlargement of the EU except for UKIP. Their manifesto promised that 'all UKIP candidates have given written undertakings which prevent them benefiting personally from their expenses and allowances as MEPs.'

Some Tories were open in their support of UKIP—sometimes too open. Dr Adrian Rogers, a parliamentary candidate for the

Tories in 1997, wrote a letter to the *Telegraph* saying that the loyal Conservatives opposed to rule from Brussels should vote UKIP. This was too much for the party chairman and Rogers was sacked from membership of the party.

As election day approached, so enemies of UKIP went to work. In the week before voters went to the polls, someone passed a photograph to *The Times* showing Nigel Farage meeting with BNP members Mark Deavin and Tony 'The Bomber' Lecomber. This was a two-year-old story, which Farage had batted away as a 'stitch-up' in 1997, but *The Times* thought it worth covering again in some detail. It repeated how the BNP had heaped praise on UKIP just before the photograph was taken. Farage admitted meeting Deavin but not Lecomber. 'I do not know him, I have never met him' he told the newspaper. 'I am at a mystery to explain how he got in the photograph. I do not and have never supported the BNP.'

Dr Alan Sked was delighted with the furore directed at Farage and was allowed to follow it up with his own article in *The Times*.

'I shall not be voting in Thursday's Euro-elections,' he told its readers. He condemned Farage and Holmes for reversing UKIP policy by saying they will take seats in the European Parliament plus their salaries and expenses. 'A party which once offered voters the chance to reject outright the undermining of Westminster now offers its leaders the chance to line their pockets in Brussels.'

Sked repeated the charges against Farage of associating with BNP racists—omitting the fact that it was he who had invited Deavin into UKIP—and attempting to get former National Front members accepted as UKIP candidates.

'In the light of all this,' said Sked, 'a betrayal of all the ordinary, decent people who worked so hard for the party I founded—I believe that it is now impossible to support UKIP in Thursday's elections. If people have to vote, they should instead vote for the Conservative Party.'

Gerard Batten was furious and wrote to Sked telling him he'd let down their cause. 'I've not joined the Tories,' Sked told Batten. 'You're not listening to what I'm saying. If you just want your own views repeated, buy a parrot.' They've never spoken to each other since.

The raking up of an old story, plus Sked's assault, infuriated many UKIP sympathisers, including Eurosceptic journalist, Christopher Booker. He told *The Times* he'd been sent the incriminating photograph over a year ago.

'I took the trouble to check the story and found that it was maliciously-inspired rubbish,' he said. 'I hope UKIP sympathisers will regard these smears as a backhanded tribute to the fears aroused in certain quarters by the support their party is attracting.'

A month after the election, *The Times* ran a brief apology to Nigel Farage for saying he had been in contact with political extremists in the BNP. 'We now understand that in 1997 Mr Farage briefly met a former UKIP member who had defected to the BNP, at that individual's request, to discuss his defection. We are happy to take this opportunity to set the record straight.'

On 10 June 1999, most of the UK electorate expressed their lack of interest in the European Union by not voting at all. Just 23% bothered to turn out, the lowest ever for a European election. When the votes were counted on the following Sunday, New Labour were the biggest losers, their 62 regional seats reduced to 29, 28% of the vote. In their core constituencies in northern England, the turnout had been especially poor. The Tories led the pack on 36% of the vote, gaining 18 seats to take them up to 36.

The Lib Dems improved their tally too, with eight more seats, giving them 10 in total and 13% of the vote, but this was disappointing for them as they had for so long argued that if PR was introduced they would do so much better, but now many of their traditional voters had gone to other protest parties. The Lib Dems had long been the protest vote party of choice for many people in general elections, enjoying a particularly loyal support in the South West where they always represented the anti-Westminster vote, but that region had been hammered by EU legislation that damaged their fishing industry. In 1997 some of their supporters had expressed this discontent by giving the Referendum Party their votes. Now, with PR on offer and an opportunity to vote for an anti-EU party—and with a higher overall turnout in the South West—they switched to UKIP. The Lib Dems were down by 15% in this region and, if it had been the general election, their leader Paddy

Ashdown would have lost his seat in Yeovil.

UKIP won three seats in the election. Their leader Michael Holmes, was elected in the South West with 10.6% of the vote; Nigel Farage won in the South East, with 9.7%; and Jeffrey Titford, a former funeral director, gained a seat in the Eastern region with 8.9%. Overall, UKIP had scooped up 696,057 votes, 7% of the voter share. It put them fourth behind the Lib Dems on 13%. Holmes was delighted. 'We were elected because so many of the electorate trusted our strident message that Britain should never give up the pound,' he said. 'It shows what a huge support there is for a Eurosceptic vote in this country.'

That was true, if you combined the Eurosceptic vote of William Hague's Tories, UKIP and the Greens, you got 49.3% of the total vote, as opposed to the joint pro-EU Labour and Lib Dems on 41%. The high level of Euroscepticism and Labour's failures to get out its core working-class voters was certainly a further nail in the coffin for any ideas Prime Minister Tony Blair might have had for winning a referendum on joining the Euro. When Michael Heseltine and Paddy Ashdown urged him to state clearly his support for the Euro, he avoided it, keeping to his mantra of campaigning for it only 'if the economic conditions were right'. The voters' lack of enthusiasm was clearly underlined by the poor performance of The Pro-Euro Conservative Party, with only 1.4% of the vote and 138,097 votes. The party disbanded in 2001 and one of its founding MEPs, John Stevens, joined the Lib Dems. In an article for the *Guardian*, Stevens invited Kenneth Clarke to leave the Tories and join him and his EU supporters. 'A new centre-right grouping,' he said, 'working in alliance with the Liberal Democrats, could be hugely successful.' He would have to wait a few more years for that.

Thanks to Proportional Representation, the Green Party finally won some of the seats they should have won in 1989. With 625,378 votes and 2.4% of the vote, they came directly behind UKIP, and this meant they were allocated two seats. Caroline Lucas, now a policy adviser to Oxfam, won her seat in the South East, while Jean Lambert, a former teacher, won in London. Lucas claimed many of their votes came from disgruntled Labour supporters. 'I lost count of the many traditional Labour supporters who have come up to me,' she said, 'and said they did not spend 20 years fighting Thatcherism only to have the Labour Party perpetuate those things.' It was a condemnation of Blair's New Labour. The Green's Eurosceptic credentials were dented, however, when they said they would work in alliance with other Green MEPs in the European Parliament, most of whom were fully behind the euro and backed the EU's institutions.

Although the trade unions were now fully behind the European project, some of their leaders were dismayed at Labour's poor performance in the European election and the distinctly Eurosceptic views stubbornly held by many of its core working-class voters.

'I always understood the new support was meant to be in addition to Labour's traditional support,' said John Monks, General Secretary of the TUC, referring to the middle class voters who had flocked to New Labour in 1997. 'The worrying Euro election results show real danger that some of it may now be at the expense of core support.' He feared that New Labour's focus on middle class concerns would alienate their older voters. 'Labour too often seems embarrassed by its traditional supporters and what they believe.' Then coining his notorious phrase, he said the party was treating them like 'embarrassing elderly relatives.'

Always one for demonising his rivals, Ashdown had hysterically derided the Tories for 'narrow nationalism'. He accused Hague of making a 'Faustian bargain with the extreme right.' Ashdown had already announced his resignation as party leader at the start of the year, but the party's disappointing performance under PR and the clear Euroscepticism of the British electorate left a bad taste in his mouth as he departed. He blamed Blair for not providing stronger pro-EU leadership during the election, as though that would stem the tide of anti-EU sentiment. He was furious at losing a seat in the South West to UKIP that he felt was Lib Dem. His just couldn't understand how so many Lib Dem supporters—the most pro-EU party—could actually be Eurosceptic at heart. Many Labour MPs were delighted at his departure as they had distinctly cooled on any further steps towards PR and were happy to see his successor,

Charles Kennedy, step away from any closer relations with Labour. Tony Blair followed their lead and confirmed his abandonment of his manifesto commitment to a referendum on PR before the next general election.

Champagne corks popped at UKIP HQ in recognition of their first electoral gains, but Nigel Farage was overwhelmed by the sudden change in his life. He was now a professional politician who would have to serve at the heart of an institution he abhorred. But, still the cheeky chappie, when a TV interviewer asked him if he would now be corrupted by an EU lifestyle of endless lavish dinners and champagne receptions, he shrugged and said 'No, I've always lived like that.'

To another journalist, he explained their purpose as MEPs.

'For us the really important reason for going over there is to find out the extent of the fraud, the waste and the corruption, to bring that information back to this country and expose that.'

Shortly after arriving in the European Parliament, Farage and his colleagues seized upon a mischief-making proposal. As Europhile Chris Patten took up his role as an EU Commissioner at a swearing-in ceremony, Farage confronted him over retaining his Rt Hon. status as a member of Her Majesty's Privy Council. Farage quoted Lord Denning, a former Master of the Rolls.

'[When] asked to rule on whether a Privy Counsellor could swear an oath of allegiance to the EU and retain his position within the British State, [Denning] said that a man cannot serve two sovereigns.'

Farage said Patten should resign at once as Privy Counsellor. (He did not.)

UKIP's success attracted a few defectors. The Earl of Bradford gave up the Tory whip to join them, saying Hague's stance on the euro was too soft. Other peers would follow. Teresa Gorman was a Tory MP for Billericay in Essex and renowned for her no-nonsense attitude. She had been a Maastricht rebel against John Major and now flirted with UKIP. Farage met her to discuss her possible defection, but a close source says they were appalled by her demands.

'She said she wanted to be leader, wanted to decide our policies and wanted to be paid,' claims the colleague. 'Do you or I tell her to f**k off?'

Gorman continued to be a draw at UKIP meetings, prompting one Tory at Central Office to say: 'It's a pain. If she is going to jump, why doesn't she just hurry up and do it?' She stood down as an MP in 2001, but has continued to support UKIP in her home borough of Thurrock.

But just as UKIP seemed to be riding a wave of popular acclaim, personality tensions within the party threatened to break it apart. It surfaced in the European Parliament. The three UKIP members had joined like-minded MEPs to form a Eurosceptic grouping called the Europe of Democracies and Diversities (EDD). This was important as it gave them access to a professional secretariat and speaking time, though Farage worked out that this amounted to just 90 seconds per person twice a week, at a cost to the taxpayer of £500 a second. He also quickly understood that MEPs were there not to question EU policy but to merely rubber-stamp it for implementation. All the decisions were made by the unelected European Commission and then presented to the European Parliament for their assent. So many measures were passed that MEPs frequently had little idea of what they were voting for and were simply instructed by Eurocrats which way to vote. Policies were hardly ever rejected.

Having done what was required of them, most MEPs then proceeded to their dinners and well lubricated meetings. It was a very comfortable lifestyle and UKIP leader Michael Holmes appeared to have gone native very quickly. Farage was appalled to see him give his maiden speech calling for an increase in powers for the European Parliament—exactly the opposite of what UKIP was about!

Back home at a party committee meeting, Holmes further enraged leading members by sacking them over alleged leaks. He survived a vote of no confidence at the following conference, but locks were changed and re-changed at their office in Regent Street as factions fought for control of the party. 'He is too combative and the wrong person to lead the party on to the next stage,' said one UKIP member. 'We need a leader capable of dealing, and striking up better relations, with other Eurosceptic groups.'

At this point, Rodney Atkinson, brother of the comedy actor Rowan best known for his portrayals of Blackadder and Mr Bean, entered the fray. Passionately anti-EU, claiming that it was a conspiracy founded by Nazis and Fascists, he put himself forward as the new leader. He had been a candidate for the Referendum Party in 1997 and stood as a UKIP candidate for the North East in 1999. He tried to indict the former Foreign Secretary Douglas Hurd for treason for signing the Maastricht Treaty.

'I am running to unite the party,' Atkinson told the press, 'and fight the notion that UKIP can work as an alternative government, which some in our party believe we can do. We must not stand against friends in other parties. I have great experience in fighting constitutional desecration on the altar of the EU.'

At a rowdy meeting in Westminster Central Hall in January 2000, Holmes was told to stand down. Furiously, he resigned and vowed to establish a rival party called Reform. 'The majority of party members are dedicated to the cause but have been badly let down by the small number of malcontents who have occupied positions of influence in the party's affairs,' he said.

'UKIP is the only vehicle through which to achieve our independence and the party will continue to prosper without Mr Holmes,' countered Farage and Jeffrey Titford. 'UKIP is conscious that our voters in the South West have been badly served and calls upon Mr Holmes to resign as an MEP in order that our supporters are properly represented.'

Holmes refused to give up his seat and sat as independent in the European Parliament.

'We are relieved that the infighting is now at an end,' said the two remaining UKIP MEPs. Some chance of that...

In April, Jeffrey Titford battled for the leadership against Atkinson and won by 16 votes. Atkinson blamed Farage for campaigning against him and said the party had lurched to the extreme Right. Over 200 fellow members resigned with him to join *Reform* and it looked as though UKIP would be fatally split.

'When UKIP was formed, it was helped enormously by being sucked into a political vacuum where no other moderate political party offered the honest policy of withdrawal from the EU,' declared a joint statement from the rebels. 'Now we fear that UKIP, through its tarnished reputation, bad organisation and structure, has become a liability in the fight for withdrawal from the EU.' Then came the usual criticism. 'Staying with UKIP tars us with an extremist brush.'

Nothing more came of Holmes, Atkinson or Reform, but Farage was very grateful that Holmes has since not spoken out bitterly against him or UKIP—unlike Dr Sked, who would continue to delight in haunting the party for many more years.

Joining the European parliamentary machine continues to cause tensions within UKIP. Tim Congdon, an influential economist and senior member of UKIP, is very much aware of this, but understands its practical purpose too.

'If you look at the history of UKIP, there is a lot of in-fighting and it is partly about the issue of how much we get involved with European institutions,' says Congdon. 'There is a paradox that it is precisely because UKIP has taken money from the European parliament that, of all the independence parties, it has been the one that has flourished. The money from the European parliament pays the party infrastructure.'

'UKIP receives no money from the British state at all,' emphasises Congdon, 'and yet look at how we have broken into British politics. For many years it has operated nationally on under half million pounds a year—outside an election year—that's less than the bonus of a City banker.'

8

OOPS, WE LET IN A MILLION!

Oops, we let in one million immigrants, when we said there'd only be 13,000 coming. That was the mistake that Jack Straw, former Home Secretary in New Labour's government, admitted in November 2013.

'One spectacular mistake in which I participated,' wrote Straw in the *Lancashire Telegraph*, 'was in lifting the transitional restrictions on the eastern European states like Poland and Hungary which joined the EU in mid-2004.' Thorough research by the Home Office had suggested there would be only between 5,000 and 13,000 immigrants per year up to 2010. 'Events proved these forecasts worthless,' said Straw. 'Net migration reached close to a quarter of a million at its peak in 2010. Lots of red faces, mine included.'

Red faces indeed! This is the narrative that the Labour party has preferred to express since losing power in 2010, that it was all a dreadful mistake for which they are really sorry. But there are those in the Labour movement who believe this is untrue and that mass immigration was a deliberate policy that has been a disaster for the working class in the UK and the Labour Party itself. It has been one of the principal reasons for the rise of the smaller protest parties

'It was a matter of deliberate policy,' says John Edmonds, former General Secretary of the GMB. 'It wasn't an accident.' It was the deliberate result of Chancellor Gordon Brown's vision for the British economy.

'Brown believed that the model for an innovative economy was the [United] States not Germany and not Japan,' explains the 69-year-old Edmonds, who, like other trade-union leaders at the time, was in constant discussions with the Chancellor. 'This was the great mistake because the model in the States is low labour regulation, low minimum wage—all that he thought was part of a fast-growing innovative economy. Now that's a bastard for us.'

Edmonds wanted to see highly skilled workers in manufacturing industries, as in Germany, but Brown and Blair said this was never going to happen in post-industrial Britain and favoured a shift from manufacturing to the service industries, especially the financial services sector.

'During this period there is a massive redundancy of people in manufacturing,' remembers Edmonds. 'Most of those people got worse jobs in the service sector, not just in pay, but in terms of security and job opportunity.'

It hit manufacturing unions badly, union membership went down and trade-union activity went down too, which had a knock-on effect on grassroots campaigning for the Labour Party. '[But] Blair is not going to get upset because there are fewer trade union activists in the Labour party. I mean this is paradise,' chuckles Edmonds. 'Blair didn't want members of the Labour party, he wanted voters.'

Then came the central role of mass immigration in this New Labour economic plan for Britain.

'The other part of the Brown philosophy is to control wages by having low entry rates,' continues Edmonds. 'The way to do this is you get as many women as possible into the labour market, you have an active immigration policy, and you make sure kids don't get the benefit of the minimum wage—and those are the three things he held to. Immigration—so there is a ready supply of labour and he knows that immigrants don't get jobs commensurate with their skills—they go in at the bottom. So the way to keep entry rates down is immigration, low minimum wage for everybody... The political consequences of that are pretty bloody obvious. It's buggered up the Labour vote. It took two elections to do it.'

'It gives a bit of a side light on the conversation with Mrs Duffy,' concludes Edmonds, referring to the embarrassing scene when Prime Minister Brown insulted a Labour voter for complaining about immigration. 'Because "doesn't she know it is part of my economic policy." Brown was all the time the driver of these policies.'

Other trade-union leaders felt there was little alternative to Gordon Brown's economic policy. John Monks, now Lord Monks, was General Secretary of the Trades Union Congress (TUC).

'It was understandable,' he says. 'We'd being trying, since the war, to keep up with Germany, as far as manufacturing was concerned and we'd not succeeded.' Oil revenues during the Thatcher years and financial services revenues in the 90s cushioned the economy. 'It was a kind of alchemy. We felt we didn't have to worry about the things we'd worried about before.'

Lord Monks does not believe mass immigration was a deliberate policy, preferring to subscribe to the cock-up version. 'I think it was a massive underestimate. The TUC at the time weren't worried about it. We tended to believe the estimate for that might be a bit more than that.' Monks believed there were more than enough jobs to go round for Eastern European workers. He saw it as positive addition to the British workplace with migrants bringing in higher productivity. 'I often said in the TUC, we never did anything for Poland in 1939, we never did anything for Poland in 1945, but we've done something for Poland now.'

Looking back at New Labour's immigration announcements in 2000, it certainly seems they were keen to push the economic argument—but perhaps not that keen to tell anyone else about it who was not a trusted apparatchik...

*

Barbara Roche is undeniably multicultural. She is a 'living, breathing melting-pot', born to a Polish-Russian Jewish father and a Spanish-Portuguese Jewish mother in London's East End—the traditional home for newcomers to Britain for hundreds of years. Her husband combines Irish, French and Yorkshire heritages.

In 2000, the 46-year-old former lawyer and Oxford graduate was MP for Hornsey and Wood Green in Haringey in North London with a large multicultural electorate. She was also Minister of State in the Home Office during Tony Blair's first term of New Labour government—when Britain was still revelling in the Cool Britannia tag that made the nation seem young and hip again after 18 years of Tory rule. Her brief was immigration and she was gung-ho about it.

'I wanted to be the first immigration minister to say immigration is a good thing,' she told a left-wing journal that year. 'We have a multiracial, multicultural society; we are a stronger country for it.'

Her opportunity came in September 2000 when she had to deliver a speech at an Institute for Public Policy Research (IPPR) conference in the City of London. It was based on a report produced by the Performance and Innovation Unit (PIU), a think tank at the heart of the Cabinet Office, full of smart young people tasked with making policy for Tony Blair's government. It was to be a major statement of the government's policy on immigration and Andrew Neather, a leading young speechwriter for the Prime Minister and other top New Labour figures, was given the task of writing it for her. Before entering government, he'd been a Cambridge graduate and edited a journal for *Friends of the Earth*.

Neather was shown early drafts of the PIU's report and later said it made him feel uncomfortable. 'Drafts were handed out in summer 2000 only with extreme reluctance: there was a paranoia about it reaching the media,' he recalled. It was eventually published in January 2001. 'But the earlier drafts I saw also included a driving political purpose: that mass immigration was the way that the Government was going to make the UK truly multicultural.'

Neather went further. 'I remember coming away from some discussions with the clear sense that the policy was intended—even if this wasn't its main purpose—to rub the Right's nose in diversity and render their arguments out of date. That seemed to me to be a manoeuvre too far.'

The New Labour government wanted to avoid any controversy on what they considered a sensitive topic. 'Ministers were very nervous about the whole thing,' remembered Neather. 'For despite Roche's keenness to make her big speech and to be upfront, there was a reluctance elsewhere in government to discuss what increased immigration would mean, above all for Labour's core white working-class vote.'

Certainly there was little in the PIU's report on the negative effects mass immigration would have on working-class communities. It concentrated on the economic benefits of immigration—said nothing about the cheap entry rates cited by Edmonds—and amusingly emphasised the wonders of a multicultural society. Among the pleasures it claimed was a boom in curry houses and a wide range of restaurants serving Indian, Chinese and Thai food. It also listed many of the Booker literary prize-winners as coming from abroad, as were three of the four artists short-listed for the Turner art prize in 2000. Residents of the sleepy Lincolnshire town of Boston who would play host to 7,000 immigrants from Eastern Europe by the end of the decade—one in ten of their population—would see Polish and Romanian restaurants sprouting up along their high street and a plunge in wages but they could at least console themselves with the hope that among these new settlers was perhaps a prize-winning conceptual artist.

Looking closely at the earlier drafts of the PIU report that Neather had seen in the summer of 2000, it is clear that those few negative aspects of mass immigration that did manage to get on paper were even too much for New Labour to contemplate and these were later removed from the final published version.

A large section on criminal behaviour among immigrants, which mentioned foreign-organised crime gangs alongside illegal trafficking of drugs and women, disappeared from the final report. As did a reference to asylum seekers 'more likely to be unemployed.' Indefensible phrases were edited out, such as 'no evidence that people feel "swamped" in a cultural sense'.

On page 60 of the July 2000 draft of the report came the shocking statement that 'as older cohorts die off, attitudes towards immigration will continue to improve.' Apparently, the death of old people was recognised by New Labour as a useful ally to the creation of a multicultural Britain. The writers of the report suggested that 'younger people and those with higher education are much less likely to be racist and hence anti-immigrant.' This sentence echoed the New Labour mantra that to be anti-immigration was also to be racist. All this did not make the final edit.

'The concentration of migrants in specific locations can also generate social effects,' admitted an original version of the report, 'for example through the competition for jobs and resources in local markets. There is at least anecdotal evidence that high concentrations of migrant children lacking English as a first language can lead to pressure on schools which lack sufficient resources to meet levels of need, and to some concern and resentment among other parents.'

That reference to 'resentment' was later edited out and a more positive spin given to the passage by saying these problems would be dealt with by 'increased funding from DfEE for schools taking on the children of asylum seekers, and by the fact that children recently arrived from overseas who have difficulties with English will not be included in the figures for school performance league tables.' Lying through one's teeth, apparently, was better than the truth.

A section about the impact of immigration on Low Skilled Workers was also removed in which the PIU claimed that foreign low skilled workers were not likely 'to significantly harm either the employment or income prospects of low-skilled natives.'

That was fundamentally wrong, argues Edmonds, Brown wanted to use immigration to keep wages low. 'What tends to happen is everything settles down[wards],' says Edmonds. 'An awful lot of employers find they can recruit on low wages, they can recruit a pound or two more than the minimum wage because there are so many minimum wage jobs about... The way to keep entry rates down is immigration, low minimum wage for everybody.'

They did keep in the admission that 'we know relatively little about migration—in particular the characteristics and motivations of different migrants and their (likely differing) economic and social impacts and experiences.' You're telling me! Should anyone dredge up the report in the future to embarrass its writers, it was a handy phrase to have to hand.

Aside from the talented young graduate researchers who wrote this report, the findings were based on two workshops filled with academics, representatives of New Labour government departments and pro-immigration pressure groups. Jitinder Kohli represented PIU. There were no councillors from deprived areas, nor union representatives, in fact, no one who might be directly affected by mass immigration.

*

When it came to Home Office Minister Barbara Roche standing up on the morning of 11 September 2000 to deliver her landmark speech about New Labour's policy on immigration to an audience of bankers, Andrew Neather had done his job well.

'Britain has always been a nation of migrants,' she declared. The government was not only there to protect Britain from external pressures, 'We also need to manage the opportunities.' She said that the first attempt at immigration controls in the 1905 Aliens Act was 'a direct response to Jewish immigration and it is difficult to deny that it was motivated in part by anti-Semitism.'

She then quoted an Edwardian MP speaking in support of the legislation, who warned his opponents 'do not live in daily terror of being turned into the street to make room for an unsavoury Pole.' That MP, said Roche with pride, 'would be spinning in his grave if he knew that their descendant would not only be the Immigration Minister but would be standing before you today making this speech.'

Roche explained that the 1971 Immigration Act was the basis of current legislation that pursued the policy that the numbers of migrants to Britain needed to be controlled and should be largely restricted to those with family ties or special skills. 'The Act, did not, of course, end all immigration, nor was it intended to do so,' she said.

From 1972 to 1998, around 60,000 immigrants arrived in Britain every year. When the UK joined the European Economic Community in 1973, European citizens of any member state were given the right to settle in Britain, but, coming from prosperous states speaking different languages, few of them took up the offer. Come 1998, however, the year after New Labour came to power, one survey estimated that there was a total of over a million foreigners working legally in the UK, almost half a million of them being EU nationals.

The headlining problem of bogus asylum seekers using humanitarian legislation to enter Britain to work had dented the debate about the positive value of immigration in 2000. Just the year before, this figure had risen to 71,000 applications and was going ever upwards. 'But, in ensuring that we crack down where necessary on misuse,' said Roche, 'we must not lose sight of the bigger picture.'

The New Labour model for the economic benefits of migration was the US—as Edmonds says. Roche quoted the Federal Reserve Chairman as saying that America's longest ever boom was thanks in part to 11 million immigrants in the 1990s. Britain could emulate that. Plus, with an aging population, who was going to do the jobs and pay the taxes in the UK in the future?

Roche put the emphasis on attracting entrepreneurs and IT workers from other countries to fill our skills gaps. She didn't mention the hundreds of thousands of low-skilled foreign workers who would take up jobs in service industries that could be filled by Britain's own unemployed if they hadn't become addicted to benefits. 'We must ensure that immigration policy continues to serve the national interest,' she concluded. 'And if we ensure that it does, then I believe that we can face a new century of migration with confidence.'

The speech was generally well received and, mercifully for Tony Blair, did not trigger anti-immigration headlines in the tabloids. The *Economist* said Roche made the economic argument for increased immigration, but quoted a demographer saying that this migration would have to take place on a massive scale to make up for the declining birth-rate and increased life expectancy. No one anticipated the UK population would grow by at least two million over the next decade mainly fuelled by immigrants and their babies. The *Economist* noted archly that her speech was light on specific policy, concluding that the 'approach of the next election may make this more reasonable debate on immigration short-lived.'

The BBC reported that Roche had said that 'the UK should consider relaxing immigration controls in order to attract "wealth creators" to meet Britain's skills shortages.' She didn't actually say 'relax immigration controls'. New Labour would never have allowed that—but that's exactly what the policy was meant to achieve.

'After announcing tax measures to drive IT professionals out of the UK when at the Treasury,' commented the Conservative shadow home secretary sourly, 'Barbara Roche is saying that we need to attract more of them into the country now she is immigration minister.'

Despite this little bit of carping, Roche and Neather had successfully achieved their aim of announcing a major new shift in government policy towards immigration—an open door policy that would transform the high streets of the UK forever—but making it seem as innocuous and uncontroversial as possible. Indeed, in perfect New Labour speak, she was merely 'calling for a debate'.

Nine years later, Andrew Neather felt this was rather sneaky. New Labour had not announced its mass immigration intentions in its 1997 manifesto—so at no time did the population have an opportunity to vote on the initiation of this policy.

'But ministers wouldn't talk about it,' he recalled. 'In part they probably realised the conservatism of their core voters: while ministers might have been passionately in favour of a more diverse society, it wasn't necessarily a debate they wanted to have in working men's clubs in Sheffield or Sunderland.'

It was also a very London argument, confirming the view that government policy was being made by a metropolitan elite. Indeed, Neather identified with their views, saying his South London family would be lost without their Eastern European nannies and he liked the fact that the richness of variety in the capital made Paris look parochial. So much so 'that it's pretty much unimaginable for us to go back either to the past or the sticks.'

Neather's openness about the secret processes behind New Labour's 'swamp 'em' immigration policy was written for the London *Evening Standard* in October 2009. It was intended apparently as a call merely to 'debate' further immigration into London.

'Of course we're too small a country to afford an open door,' concluded Neather, 'but, by the same token, if the immigrants dry up, this city and this country will become a much poorer and less interesting place. Why is it so hard for Gordon Brown to say that?'

Well, the centre-right pounced on this admission by someone at heart of the New Labour policy machine.

'The huge increases in migrants over the last decade were partly due to a politically motivated attempt by ministers to radically change the country,' raged the *Telegraph* later that day. They then quoted Sir Andrew Green, chairman of Migrationwatch. 'Now at least the truth is out, and it's dynamite,' he said. 'Many have long suspected that mass immigration under Labour was not just a cock up but also a conspiracy. They were right. This Government has admitted three million immigrants for cynical political reasons concealed by dodgy economic camouflage.'

Labour MP Frank Field and Tory MP Nicholas Soames, chairmen of the cross-party Group for Balanced Migration, agreed: 'We welcome this statement by an ex-adviser, which the whole country knows to be true. It is the first beam of truth that has officially been shone on the immigration issue in Britain.'

Such was the outrage at the admission that New Labour had deliberately and irrevocably transformed Britain for political purposes that the New Labour Home Secretary, Alan Johnson, had to make a speech on the subject and apologise.

Just over a week after the revelation in *The Evening Standard,* Johnson stood up before an audience at the Royal Society of Arts in central London.

'Whilst I accept that governments of both persuasions, including this one, have been maladroit in their handling of this issue,' he said. 'I do believe that the UK is now far more successful at tackling migration than most of its European and North American neighbours.'

'There are communities which have been disproportionately affected by immigration,' he admitted, 'where people have legitimate concerns about the strain that the growth in the local population has placed on jobs and services.'

He refuted strongly the implication of Neather's claims that there had been a conspiracy in 2000 to inflict mass immigration on the UK population.

'As I've said, our record is not perfect' he continued. 'When we came in to government in 1997, there was no magic button we could push immediately to resolve all the historic, political and operation problems associated with immigration. The legacy problems with unreturned foreign national prisoners and asylum seekers may have accumulated under previous administrations, but they continued to be ignored for far too long on our watch.'

The problem was that when Johnson had first got his job a few months earlier he'd said he did not 'lie awake at night' worrying about the UK population heading towards 70 million thanks to immigration, but now, following 'Neather-gate', 'I want to talk about immigration today, tomorrow, next week and on any occasion I can.'

Government critics were far from mollified.

'This apology is three million immigrants too late,' said Sir Andrew Green. 'We now know that some of his colleagues deliberately encouraged mass immigration so as to engineer a multicultural society in the full knowledge that they were flying in the face of public opinion, especially their own working-class supporters.'

Somewhat distraught at having opened up this disastrous can of worms for New Labour—and maybe fearing he'd plunged down to the bottom of any metropolitan dinner party guest list—Andrew Neather rapidly explained his reasoning behind his admission. He did it by repeating his initial accusation that 'my sense from several discussions was there was also a subsidiary political purpose to [mass immigration]—boosting diversity and undermining the Right's opposition to multiculturalism. I was not comfortable with that. But it wasn't the main point at issue.'

He felt that had now been distorted by the right-wing press into a rage about a plot to inflict multiculturalism on Britain. 'There was no plot,' he stated. 'I've worked closely with Ms Roche and Jack Straw and they are both decent, honourable people whom I respect.'

He did feel, however, there was a certain 'nervousness' that came from Tony Blair who did not want to be associated with the report. 'According to my notes of one meeting in mid-July 2000, held at the PIU's offices in Admiralty Arch,' he recalled, 'there was a debate about whether the report should be published by the PIU or by the Home Office: the PIU didn't think the Prime Minister wanted his "prints" on it.'

John Edmonds believes that the political element to the

immigration policy may well have been bandied about to appeal to Labour MPs, but it was not the core reason for it. 'That was a political justification,' he said, 'that I am certain had an economic motive.'

Just over a month after this scandal burst came the official figures that revealed that Britain had indeed been 'swamped' by immigrants during the New Labour years. The Office for National Statistics said that one in ten of the UK population had now been born abroad. This portion had doubled in the past two decades to 11% or 6.7 million people. The major factor in this increase had been the arrival of migrant workers from Eastern European countries newly admitted into the EU. They had increased from 114,000 in 2001 to 689,000 in 2008. A tenth of them were children. In addition to this, those children born to foreign mothers had also reached a peak of 24% of total births in England and Wales—that is, 170,834—the highest level since records began in 1969.

'This is a measure of the way in which our society is being changed without the British public ever having been consulted,' said Sir Andrew Green of Migrationwatch. 'Immigration on this scale can only add to the strains in our society and the pressure on our public services. These figures confirm the enormous impact of mass immigration on our society.'

It did indeed and this succession of facts and revelations was a gift to those politicians who had long campaigned against open-door immigration. But the curious thing was that the ultimate beneficiary of this at the ballot box would not be those hard-right groups who marched through decaying town centres but that gentleman with the fag and a pint who'd been banging on about Europe for so long.

In the meantime, Barbara Roche had lost her job as an MP. She had found out what 'we know relatively little about migration' meant when she was kicked out in 2005 by immigrant voters angry at Tony Blair's invasion of Iraq. She remains a keen advocate of immigration and supported the creation of a museum devoted to migration. 'I have never been in favour of unrestricted migration,' she surprisingly told the *Guardian* in 2011. Undaunted, she continues to defend the shambolic government record, arguing, '[I]t was a landmark speech. When I arrived at the Home Office there was no coherent migration policy.'

Andrew Neather continues at the *Evening Standard* as its Comment Editor and has branched out into wine criticism.

*

The beauty of an open-door immigration policy, from the point of view of New Labour, was that aside from discreetly announcing it in Barbara Roche's speech, they had nothing else to do. Geopolitical forces just took over and sent hundreds of thousands of people their way. It was laissez-faire economics at its most efficient. In the 1990s, thousands of economic refugees from the world's trouble spots exploited the UK's asylum system. In 2004, eight Eastern European countries joined the EU and hundreds of thousands of their citizens came to work and settle in Britain. Of course, the converse to this was that if any of this generated negative headlines for the government, there really was nothing they could do about it!

Another brilliant dimension of open-door immigration, from New Labour's point of view, was that any objectors to this massive influx of foreigners could be called 'racist'—a term which had grown more and more damaging to anyone's reputation and career from 1997 onwards. So cowered were traditional critics of immigration in the Conservative party that any debate on immigration in the early 2000s could barely get off the ground. Indeed, by the time Cameron took over the party in 2005 it was virtually off limits and reserved for only the nuttier elements of the party who stood no chance of advancement.

This was largely down to associations with a speech made nearly four decades earlier by the senior Conservative politician Enoch Powell in Birmingham in April 1968. Dubbed the 'Rivers of Blood' speech, he had spoken out against Commonwealth immigration and its impact on future generations.

'We must be mad, literally mad, as a nation to be permitting the annual inflow of some 50,000 dependants, who are for the most part the material of the future growth of the immigrant descended population,' he thundered. 'It is like watching a nation busily engaged in heaping up its own funeral pyre.'

He feared that parts of Britain were being transformed beyond recognition and that immigrants would soon occupy a privileged position in British society, competing for services that would breed resentment among the native population.

'For reasons which they could not comprehend, and in pursuance of a decision by default, on which they were never consulted, they found themselves made strangers in their own country,' he said. 'They found their wives unable to obtain hospital beds in childbirth, their children unable to obtain school places, their homes and neighbourhoods changed beyond recognition, their plans and prospects for the future defeated….they began to hear, as time went by, more and more voices which told them that they were now the unwanted.'

It was a vision of the future that many working class might agree with today. Indeed, at the time, a poll claimed that 74% of people agreed with him. The problem was that many of the people he quoted saw immigration at that time in terms of skin colour. One of the most incendiary phrases in his speech was when he quoted a constituent saying 'In this country in 15 or 20 years' time the black man will have the whip hand over the white man.' It conjured up images of slavery and imperialism and seemed horribly locked in a dubious past.

This only got worse when Powell alluded to race riots in America, but being a classical scholar, he gave it a Latin twist. 'As I look ahead, I am filled with foreboding,' he said 'Like the Roman, I seem to see "the River Tiber foaming with much blood".'

These vivid but hyperbolic sound bites sealed Powell's fate. Within days, he was sacked from the shadow cabinet, condemned by the press, and most senior politicians of all parties distanced themselves from him. His speech did, however, have some currency with working-class voters and a thousand East End London dockers marched in support of him to Westminster, carrying banners that said 'Back Britain, not Black Britain.'. We are representatives of the working man,' said their leader. 'We are not racialists.' Many others went on strike, demanding his re-instatement, but events took a nasty turn when an immigrant family reported being attacked by yobs chanting 'Powell' and 'Why don't you go back to your own country?'

It all meant that any discussion of immigration in Britain for the next 40 years would be framed in Powell-ite terms of racial conflict. It seemed increasingly old-fashioned, like the character of Alf Garnett in the popular late 1960s and early 1970s BBC TV comedy series Till Death Us Do Part. The show satirised its lead 50-something working-class character as a bigot and racist and yet, perversely, by putting the most colourful language in his mouth made him a popular comedy star. The series was dropped in 1975 and is never repeated now, despite its comic cult status.

More importantly, it meant that as the mainstream political parties stepped away from such an attitude, it was left to fringe parties to express the discontent of the electorate towards immigration—and they were openly racist.

The National Front (NF) had been founded in 1967 and by the early 1970s was attracting a membership of around 20,000. It was not originally a neo-Nazi party as its critics liked to claim, but it did demand the compulsory repatriation of all non-white immigrants—it did not oppose whites from abroad already settled in the country. It had 50 local branches and the majority of its membership was working class. People concerned about competition with immigrants in the job market and for council housing, as well as those who just didn't like 'black faces'. It also campaigned against the European Economic Community and for Ulster loyalists. Its banner was the Union Jack—establishing a link between the Union flag and racist parties which many resented. Its clear anti-immigrant stance attracted voters in the early 1970s. At the West Bromwich by-election in 1973, the NF candidate won 4,789 votes—16% of the poll—raising eyebrows in Westminster.

The National Front continued to attract nationalist voters throughout the 1970s, despite its leadership being taken over by John Tyndall and Martin Webster, who were exposed as having genuine neo-Nazi links. In 1976, in local elections in the heavily Asian populated Leicester, their candidates won 14,566 votes, nearly 20% of the total. In Greater London Council elections the following year, the NF attracted 119,060 votes and beat the Liberal party in several wards. Provocative marches and riots followed, with punk bands reflecting the racial tension of the time in their raucous music.

'White riot—I wanna riot,' sang *The Clash*. 'White riot—a riot of my own.' In 1978, however, Margaret Thatcher, the newly elected leader of the Conservative party—taking over from the liberal Edward Heath, who had sacked Powell from the shadow cabinet—made a major public statement about immigration. She had no truck with racism, she said, but did she understand some of the frustration felt by NF supporters.

'In my view, that is one thing that is driving some people to the National Front,' Thatcher told the ITV political programme *World in Action*. 'They do not agree with the objectives of the National Front, but they say that at least they are talking about some of the problems. Now, we are a big political party. If we do not want people to go to extremes, and I do not, we ourselves must talk about this problem and we must show that we are prepared to deal with it.'

'We are a British nation with British characteristics,' she continued. 'Every country can take some small minorities and in many ways they add to the richness and variety of this country. The moment the minority threatens to become a big one, people get frightened.'

She said her Tory party was committed to reducing the level of immigration into the UK.

'So, either you go on taking in 40 or 50,000 a year,' she said, 'which is far too many, or you say we must hold out the prospect of a clear end to immigration and that is the view we have taken and I am certain that is the right view to keep good race relations and to keep fundamental British characteristics which have done so much for the world.'

'So,' wondered the interviewer, hoping for a Powell-like blunder, 'some of the support that the National Front has been attracting in recent by-elections you would hope to bring back behind the Tory party?'

'Oh, very much back,' said Thatcher assuredly, but then added cheekily 'I think that the National Front has, in fact, attracted more people from Labour voters than from us, but never be afraid to tackle something which people are worried about. We are not in politics to ignore peoples' worries: we are in politics to deal with them.'

It was a skilled performance that walked the tight rope of racial controversy but it showed she was reaching out to voters who felt they had nowhere else to go to vent their anger than the NF. Come 1979 and the general election, and some of those working-class NF supporters shifted their votes to the Tory party and Thatcher was in.

The NF did not go away in the 1980s but its appeal was much diminished and it split into bizarre factions. One of its leaders, John Tyndall, formed the British National Party (BNP) in 1982. It was this that now took up the banner of anti-immigrant working-class resentment in the 1990s. Young racist football hooligans were attracted to it as a vehicle for fighting and it seemed unlikely to win any major support from the electorate. Many of the working class that had voted for Thatcher in the 1980s now cast their votes for a New Labour party more in tune with their aspirations in the late 1990s.

For a moment, immigration seemed to be less of a problem. Many more people were relaxed now about a multicultural Britain— it seemed part of the modernising of their country, which on the whole they seemed to enjoy. There was also a revolution in attitudes among the younger working class towards racism. No longer influenced by the 'colonial' prejudices of older generations, many young people, especially those living on council estates, were fans of American black culture. It was tough, fit and cool and they began to ape the manners and style of hip-hop groups. They integrated more easily with the descendents of West Indian immigrants and no longer saw them as rivals for jobs. This was partly because many of the young living on council estates were now supported by state benefits—not jobs—and they had relatively little to complain about.

It was against this background that Tony Blair and New Labour felt confident enough to take their foot off the pedal of immigration control in 2000. Young people were essentially cool with immigration and those grumpy old voters who'd dallied with the NF were dying off—according to their own report. Tories were terrified of sounding Powell-ite. Roche made her speech and Neather said nothing about his doubts. Then came 2004 and the accession of Eastern European countries to the EU. That would significantly change the whole debate about mass immigration— and would mean that the BNP and UKIP would go head-to-head on this touchy subject.

9

MARCHING ON THE STREETS

Like any party, you wonder, will they come? The 52-year-old blonde, strikingly good-looking Baroness Mallalieu wondered this in July 1997 in Hyde Park when she helped organise a rally for country folk appalled by New Labour's proposal to ban hunting.

'Would they come?' she recalled. 'I still never forget how they came, streaming in though every gate of the park—country people totally distinctive from their city cousins, flocking towards those giant balloons.

'The marchers, the speakers, the singing and I shall never forget a sound engineer—a West Indian—hanging off the stage gantry staring in astonishment at tens of thousands of people as far as the eye could see singing John Peel at the tops of their voices. His expression was that of an explorer who had unexpectedly come across an undiscovered tribe engaged in some strange rituals in a forest clearing.'

As the years of Tony Blair's government progressed, it appeared to many that a metropolitan elite was foisting its views on large swathes of the country, fuelled by an urban prejudice against a way of life it knew little about. The interesting thing was that many of its opponents, including the Baroness Mallalieu, were not typical hunting and fishing conservatives.

Ann Mallalieu came from a distinguished family of left-leaning politicians. Her grandfather had been a Liberal MP for Colne Valley while her father, Joseph Mallalieu, was Labour MP for Huddersfield. At 16, she pinned on her CND badge and marched off to the Aldermaston anti-nuclear weapons protests in the early 1960s. The first woman president of the Cambridge Union, Ann had a successful career as a top barrister. Married to an equally successful QC, they were a golden couple. She continued to be interested in protest politics, campaigning for women's rights, and in 1991 she was made a Labour peer. Her great love, however, was the countryside and she made it a condition of marrying her husband that he take up hunting. On his first outing, he broke his leg. She loved living in their second home near Exmoor and was a regular rider with the Exmoor Hunt and the Devon and Somerset Staghounds.

When New Labour swept into power in May 1997, one of their manifesto pledges was to introduce a free vote in Parliament about banning hunting with hounds. Mindful of their enormous majority, the leaders of three organisations—The Countryside Business Group, the British Field Sports Society and the Countryside Movement—had already come together a few weeks earlier under the umbrella of a Countryside Alliance (CA). Ann Mallalieu was not part of the initial discussions that led to the three groups coming together, but it was at the Hyde Park rally on 10 July that she demonstrated her talents as a figurehead for the campaign. She became the CA's President, partly because she was a Labour peer and partly because she had the media skills.

'I think the combination of somebody who was Labour and supported hunting was useful,' she recalls, 'but also they quite wanted a younger woman rather than an elderly military type, which at one stage was the image the Alliance had.'

In the days running up to the Hyde Park rally, the CA invited a cabinet minister to speak—Jack Straw being their first choice—but no one was available. On the morning of the rally this suddenly changed.

'I got a call from Downing Street,' says Mallalieu. 'They said what can we do now. I said at least you can send a message. "What would you like it to say?" I dictated the message and it was read out to the crowd, who were deeply unimpressed. [The government] missed a serious opportunity to come forward and be part of it.'

As tens of thousands of people poured into the central London park, William Hague, the newly elected leader of the Conservative Party, could see its value and so could Michael Heseltine, the former

Tory Deputy Prime Minister. When Heseltine addressed the crowd, he said the proposed hunting ban would only satisfy the 'bigotry and prejudice of people whose concept of rural life owes more to Walt Disney than to any appreciation of the world as it is.'

Actor Robert Hardy read the G.K. Chesterton poem 'The Secret People', which boomed out over the loudspeaker system with the refrain: 'For we are the people of England, that never have spoken yet.'

When Baroness Mallalieu took to the stage, her speech moved away from the narrow interests of hunting—to which most people would probably object or feel neutral about—towards a more overarching concern about an assault on lifestyle and freedom. If a government can choose to ban something because they simply don't like it, what else could they do?

'We cannot and will not stand by in silence and watch our countryside, our communities and our way of life destroyed for ever by misguided urban political correctness,' she told the audience. 'This rally is not just about hunting. Many people, perhaps most of those here today, don't hunt. It is about freedom, the freedom of people to choose how they live their own lives.'

'It is about tolerance of minorities,' she continued, 'and sadly those who live in and work in the countryside are now a minority. It is about listening to and respecting the views of other people of which you may personally disapprove. Many people don't want to fish or shoot or hunt—some dislike these things. Let them try and persuade those who disagree with them by reasoned argument but do not try to pass laws to make those you have failed to convince into criminals.'

It was the first major shot across the bows of the New Labour government and its urban liberal elite, but it was not just coming from some angry conservative opponent, far from it. Towards the end of her speech, she made it clear she was a Labour supporter. She blamed the bill on rogue Labour MPs and hoped that Tony Blair's government would see the bigger picture

'We do not want this fight,' she said. 'It is not of our own making. We do not want conflict between the town and the country. We do not want a nation divided. We want others to share and enjoy the countryside with us. To our newly elected Members of Parliament we say this: we elected you in the hope that you would provide more of our people with new and better opportunities to do more with their lives. We did not elect you to lecture us on morality or to criminalise hundreds and thousands of our decent law-abiding people.'

The response of the crowd was summed up by one Devon farmer. 'I went there feeling this small,' he later told the Baroness. 'I came away feeling 10 feet tall.'

Mallalieu had brilliantly articulated the voices of thousands of people—not just in rural communities—who would feel increasingly ignored by the New Labour government. With 418 MPs behind him, however, 145 of them newly elected, Tony Blair could afford to shrug off the Baroness' warning. What did he care about the rural electorate, when most of them returned Conservative MPs? It was a battle he could press forward without losing too many casualties. Besides, after 18 years in opposition, many Labour MPs were keen to inflict a cultural blow on supposedly Conservative voters and their MPs, equivalent to that dealt by Thatcher against the trade unions and working-class communities. But the Labour Baroness Mallalieu believes this was not a battle that Tony Blair wanted.

'I think they walked into it,' says Mallalieu. 'They did not want a battle at all. They had accepted money.' This was the £1m given to the Labour Party in 1997 by the Political Animal Lobby (PAL), closely linked to the International Fund for Animal Welfare, both founded by the Canadian animal rights activist Brian Davies. In London, PAL's office was run by Angela Beveridge, sister of the outspoken anti-hunting Labour MP Tony Banks.

'They had put over £1m into the Labour Party and they had bought off the other parties with smaller donations,' says Mallalieu. '[Labour's] animal welfare spokesman was Elliot Morley. His office had been funded by them. There were financial reasons behind the pressure, but nonetheless those at the centre of government at that time did not want this—certainly Peter Mandelson was opposed to it. Tony Blair had no real interest at all. I remember them saying "oh, we leave animal things to Elliot" so that meant leaving it to the animal rights pressure groups.'

Blair then accidentally trapped himself into personally supporting the ban when he 'misspoke' on BBC TV's Question Time programme in July 1999. Responding to a question on hunting, he unguardedly said his government would have a vote to ban it as soon as possible. 'From that moment on they were trying to backtrack,' says the Baroness, 'but he'd got himself locked in.'

Jack Straw, then Home Secretary, backs this up in his memoirs. 'To me, banning it was a nonsense issue for a serious party making a determined bid for government after 18 years in opposition,' wrote Straw. 'It was best left alone. But it crept into the manifesto in a suitably ambiguous form—until Tony, who didn't think it important either, went on Question Time, was put on the spot and announced he'd support a ban. I went to see him the next day to ask him why. "I'm very sorry, Jack," he said. "I misspoke."'

'They got themselves in a position where the Parliamentary Labour Party saw it as a totemic issue,' says Mallalieu, who remembers attending a meeting held by Jack Straw. She noted the biggest cheer came when one of the backbenchers stood up and said 'This isn't about foxes, it's about who rules Britain—us or the Tory toffs.' Straw robustly rebuffed this. 'But that was the mood of the Parliamentary Labour Party. Then it became an issue of who makes the policy—do we do it or does Tony Blair? That was the point at which [Blair] gave in—very weakly.'

The CA had several private meetings with New Labour to resolve this issue.

'There clearly came a point when Tony Blair realised he'd made a dreadful mistake and there were meetings to try and alter things,' says Mallalieu. 'We went in repeatedly. We would see Jonathan Powell [Blair's Chief of Staff] on each occasion. We would take him an analysis of where we were and what the Labour party should do to avoid the problems. They were very courteous and pleasant and they would never follow what we said.'

A second reading of a private member's bill against hunting, introduced by Labour MP Michael Foster, got 411 votes in support, but ran out of parliamentary time in 1999. Then followed the government's attempt to kick the subject into the long grass with the Burns Report in 2000. A second bill also ran out of time as the

House of Commons voted for an outright ban, but the House of Lords called for self-regulation. With New Labour re-elected in 2001, Labour MPs resumed their campaign with Margaret Beckett, newly appointed Environment, Food and Rural Affairs Secretary, making it clear that she wanted to see it in the Queen's Speech.

'It's a free vote,' she said. 'I have always voted to ban hunting but it's a free vote and everyone will vote as they think is right.'

Emboldened by their second election victory and a survey that showed that two out of three people wanted fox hunting banned, Labour MPs wanted to press ahead with it and not run out of time. For the Countryside Alliance, it was the moment to bring more people on to the street and they organised a rally for September 2002. It would be an historic occasion. They called it the Liberty and Livelihood March.

'The marchers will demand answers to the countryside's problems,' said the CA's Deputy Chief Executive David Lowes, 'in place of this destructive political obsession with ending an innocuous tradition whose demise would not help a single rural— or urban—family, with no gain to animal welfare. They will demand constructive policy rather than destructive politics. That is what this march is all about.'

Sensing that this protest was becoming a broader critique of his government, Tony Blair announced he would embark on a countryside tour to reassure rural communities that his policies weren't a threat, but would create jobs and affordable housing. He supported a compromise clause in the new anti-hunting bill allowing some regulated fox hunting, but many Labour MPs wanted that clause struck out. Blair encouraged his rural advocate, Ewen Cameron, chairman of the Countryside Agency, to attend the march, but no government minister would.

'It would be good if [Blair] could get out,' said Ewen Cameron. 'In some places, though, he would be wise to let things cool down. After the march, people will have their tails up and it could become quite aggressive.'

Certainly some hunt supporters were planning more aggressive action, such as pouring dye into Welsh reservoirs that supplied the Midlands. The water authorities took the threat seriously and bolstered their security. These militants called themselves the Real Countryside Alliance and embraced a Green Union Flag as their symbol. Most of their members had never been in trouble with the law before but were willing to clash with the police if it meant protecting their traditional ways.

The problem was that every new law introduced to nudge people towards behaving in a more politically correct way—whether it be smoking bans, controlled parking zones or stopping hunting—meant that more and more previously law-abiding citizens were becoming criminalised. It encouraged them to take action and once they'd become used to protesting, it became easier for them to object more and more to government restrictions. It also saw a shift away from regular left-wing protestors to those people who'd never really seen themselves as the protesting type.

Even mild-mannered vicars were taking the bait. 'While we respect the diversity of views among Christians on hunting,' wrote a group of clergy to *The Times*, 'we are convinced that it is an integral part of balanced and sustainable countryside management and a legitimate recreation compatible with Christian belief... Those of us who can will be at the march to walk alongside those who feel marginalised and misunderstood.'

The march was very well-organised. Two and a half thousand coaches and 31 chartered trains were ready to transport supporters to London. Parking places were secured for the coaches to deposit their travellers. Many of them got up as early as 3 a.m. to ensure they were there on time—these are farmers after all. Some 1800 Countryside Alliance stewards were ready to ensure their supporters behaved well and the protest could be funnelled safely through the streets of the capital. But still Baroness Mallalieu wasn't sure if enough of them would turn up.

James Stanford was the march director. A former director of a charity, he had begun preparation for the march months beforehand. He visited 11 key groups of supporters across the country from Dartmoor to Edinburgh. He reassured them over every little detail, including wheelchair access and sufficient toilets. The Metropolitan Police had been impressed with previous events like the Hyde Park Rally and so offered a light touch to their policing of the march. There would be two streams of marchers, one 'Liberty' and one 'Livelihood', and the first set off from Hyde Park and the second from Blackfriars. They would converge at the south end of Trafalgar Square to march along Whitehall. The police set up a counting zone to monitor the number of the crowds as they entered Parliament Square.

The day of the march was clear of rain and Stanford felt pretty confident that it would proceed smoothly, until he arrived in Westminster. The council had insisted that the organisers only dress the route with banners early that morning.

'That nearly led to a heart attack for me when I arrived in Whitehall,' recalled Stanford, 'less than 30 minutes before the agreed start time to find the huge End of March banners pointing the wrong way. Somehow an army of cranes and gangers materialised and with seconds to spare the route was clear... Even at that stage, with buses and trains disgorging their cargoes all around the capital, we had no idea how large the attendance might prove to be.'

The 'Liberty' marchers set off at 10 a.m. behind an enormous 30 foot Liberty and Livelihood banner. They cheered, blew whistles and horns and carried placards. 'For fox sake, fox off Blair,' said one. Many were farmers and agricultural workers—from lords of the manor to rat-catchers—but many others were not. 'It's exercising our right to democracy,' said one teenage girl. 'It's a freedom issue.' Tweed and barbours appeared sided by side with more militant camouflage gear.

Media-friendly people joined the throng, including comedians Rory Bremner and Jim Davidson, footballer Vinnie Jones, explorer Sir Ranulph Fiennes, actor Edward Fox, writers Frederick Forsyth, Julian Fellowes, Lord Bragg and Sir Max Hastings, editor of *The Ecologist* Zac Goldsmith, sportsmen Willie Carson and Allan Lamb, and General Sir Peter de la Billière. Some of them spoke at a press conference at the Institute of Directors in Pall Mall.

'I just wish Tony Blair had the balls to come out and see us,' said Vinnie Jones, summing up the essence of the protest. 'People should not poke their noses into other people's business.'

UKIP MEP Nigel Farage was among the marchers and thoroughly enjoyed the day. He'd been a member of the CA for years, having attended its opening rally in Hyde Park five years earlier.

Baroness Mallalieu was delighted with the turnout. 'That incredible silence as the March passed the Cenotaph—tears in many eyes, including mine. The incredible euphoria of standing on the platform in Parliament Square when the figure 400,000 went up. I shall never forget it. Or going back to the start where thousands upon thousands were waiting to start—urging them to be patient and being told time and again "we are not going away until we are counted".'

Neither James Stanford nor Baroness Mallalieu could be disappointed. The final figure for the march was 407,791. It was the largest ever protest in British history—and would only be topped by a Stop the War gathering the following year.

But still the anti-hunting Labour MPs were unimpressed. A bill allowing some licensed hunting was rejected by the House of Commons in favour of an amendment proposed by Tony Banks MP calling for a complete ban, which was passed with a majority of 208 in July 2003. This was rejected by the House of Lords. An identical bill was reintroduced in 2004 but again rejected by the Lords.

The CA kept up the pressure with smaller, more quirky events, such as their Pants against Prejudice protest in Parliament Square in 2004. Organised by the Ladies of the Vale of White Horse Hunt, it was a women only event in which they erected clothes lines around the square hung with over a thousand pairs of knickers. 'We are trying to show we are not all murderous men and this is a very important part of our lives and our families' lives,' said one of the protestors.

'That was one of the best nights I've ever had,' said Mallalieu. It was pouring with rain but they'd come well stocked with bottles of drink and TV cook Clarissa Dickson Wright rustled up some food. 'At midnight there were two American girls with the longest legs you've ever seen. They were mink hunters. They did a pole dance. We had a deafening sound system. They danced to It's Raining Men and all the traffic came to a halt and everybody cheered.'

In the end, with Commons and Lords unable to reach

agreement, the Speaker of the House of Commons Michael Martin MP invoked a rarely used act that allowed the Commons to overrule the Lords. The Hunting Act passed into law in February 2005.

So, Baroness Mallalieu and the Countryside Alliance had failed in their principal purpose, but their campaign had awakened a spirit of active protest among a large part of the population that had never considered such action before.

'The irony is,' says Mallalieu, 'with the two biggest protest groups in recent times—ours and Stop the War—they both failed. And they were both right.' That spirit would feed into other causes in subsequent years. It also widened the gap between the political establishment and many voters who normally considered themselves conventional voters tied to the main parties. Seeing that there were many people like them out there—marching along Whitehall in their hundreds of thousands—they were willing to be more adventurous with their votes and back smaller parties who spoke more clearly for their concerns. They could no longer be depended on to renew their traditional party memberships so readily.

'Was it all worthwhile?' wondered march organiser James Stanford. 'The Liberty and Livelihood March showed the world at large and politicians in particular the strength we can muster when roused to defend our cause.'

'Should we have done things differently?' asked Baroness Mallalieu. 'We could have been more militant and less law-abiding, but that is not the nature of our people and would have lost us public sympathy and political support. As it is, I believe that public perception now is that a bad law was enacted for the wrong reasons as an act of political spite, and that is the strong reason we need to change it.'

In 2010, Tony Blair finally admitted to an error of judgement over the Hunting Act, saying it was one of his biggest regrets. 'If I'd proposed solving the pension problem by compulsory euthanasia for every fifth pensioner I'd have got less trouble for it,' he said. 'By the end of it, I felt like the damn fox.'

As New Labour went on an enormous spending spree in the first decade of the 21st century, with billions of taxpayers' pounds on capital projects and public sector expenditure, it seemed there was no one really to question this lavish use of the voters' own money. Overwhelmed by the political success of Tony Blair, both the Conservatives and the Lib Dems were wedded to big government and matching the Chancellor's expenditure. Margaret Thatcher's quest for reducing the role of the state and cutting taxes was distinctly out of fashion.

This lack of concern for the voters' hard-earned pounds provoked a group of young people to form another kind of alliance—the TaxPayers' Alliance (TPA). No mass rallies or marches for them, but a different kind of organisation that married a Westminster think tank with a grassroots pressure group. It would, arguably, be more successful than the Countryside Alliance at getting change from government and represented yet another move away from conventional party politics as many people felt that politicians no longer adequately represented their concerns.

Founder Matthew Elliott was born in 1978 in Leeds and went to Leeds Grammar School. There, he was inspired by his sixth form economics teacher, who taught him using Milton Friedman's 1980 *Free to Choose* book and 10-part US PBS TV series. He was also taught French by Joanne Harris, author of the best-selling novel *Chocolat*. At the London School of Economics, where he took a degree in Government, Elliott met Allister Heath, who was born and raised in France, and they shared a passion for free market politics. It was at the LSE that Heath founded the Hayek Society— devoted to the great free market philosopher. Afterwards, they did a stint of work experience together at the Eurosceptic European Foundation.

With a First Class degree, Elliott proceeded to work as a researcher for MPs in the House of Commons. It was the tried and tested way of getting into politics, but when he was pipped to the post as chief of staff to a shadow cabinet minister, it gave him the spur to do something different. It was in 2002 that he and his like-minded friends first got the idea for the TPA.

'There was a feeling, after the 2001 general election,' recalls Elliott, 'when the new leadership came in. There were lots of noises in the Conservative Party about how they needed to start matching Labour's spending plans, how they had to do exactly what Brown had done to get Labour elected in 1997 by matching Ken Clarke's spending plans, so therefore the Conservatives needed to go along with Gordon Brown's spending increases. We felt that was wrong. We felt that point of view was not represented in politics and therefore needed a voice to express that.'

Elliott was inspired by the work being done in the USA by groups such as Americans for Tax Reform and the National Taxpayers Union, as well as similar groups in France and Germany. 'The UK hadn't really needed one because Thatcher was such a tax-cutter and her legacy lived on.' But in 2002, thanks to the crisis of confidence in the Tory party following their 2001 defeat, that legacy was suddenly in danger.

Existing free-market think tanks in the UK, the Institute for Economic Affairs (IEA)—a key influence on Thatcher's economic reforms in the 1980s—and the Adam Smith Institute (ASI), were doing fine work but had become mainly bodies for publishing academic research and did not engage with the broader media. Elliott saw there was a gap for a grassroots campaign group.

'If we were in the US we'd have called that campaign Freedom Works or Britons for Prosperity, but we didn't feel that worked. TaxPayers' Alliance got to the nub of what we were doing.' He had also been impressed by the Countryside Alliance's big march in 2002. 'That gave us the Alliance part of the name, rather than going with Taxpayers' Union which was the name used in the States or Germany.'

The four key players in the early days of the TPA were the 24-year-old Elliott, Allister Heath, who was working as a journalist at the Barclay brothers owned the *Business* newspaper, his sister Florence Heath, a student at Imperial College, and Andrew Allum, a graduate of Imperial who was beginning his career in management consultancy. They met every Tuesday morning at 7.30 a.m. at a Starbucks near Embankment station.

'It was hugely exciting,' says Elliott. 'None of us knew that many journalists, none of us knew any donors, we don't know where to start, we had the energy, we had the vision, we just pushed on.'

Most of 2003 was spent pulling together information for their *Bumper Book of Government Waste*, building a website, registering a bank account, and creating a logo. The TPA was launched in February 2004. Part of its initial success was down to its ability to produce information in a form that appealed to newspaper journalists, especially at the popular end of the market. Elliott saw himself as similar to a newspaper editor, guiding research towards making it newsworthy.

'Our frustration with the existing groups in the UK,' says Elliott, 'partly came from the fact that they were still quite learned and academic and publishing high quality monographs, but perhaps not getting the media attention. Although it has to be said the ASI came up with the first non-jobs report [and] they imported tax freedom day to the UK. But we felt we could add something there. Andrew as a consultant likes to be able to simplify things. Allister definitely has an eye for what makes a good story. But basically we wanted to bring a campaigning approach to the UK, partly inspired by what we'd seen in the US. We wanted to influence the media climate'

Elliott is a 'huge fan of Hayek', he was president of the LSE's Hayek Society, after Allister Heath, but felt Hayek's book *The Intellectuals and Socialism* was very much of its time in that it believed that intellectuals could influence society and thus think tanks were the engine of policy making.

'My view, and this is a slight exaggeration, is that the media doesn't care about intellectuals. In this age of celebrity culture, if you pitch anything intellectually you won't get anywhere. What the reader is interested in is 'who do you represent?' That is more important now than what set of ideas you represent or which university you come from.'

The TPA has been called a 'vertically integrated campaign and think tank'. What that means, as Elliott describes it is, 'we've picked a subject, broadly speaking tax and spend, fiscal policy, and we do everything from the thinking right through to the grassroots, the internet and the media.'

They soon made waves. In 2006, Conservative Home—the grassroots website—gave it their 'One to Watch' Award and their *Bumper Book of Government Waste* won the Atlas Sir Antony Fisher Memorial Award—Fisher had founded the IEA. In 2008, the TPA was named 'Pressure Group of the Year' by readers of Iain Dale's Diary. It is widely quoted in the media and the *Sun's* Page Three models have been noted spouting pithy comments in support of their research as well as featuring in some of their 'white van man' campaigns against fuel duty and alcohol duty.

Their number of supporters rose from 18,000 in 2008 to 80,000 ten years after their founding. To counter the criticism that they are an 'astroturf' organisation, they have been keen to push genuine grassroots activities around the UK, including action days where local supporters hand out leaflets and raise signatures for petitions, alongside protests outside high spending council offices. They link these traditional forms of protest with websites that enable people to click on an issue and automatically sign an electronic petition or send a letter of protest to their MPs.

For their campaign against the beer duty escalator in early 2013, the TPA printed hundreds of thousands of beer mats featuring their campaign website. These were distributed in pubs, allowing beer drinkers to use their mobile phones to click on the link and send a letter of complaint to their local MP—while continuing with their drinking! Shortly afterwards, the Coalition government abolished the beer duty escalator and knocked a penny off the pint.

'It made it easy for people to engage in the political process,' says Andrew Allison, the TPA's former National Grassroots Co-ordinator. 'Many of the people who attended our Mash Beer Tax parties had never written to their MP, and here they were sat in a pub doing just that. Looking back, you can see just why the campaign was successful. It reached the parts other campaigns and campaign groups cannot reach!"

The TPA have been criticised for being too close to the Conservative Party and many of their members have close links with the Tories. Elliott is quite open about this. 'Yes, broadly speaking we are more on the centre right of British politics if you define low-tax, low-spend as being a centre right position. So, yes, the Conservative Party is the closest political party to us, but over the last few years we have taken them on over HS2—a very touchy issue for the Conservative Party leadership—we have pushed really hard on that. The deficit is still huge, government spending is still going up, cuts have not been substantial... Are we closer to them than the other political parties? Yes. Are we brave enough to take them on? Certainly. We aren't one of these patsy think tanks that won't say anything controversial in order to get ministers around their lunch table and impress corporate donors.'

The TPA is funded by a variety of individual and business donors giving small and large sums of money. It is not supported by the government with grants of taxpayers' money. This gives them tremendous independence, but also puts them at odds with many left-of-centre think tanks and campaign groups who have benefited tremendously over the Blair-Brown years from government patronage. Matt Sinclair, a former Chief Executive of the TPA, made a study of this.

In 2007-8, at least £37m of taxpayers' money was spent on funding a multitude of campaigning groups that coincided with New Labour's political philosophy. Many of these included environmental and lifestyle pressure groups, but £1.6m of taxpayer funding went to major political think tanks such as Demos, the New Economics Foundation, and the Institute for Public Policy Research.

'Funding of lobbying and political campaigning by government bodies has a number of negative effects,' concluded Sinclair. 'It distorts decision making in favour of the interests and ideological preoccupations of a narrow political elite. It slows adjustments in the direction of policy in reaction to new evidence or circumstances. It increases political apathy among the public [and] taxpayers are forced to fund views they may seriously disagree with.'

In the first decade of the 21st century, the TPA has very much been part of a shift away from conventional party politics with the most successful campaigning groups providing that sense of community with a purpose that used to be the preserve of the leading political parties.

'It's a long-term trend, 'says Matthew Elliott. 'Basically, the trend is that all political parties don't want to give their activists much of a say. Frankly, they're embarrassed by them. They don't like debates at party conference because they can't control what people are going to say. They would much rather activists pay their subs, give their donations, deliver their leaflets and have no opinions of their own. Which is why membership numbers for all political parties are going down. What people like about everything from Conservative Home to the TPA is that there is a vibrant debate there. If you're just there as fodder for delivering leaflets, why do it?'

The view has always been that the party leadership could take their supporters for granted as they had nowhere else to go, but the rise of the smaller protest parties and pressure groups has shown there are other ways to alter the political climate.

'When parties started clamping down on dissent within parties, that's when pressure groups became more appealing,' argues Elliott. 'People would go for single-issue pressure groups. They could see how they make a difference in politics, they satisfy their interest in politics, and they don't have to sign up to all the things they disagree with within a political party.

'Now, I think we've gone one step further when people are slightly nervous about pressure groups because again they will represent a group of issues, some of which they may or may not agree with. That's why at the TPA we are going for micro-campaigns, which appeal to a niche for people who are with us on one issue but not on another. Politics is becoming hyper-issue based rather than generalist.'

Matthew Elliott proved his effectiveness at just this kind of politics when he took a sabbatical from the TPA to direct the 'NO to AV' campaign in a referendum on changing Britain's electoral system—part of the Lib Dem deal for being in the Coalition and their drive towards proportional representation. Elliott's cross-party campaign won the referendum by a resounding two to one in May 2011.

In November 2013, Elliott flew to New York to receive the Prestigious Templeton Freedom Award from the Atlas Foundation, which came with a cheque for $100,000. 'The TaxPayers' Alliance has become such a force of nature in a relatively short amount of time,' said the Atlas Network chief. 'From impeccable research to clear messaging, they've really raised the bar for think tanks.'

In February 2014, the TPA celebrated its tenth anniversary. One central achievement stood at the core of its work. 'We've managed to make the issue of how the government spends our money a significant issue in public debate and an issue that goes cross-party,' says Elliott. 'No politician will now stand up and defend wasteful spending. Even the Labour Party now in some press releases and attacks on government are based on "haven't you wasted this money?"'

This is why many politically engaged people are choosing to join pressure groups rather than stand as conventional politicians. 'If you look at my school yearbook for 1996, it does say my ambition was to become a Member of Parliament,' says Jonathan Isaby, current chief executive of the TPA. 'But I've assessed in my jobs in journalism and at the TPA I can have influence on the political agenda, on public opinion and the policies that politicians take on board without the demands from the Whip's office that you have to vote a certain way every night of the week unless you want to be frozen out from the hierarchy.'

*

In the footsteps of the TPA, others have followed with web-based campaigns that are motivating previously apathetic voters. One other leading campaign group is 38 Degrees. 'They had a good success over the privatisation of forests,' says Elliott. 'A good success at watering down the NHS reforms.'

Set up in February 2009 by Gordon Roddick, co-founder of The Body Shop, Henry Tinsley, ex-chairman of Green & Black's and David Babbs, its current Executive Director, 38 Degrees claims over 1.9m members. Its name comes from the critical angle at which an avalanche is triggered. It calls itself progressive with a great interest in environmental and social issues. Although essentially web-based, inviting people to sign their online petitions, it has also organised grassroots events around the country. It first came to public attention when it successfully opposed the Coalition government's intention to sell off woodland in 2010, which was then subsequently dropped.

Conservative MP Douglas Carswell has written about this new political landscape in two keys books, *The Plan: Twelve Months to Renew Britain*, with Dan Hannan, and *The End of Politics and the Birth of iDemocracy*.

'The two and a half party system is disintegrating,' says Carswell, 'because the two and a half brands are losing market share and that is because the nature of the electorate is changing. The electorate is much less tribal. The new political force is the rise of the citizen consumer. In order to buy into a political party you need to give them an attractive retail proposition.'

Many of these voter consumers have been put off the main parties by their attempts to iron out any awkward moments or differences in opinion within the parties.

'The two-and-a-half party brands are very centrally controlled,' explains Carswell. 'There has been a huge extension of power over party machinery by those at the top. In the 1990s it was at its apogee where you had lines to take fed through to politicians on pagers. You controlled the selection of candidates. In effect, the parties became almost the private property of a clique. Politics was reduced to being a competition between two cliques in charge of their parties in order to get the right to sit on the sofa in Downing street.'

On the Left, in the late 1990s and into the first decade of 21st century, this process was noted by trade-union leaders who felt they and their supporters were being left behind. 'The centre ground is where the action is,' recalls John Monks, former head of the TUC. This was reinforced by the political technique of 'triangulation,' adopted by New Labour from Bill Clinton and the Democrats in the US, who used opinion polling to determine their policies and how best to tackle those of their opponents. It frequently meant taking on the popular policies of rival parties to reduce their potency for the opposition.

'It prompted the charge that there are no differences between the parties' says Monks and, when it came to maintaining links with core supporters, he believes 'triangulation didn't help.'

'It's demeaned politics,' says the former TUC chief. 'The fact that there's not [many] people of strong convictions trying to persuade you of the rightness of their convictions. Instead we go wherever the public are, we follow.'

For the Conservatives, their version of this process would become known as 'de-toxifying' their brand.

The revolution in social media has also given voters a greater choice.

'It allows people as candidates and MPs to create their own communication directly with voters,' says Carswell. 'You've got the democratisation of the media. This allows individual MPs and candidates to go directly to the voters and create their own brand.'

Curiously, it takes voters back to the time before 1968 when candidates were not allowed to put their party affiliations on ballot papers—because you were supposed to vote for the quality of the person and not the party. It means voters can reject a party in favour of more authentic politicians who speak their language and voice their concerns.

'If I was to send out a tweet everyday that echoed what Tory central office was saying I would look ridiculous,' says Carswell. 'I have to say what I think otherwise people just aren't going to follow me. The challenge for the parties is to adapt to this new technology. They're pretty slow and flat-footed.'

'The extraordinary thing is you don't need a big costly political structure based in London funded by multi-millionaires donors to do that,' concludes Carswell. 'The internet allows you to do that very cheaply.'

10

TOXIC TORIES

The shock of repeated defeat can make you change your character—completely. After three defeats at the hands of Margaret Thatcher, the trade unions and the Labour Party ditched their Euroscepticism and embraced the EU. After two defeats at the hands of Tony Blair, the Conservative Party was determined to change its spots too. But whereas the Labour movement sought a patron outside the UK, the character transformation of the Tories began with a masochistic affection for the man who beat them.

Michael Gove, a leading writer for *The Times* from 1996 onwards but soon to become a Tory MP in 2005, expressed this emotion in 2003.

'You could call it the Elizabeth Bennett [*sic*] moment,' he wrote. 'It's what Isolde felt when she fell into Tristan's arms. It's the point you reach when you give up fighting your feelings, abandon the antipathy bred into your bones, and admit that you were wrong about the man. By God, it's still hard to write this, but I'm afraid I've got to be honest. Tony Blair is proving an outstanding Prime Minister at the moment.'

Aside from showing a good knowledge of high-end literature as to be expected from an Oxford English Lit graduate (though it is 'Bennet'), it crystallised a moment when a new generation of Tories had fallen under the spell of their vanquisher. Gove, 35 at the time, was a rising member of the Tory elite. President of the Oxford Union, columnist and assistant editor on *The Times*, he was chairman and co-founder of Policy Exchange, the right of centre think tank established in April 2002, devoted to a modernising agenda for the Conservative Party. Many of its members would become key players in David Cameron's future transformation of the party.

To be fair, Gove's public declaration of love for Blair was mainly based on the Prime Minister's intervention in Iraq in the face of tremendous opposition from the Left. Gove compared it to Thatcher standing up to tyranny in the Falklands War—although the error in this analogy was that she was fighting to defend British territory and not effect regime change. Gove's affection for Blair was also based on an array of domestic policies, including his introduction of university top-up fees and the handling of a firefighters' strike. Essentially, at that moment, Gove and his conservative colleagues were in thrall to Blair and saw few points of dispute with him and his immediate coterie. Of course, they hated the hard-left characters in the New Labour government but thought that Blair was doing a good job containing them. Gove felt he could say this because he was not a Tory 'tribalist' but 'in so far as I'm sympathetic to Tory politicians, and their arguments, it's because as a right-wing polemicist I find them persuasive. And as a right-wing polemicist, all I can say looking at Mr Blair now is what's not to like?'

Two years later, he would become a Tory MP and in 2010 a Coalition government minister. It is perhaps not surprising to hear that when Gove had earlier applied to join the Conservative Research Department, he was turned down because he was 'insufficiently Conservative'. Certainly in 2005, he was happy to chat to *The Guardian* putting the case for 'greater immigration'—an increasingly contentious aspect of the Blair years—saying a 'precondition of securing support for greater immigration is having a sense that it's controlled.' (Not that it is *actually* controlled—just a 'sense' it is—classic Blair-era spin.) But, sitting in the Westminster office of Policy Exchange, he was gung-ho about winning power.

'You've got to focus on trying to win,' he said, 'because once you believe, going into an election, that you won't win, that communicates itself to everyone. Football teams that play for a draw are more likely to get beaten.' In retrospect, it could be argued that the new set of modernising—and moderating—beliefs Gove and his colleagues would embrace for the Tories would end up in a draw rather than a win.

Another co-founder at Policy Exchange was Francis Maude. He had been an MP and minister in Thatcher's government and was one of those who told her to exit the fateful leadership race in 1990 in the first round because he felt she could not win it. He would later disavow her government's Section 28 rule, which banned councils from promoting homosexuality. 'It took me some time to realise what an emblem of intolerance Section 28 had become for gay people,' he told the *Telegraph*. 'It was the tip of a deep iceberg—the iceberg below the surface being a host of anti-gay social attitudes.' He felt the law did not make it any easier for his gay brother to be open about his homosexuality and Maude became a strong advocate of gay marriage. He believed it would help curb gay promiscuity and may have saved his brother dying from AIDS.

Maude lost his seat in 1992, but re-entered parliament in 1997 and became a key member of the shadow cabinet. Not only did he help found Policy Exchange in 2002 but he also established Conservatives for Change, which shared the same offices as Policy Exchange, and became its chairman. 'We work to modernise the Conservative Party and to ensure that it reflects the realities and complexities of contemporary Britain,' says its mission statement. 'Through a programme of constructive activity C Change seeks to play a full part in the process of Conservative recovery.'

Maude made his own views clear in an article for the *Spectator* in March 2002. 'It is five to midnight for the Tories,' warned the 49-year-old Maude. 'Yet the Conservative party is a phoenix, not a dodo.' There was no guarantee, however, it would rise again if it did not get with it—if it did not become more in tune with Tony Blair's open-collar electorate.

'For some years now we have simply not seemed to be in touch with the way people live, or attuned to their aspirations and fears, their anxieties and their hopes. At the election last year, fewer people voted Conservative than voted for Michael Foot's Labour party.' And that's about as bad as it gets!

So what did he advise?

'First, we must again become a genuinely national party, as Disraeli insisted. We must show real respect for all: male and female, rich and poor, old and young, black and white, gay and straight. This is not about "pandering to minorities." It is about being a decent party.'

He said the Tories must embrace alternative lifestyles and recruit beyond their usual list of straight, white males for parliamentary candidates. They needed to recognise the importance of groups to society—'the fantastically complex tapestry of voluntary organisations'—the first hint of David Cameron's Big Society. They needed to ditch the characterisation of their party as 'selfish' and focus on social justice and welfare reform. He favoured localism and de-centralization of power away from central government—'diversity is to be celebrated'. Finally, he dismissed the party's 'Little Englanders'—code for the Eurosceptics—saying modern Tories must be internationalist.

'We can retreat further into a reactionary redoubt and try to hold the modern world at bay,' he concluded, 'or we can rise up and embrace it. Stagnation and oblivion or radicalism and revival? Modernise or die? It's obvious, isn't it?'

It was a manifesto for a new Tory party and went down a storm with the younger metropolitan clique conservatives that became known as the Notting Hill set, which included Gove as well as the youthful David Cameron and George Osborne. Good at outlining the parameters of this revolution, Maude's article lacked the zingy catchphrase. That came with a speech delivered by Conservative party chairman Theresa May at their party conference in Bournemouth in October 2002.

From her very first words she said 'this conference marks a new approach from a party that is changing... Reforming ourselves so that we can reform Britain.'

She said politicians of all main parties were regarded as self-seeking and untrustworthy. The electorate had become cynical of their Punch and Judy politics and fewer and fewer of them were voting. 'When they start voting for the BNP then it's time to admit that things have gone badly wrong,' she said. She then referred to marching with the Countryside Alliance against New Labour's ban, but without mentioning the group by name.

It was not just Labour that was failing, but also the Conservative party, argued the 46-year-old May, who spruced up her own public image by wearing stylish designer shoes. 'What do I mean when I talk about the party changing? Well, one of the ways in which we're changing is by being proud of the right things.' She then echoed Maude by mentioning the work of local charities run by Tory party members. That was the caring face the Conservative party must present to the British people.

'Twice we went to the country unchanged, unrepentant, just plain unattractive. And twice we got slaughtered. Soldiering on to the next election without radical, fundamental change is simply not an option…

'In 1979 the challenge was reform of the economy. Today the challenge is reform of public services,' she said, again repeating Maude's policy shift from free market economics to social justice. Then came the memorable phrase that summed up the whole enterprise.

'Our base is too narrow and so, occasionally, are our sympathies. You know what some people call us—the nasty party.'

That was it, she said it, said what every sophisticated pinot grigio quaffing Tory moderniser thought when they sat down to dinner. Not, are we doing or saying the right things—but are we liked? Why do people think we're nasty?

'I know that's unfair,' said May, playfully backtracking. 'You know that's unfair but it's the people out there we need to convince—and we can only do that by avoiding behaviour and attitudes that play into the hands of our opponents.'

So, open up those prospective parliamentary candidate lists to women and ethnic minorities. 'Our forebears never flinched from modernising the Conservative party, so why should we?'

It was a full faced blast at the grassroots by the new generation of Tory leaders because it was *they* who were the 'nasty' party and their old ways and prejudices were holding back the 'nice' section of the party—the Notting Hill set. Of course, May's comment was also an own-goal in that it crystallised in the minds of swing voters that the something indefinable that held them back from voting Tory was, yes, the fact they were 'nasty'. It became a useful cudgel for the Left as well as the Tory modernisers. But the Tory modernisers so loathed their own old-fashioned grassroots that they'd seemingly rather demonise the whole party so long as they could diminish its influence.

If a 'coup' had occurred in the Labour Party over a matter of months in 1988 with its *volte face* on the EU, then this was a beerhall putsch with Gove, Maude and May standing on tables and firing shots in the ceiling in 2002. It was the beginning of a process that would see David Cameron elected as party leader in 2005.

Cameron had come from studying PPE at Oxford to start his political career working in the Conservative Research Department (CRD). Fellow modernizers who passed through the CRD included George Osborne (his future Chancellor), Steve Hilton (his Director of Strategy), Edward Vaizey, Rachel Whetstone (Hilton's wife), Edward Llewellyn (his future Chief of Staff), and Daniel Finkelstein. Many of them were also part of the Notting Hill set, along with Gove and third co-founder of Policy Exchange, Nicholas Boles.

Finkelstein was director of CRD before becoming a *Times* leader writer and editor. There, he was chief cheerleader for the modernising project, articulating the case for change in articles and speeches. He is now chairman of Policy Exchange and been elevated to the Lords as Baron Finkelstein of Pinner. As a young man, however, he was a high flyer in the SDP, an adviser to its leader David Owen and headed SDP think tank the Social Market Foundation before leaving them in 1990 to join the Tories.

A third defeat to New Labour in 2005 ended the grip of the older generation on the Tory Party. Michael Howard stepped down as leader and David Cameron put himself forward, but the more traditionalist Tory David Davis was the initial front runner. Robin Birley, Jimmy Goldsmith's stepson and formerly of the Referendum Party, helped finance Davis' bid for leader.

'He's a sound Conservative,' says Birley, 'a libertarian. I like his background, his earthiness. He's a proper Conservative. Cameron is a man on the left. He's a left of centre Conservative. I don't believe his utterances on Europe. He doesn't understand the dynamics of low tax. He's essentially a go with the flow Conservative, which dispirits me.'

At the party conference in October 2005, it largely turned on the speeches the two leadership candidates gave to their supporters.

'[Davis] was very lazy when it came to making that speech,' recalls Birley. 'If he'd really prepared for that, he could have won. Whereas Cameron was super organized, courageous and really prepared for it.'

In his speech, delivered impressively without notes, Cameron very much flew with the modernising, detoxifying creed, declaring he wanted to 'switch on a whole new generation' and make people 'feel good about being Conservatives again'.

In the first ballot, Davis came top with 62 votes but that was short of his declared supporters; Cameron came second with 56. In the second ballot, Cameron triumphed with 90 votes to Davis' 57.

'I'm very sad about it,' says Birley. 'I think [Davis] would have made an infinitely better leader.' Birley has since switched his allegiances to UKIP.

What also helped Cameron's cause was the speech Francis Maude made at the 2005 conference, quoting the results of two opinion polls by Populus and ICM. He showed the findings to the audience.

'People liked our policies—until they found out they were ours,' he said. 'Look at this chart. It shows the approval of our immigration policy before it was identified as a Conservative policy and then once they knew it was ours, support halved. This chart tells its own story.'

There's nothing quite as persuasive as data and charts. In the same year, Lord Ashcroft, an immensely wealthy donor to the Tory party and highly influential patron of Conservative research, published a report called *Smell the Coffee: A Wakeup Call to the Conservatives* in which he also concluded that the 'Conservative label was undermining its ability to sell its policies.' Daniel Finkelstein made sure this message got out to a wider public by citing the poll results in *The Times*.

It would only be five years later that the very data quoted by Maude would be questioned. Journalist Janet Daley made the point in *The Telegraph* that a polling expert had said that the very same brand disapproval was noted when a popular policy was ascribed to the Labour Party.

'When the public was offered what were in fact Labour policies but which were not identified as such, they approved of them,' she wrote. 'When told that these were official Labour policies, they said they disliked them. So where exactly does that leave us?'

It meant that the leading political parties in general were not popular with the electorate, not just the Conservatives. Authors Anthony Scholefield and Gerald Frost in their book *Too 'nice' to be Tories?* poured further doubt on the value of the polls when they revealed that voters of all parties had commented on the policies in the polls so clearly non-Tory voters would not support a policy once it was revealed as such.

Maude had skewed the debate by quoting these polls, but it served the purpose of the modernisers and, once Cameron was in power, they pressed ahead with their campaign to confound peoples' expectations of what a Tory is. In came a passion for fighting Climate Change with expensive green policies, in came social compassion, 'hug a hoodie', in came strident support for gay issues, including gay marriage. Out went a commitment to a smaller state and lower taxes, out went Euroscepticism. In 2006, Cameron made a speech in San Francisco in which he derided past politicians for their concern with economic growth and budgets—all the hardcore stuff that Thatcher knew was central to a healthy nation. Instead, he was concerned about happiness.

'Wealth is about so much more than pounds, or euros or dollars can ever measure… It's time we admitted that there's more to life than money, and it's time we focused not just on GDP, but on GWB—general well-being.'

Such as an argument is always so much more convincing when it doesn't come from the multi-millionaire son of a wealthy stockbroker. Still, it set the tone for a new style Tory party that was desperate to escape from its supposedly toxic past to get elected. Whether it would achieve that purpose—and whether it was worth the sacrifice of traditional Tory values—would be challenged over the following five years. Not least by members of its own party.

'One of the great tragedies of modernisation is we've had lots of modernisers but precisely the wrong sort of modernisation,' says Conservative MP Douglas Carswell. 'Modernisation has been about imposing the faddish obsessions of a small clique in London on the wider Conservative movement. Actually modernisation should have been about not having the Tory party run by a clique at all.'

*

As Cameron's detoxifying Tory party pulled away from many of its grassroots supporters, those organisations that remained unashamedly Thatcherite saw a boost in their membership and would provide a platform for forays against the modernisers. One of the most notable of these was the Freedom Association. At the beginning of the noughties, it had seemed that its glory days were behind it. Founded in 1975 as the National Association for Freedom by Ross and Norris McWhirter, it had the unfortunate acronym of NAFF, but despite this its popularity leapt as it took on the all-powerful unions with a series of campaigns. Tragically, Ross McWhirter was murdered by the IRA a few months after its founding.

NAFF—finally changing its name to The Freedom Association (TFA) in 1978—gave support to employers and non-unionised workers during several high profile industrial disputes in the late 1970s, such as the Grunwick strike. This was just as the British public were finally getting fed up with trade-union dominance of the economy, paving the way for Thatcher's election in 1979. Its current chief executive director, Simon Richards, was part of this turmoil. As a history student at King's College, he took over his college Conservative Association in 1977 and made it a force to be reckoned with. A friend at the time remembers his impact.

'Simon was a figurehead of right-thinking students at King's. He masterminded the campaign to save the student body thousands of pounds by disaffiliating from the National Union of Students, while proving his worth for greater things with his diligent work as Secretary of the student union.'

These were politically fraught times and Richards remembers when left-wing students from the LSE broke up a meeting to which he'd invited Rhodes Boyson MP to speak. 'It caused a great deal of outrage at the time,' says Richards. 'Rhodes Boyson called them "red fascists". We broke off relations with the LSE and stole their mascot—a beaver.' Richards got elected to be sabbatical secretary on a strongly Thatcherite ticket—the only Thatcherite student union secretary in England at the time—and cheerfully acknowledges he has been a fan of the Iron Lady ever since.

During the 1980s, with Thatcher in power, there was little for the TFA to protest about, but they did campaign against sports sanctions stopping England cricketers from touring South Africa. Simon Richards veered away from a career in politics to get 'a proper job' and worked in retail management. Settling in Cheltenham, he set up his own retail business but this got into difficulties during the recession of the early 1990s when John Major's ERM debacle destroyed the Conservative party's reputation for economic competence. Up until this point, Richards had been a loyal Tory, although his faith had been shaken by the deposition of Thatcher. When former party chairman Norman Tebbit spoke at the 1992 Tory party conference, calling for Britain to withdraw from the ERM, he was not allowed to speak from the platform.

'He came from the back of the hall,' remembers Richards, 'to a standing ovation, made a marvellous speech.' Richards was vice-chairman of his local Conservative Association and its members had mandated their chairman to support Tebbit's view, but the chairman ignored them and accused Tebbit of rocking the boat. 'It was the final straw,' says Richards, and he resigned from the party. He wouldn't re-join the Tory party until Hague took over as leader and apologised for the errors of the Major era.

In the meantime, Richards had found a new political passion and got more involved with the Freedom Association, of which he'd been a member since his student days. He edited their magazine, *Freedom Today*, and developed their website for several years before becoming its director in 2008. He helped re-invigorate the organisation, bringing it up to date and giving it a new sense of relevance. He extended its membership among students with several Freedom Societies established in British universities and has successfully incorporated a younger generation of libertarians with older more established figures.

With Cameron's modernising triumph over the Tory party in 2005, TFA's moment had come and resolute Thatcherites and robust libertarians had the perfect meeting place to air their views and formulate campaigns. Rebellious Tory MPs mixed with fractious UKIP supporters. Conservative commentator Iain Dale has since called the TFA under Richards' leadership 'one of the most valued pressure groups on the Right, acting as a forum of communication between those on the Right of the Conservative Party and those in UKIP.'

In 2006, provoked by a new treaty pressing for further integration in the EU and fearing the Tory modernisers drifting away from Euroscepticism, the TFA started *Better Off Out*, a cross-party campaign aimed at British withdrawal from the European Union. 'The Better Off Out campaign believes that we can break free of the EU's control,' says its website, 'and embrace a global future based on the rules formed by a forward thinking and confident country.'

It gained the support of several Eurosceptic Tory backbenchers. The leading figure among these was Philip Davies. MP for Shipley in West Yorkshire, the former supermarket manager overturned a Labour majority in his seat in 2005 and made it clear in his maiden speech that he was not looking for advancement in the shadow government, preferring to remain a backbencher and retain the freedom to speak for his constituents. A staunch libertarian and member of the Freedom Association, he had spoken out at a party conference in 2005 about Britain leaving the EU. Despite getting 'a pasting from the chief whip at the time' he was determined to carry on representing this view.

'For parliamentary democracy to work,' says Davies, 'everyone in the country has to feel that somebody is speaking up for them. It astonished me that in 2005 at that time 40% of the public said they wanted to leave the EU and yet there wasn't one MP who would stand up and say the words "we should leave the EU". It was a failure of democracy.'

When it came to launching *Better Off Out* in parliament in April 2006, Davies invited the press and all MPs to attend the event but feared he would be the only MP to actually turn up at the committee room. 'I was certain there would just be me,' he recalls, 'and was actually quite astonished that eight or nine of my colleagues came along to support, Ann and Nicholas Winterton, Peter Bone, Philip Hollobone, Eric Forth…' Other MPs to join the campaign included Douglas Carswell and David Nuttall as well as Labour MP Austin Mitchell. MEPs David Campbell-Bannerman, Roger Helmer and Daniel Hannan pledged their support, along with the explorer Ranulph Fiennes and economists Alan Walters and Ruth Lea. Its chief patron was Lord Tebbit, Simon Richards' hero from 1992. It created ripples in the European Parliament too.

'The realisation began to dawn on me that we'd been talking about reforming the EU for 40 years,' remembers Conservative MEP Roger Helmer. 'I joined *Better Off Out* and said I don't think this renegotiation is going to work. I think it's beyond reform and deserves to be put out of its misery. This was extremely uncomfortable for the party.'

In an article for the *Sun* in September 2007, Cameron seemed to me more in tune with his Eurosceptic colleagues when he declared 'Today, I will give this cast-iron guarantee: If I become PM a Conservative government will hold a referendum on any EU treaty that emerges from these negotiations. No treaty should be ratified without consulting the British people in a referendum.'

Two years later, when the Czech president signed up on the latest round of EU integration—having held out for as long as he could not to sign it—William Hague had to admit that 'What has happened means it is no longer possible to have a referendum on the Lisbon treaty.' Cameron's empty 'cast-iron guarantee' would haunt him ever after, being held up by UKIP as a reason not to trust the Tory leader on Europe. In October 2011, David Nuttall MP, chairman of the *Better Off Out* group of MPs proposed an EU Referendum Bill in the House of Commons. Despite it being opposed by all main parties, the motion gained the support of 113 MPs. This helped trigger a chain of events that led to Cameron making another promise to offer a referendum on EU membership in 2017.

Nuttall and Davies believe the steady pressure of backbenchers like them will ultimately deliver what the nation wants—rather than what their party elite wants—and it is better achieved within the Tory party than outside.

'The best way to do it,' says Nuttall, 'is by staying within the Conservative Party because for all their huffing and puffing UKIP do not have a single MP, they have very few councillors, control of virtually no councils of note in the country. They are essentially a pressure group with a political arm.'

Davies has no wish to jump ship either and join UKIP.

'I agree with UKIP on virtually everything,' he says, 'and I might not be loyal when it comes to a vote on a policy issue, but I am a Conservative, always have been, and they gave me a massive opportunity to become an MP and I wouldn't want to kick them in the teeth. I have my own loyalties. The Conservative Party is a broad church, always has been.'

'I don't want to be critical of UKIP,' says Douglas Carswell, 'but I think perhaps it is slightly too authentic at times. UKIP wouldn't exist if the Tory party was the kind of Tory party I think it ought to be and will be—a broad based movement in touch with the grassroots and run by the grassroots.'

He then makes the point that Nigel Farage and UKIP might be setting the agenda for many of those grassroots members, but that doesn't mean he will become their leader.

'The catalyst for change might be the insurgents,' says Carswell, 'but ultimately the people who prevail will be the established parties adopting the tactics of the insurgents. The Tory party needs to become an insurgent force. I can best make that happen by being a member of the Conservative party and advocating these changes.'

The need for a voice to express grassroots concerns inside the Conservative Party was met most importantly by the founding of ConservativeHome in April 2005, a website first edited by Tim Montgomerie, a 35-year-old former director of the Conservative Christian Fellowship and speech-writer for Tory leaders. Its purpose says its website is 'to champion the interests of grassroots Tory members and to argue for a broad conservatism that is as serious about social justice as it is about economic competitiveness.' It very much owed its beginning to battling against a leadership that wanted more control over the party.

'The thing that started it,' says Jonathan Isaby, a former co-editor of the website, 'was that the Michael Howard leadership wanted to take away the right of the party members to choose the party leader. Tim said no that's wrong, the party members vote for the leader and to take that right away would be a backward step. It was very much standing up for party democracy.'

ConservativeHome helped co-ordinate resistance and defeated the proposed change. It next took on the party leadership over insisting that it continue to support grammar schools as well as tackling it over its secret A-list of preferred candidates. 'Within 48 hours,' says Isaby, 'Tim had all 100 names and published it. Two fingers to the party leadership and also a demonstration that in the age of the internet and blogs that any attempts to stifle people and cover-up is in vain.'

Tighter control over the party had very much developed over the first decade of the century. 'The party conference became an unashamed rally where it was all stage-managed,' says Isaby. 'For a long time now there have been very few opportunities for ordinary party members to have their say.' But Isaby does not blame any party for trying to control its conferences as journalists are only too happy to seize on points of debate as potential splits in that party.

'At the 2001 spring conference—six weeks before the general election—I remember one 20-year-old student who got up on stage and said it's time to legalise cannabis. Obviously this did not go down well with Ann Widdecombe, who was the shadow home secretary at the time, and coverage in the papers the next day was Tory student calls for drug legalisation, which was not the message the Tories wanted to come out of that conference.'

So, some stage-management is essential for a cohesive and effective political message, but this process seems to have gone too far and can make grassroots members feel undervalued and that their views do not matter if they fail to coincide with the party line.

'There is increasingly a sense from people I talk to in the Tory party,' says Isaby, who is now chief executive of the TaxPayers' Alliance, 'that even behind closed doors there is very little opportunity for discussion that disagrees with the line being taken by the party leadership.'

It was largely for this reason that Simon Richards and the TFA set up their Freedom Zone fringe meetings and talks outside

Conservative Party Conferences from 2008 onwards to allow such open discussion among Tories and other right of centre politicians. The TFA had been banned from running their stall within the conference previously because of their support for the *Better Off Out* campaign.

ConservativeHome was certainly welcome for opening up its party processes and putting a halt to some dictatorial tendencies, but it was not a bastion for all those opposed to the modernisation of the party, even though it was open to them to express their views. The modernisers soon seized upon it as a useful tool. Francis Maude described it as 'the only place to find out what's going on,' and a deputy editor was recruited as one of Cameron's speechwriters. But Tim Montgomerie did continue to press some sensitive buttons for the Tory leadership, criticising Cameron's failure to make a pledge on cutting taxes and his disconnection from working-class voters. He is now comment editor for *The Times*.

The triumph of the Tory modernisers may have been countered in part by moves within its own party to represent more grassroots views—Carswell has been a champion of open primaries to select candidates—but that has not patched over the great rift that many old-style Tories and disappointed Thatcherites feel now separates them from their party. Their core views have been trashed and they are not afraid to look elsewhere for someone who might listen to them. It should have been a great opportunity for UKIP but in 2005 its future was looking distinctly wobbly as it faced an embarrassing interlude with a perma-tanned chat show host.

11

CHASING CELEBRITY

When St Antony, alone in the desert, surrounded by devils, was tempted away from his path of godliness, a sparkling vision of the Queen of Sheba tried to seduce him with offers of riches and unbridled sensuality. When Nigel Farage faced his own temptation, he was offered Tunbridge Wells.

'It was terribly cleverly done,' recalls Farage. 'Somebody who I'd worked with in the City and had been a mate for some 20 years said to me you must come round for dinner. An important local councillor wants to meet you. If you say yes, the local MP will come. They've got some things to talk to you about.'

It was early 2005 and UKIP had done rather well in the European parliamentary elections in June the previous year. They'd won 12 MEPs, coming third overall with 2,650,768 votes and 16% of the vote. In the London Assembly elections held at the same time they'd won two seats. Whenever proportional representation was applied, UKIP was doing well. It was during this campaign that a leaked briefing document from the Conservative Research Department delivered another memorable political insult.

'The United Kingdom Independence Party claims to be a home for Eurosceptics,' said the document, 'but in reality it is full of cranks and political gadflies.' UKIP has ever after rejoiced in this phrase, providing its members with ties bearing madmen and buzzing insects. 'You only have to go to a public meeting of theirs,' said a Tory spokesman shortly afterwards, 'and they end up talking about Napoleon, the Spanish Armada or the Luftwaffe. They certainly have their share of oddballs.'

A few months later the Tories had decided to take a more subtle approach to subverting UKIP and were keen to flatter Farage. He remembers the flow of the conversation at his meeting in west Kent. He couldn't stay for dinner, but he enjoyed a glass of red wine as the blue imps danced around him saying he was doing marvellous things and UKIP had some very good points. Then it got down to business.

'Archie Norman has decided that politics isn't really for him,' said one of the Tories, 'and he'll be standing down in the next couple of days. Michael thinks that you'd be very well suited to Tunbridge Wells. It's your home county. A hunting, shooting, fishing type of constituency and at your age you'll be there for the next 30 or 40 years. A great chance for advancement...'

The offer of an easy, secure seat came straight from Michael Howard, then leader of the Conservative Party.

'I'm incredibly flattered,' said Farage. 'What is the price?'

'Oh, well, of course, we'd be very happy for you to carry on campaigning for a referendum,' said the Tory seducer. 'Perfectly justifiable, understandable position for a chap to take, but of course, it's less than helpful to have somebody as part of a team advocating full withdrawal. Obviously, there'd be reform and repatriation of certain rights...'

'This really isn't very interesting,' interrupted Farage with a broad smile. 'This relationship will be over in a fortnight. I won't even make it to nominations on this basis.'

The interview was over and Farage didn't even have to think about it.

'Of course, it is tempting in some ways,' he says now. '[But] I haven't ploughed this furrow for all this time, against impossible odds, to give it up. That would be a most awful thing to do.'

Farage, however, was less resolute when he was tempted by the prospect of a celebrity joining his party. Robert Kilroy-Silk had been the presenter of a popular BBC TV morning chat show—Kilroy— in which members of the audience gave their views on topics of the day. A handsome, charismatic figure with a permanent tan, he had an easy charm that made him good on TV and kept the show going for 18 years, but this was only one personal triumph among many.

Kilroy came from a working-class background in Birmingham,

went to grammar school then onto the LSE. From there he became a lecturer in politics at Liverpool University and then a Labour MP for 12 years. At one time he was Shadow Home Affairs spokesman, but he fell out with the hard-left Militant Tendency and resigned from the party to take up a career in TV in 1986.

A strongly opinionated article he wrote for the *Sunday Express* in January 2004 brought all this success crashing down. Entitled 'We Owe Arabs Nothing', the article attacked Arab culture and Middle Eastern regimes for their repressive regimes and support for terrorism. It was not delicately written and some people found it offensive, not least the BBC, which soon after dropped his show.

Casting around for his next project and having established a new non-politically correct reputation, he was receptive to an approach from UKIP. His wife had voted for the party and they were invited to several meetings. Nigel Farage could see Kilroy's value in attracting considerable coverage and so within weeks he was incorporated into the party. He delivered on that publicity too, especially when he got movie star Joan Collins to attend a UKIP press conference. Glamour was one demon not even Farage could resist.

'The people in middle Britain are fed up with being lied to,' Kilroy told a newspaper interviewer. 'They know they have been lied to over the European Union and the proposed European Constitution.' He then took the appeal of UKIP beyond its Euroscepticism. 'They know they were lied to over the war in Iraq. They know they are being lied to about asylum-seekers and immigration.' It was fertile territory.

Kilroy stood for the East Midlands region and won his seat as an MEP with 26% of the votes, a fraction just behind the Tories. So far so good—the only problem was that the 62-year-old Kilroy was used to running the show and somewhat assumed UKIP would be so grateful for his intervention that they would soon after make him their leader. It has been suggested that Farage promised him the leadership as an enticement to joint the party, but he denies this. Gerard Batten, who had also become a UKIP MEP in June of that year, had some sympathy with Kilroy's views.

'It was perfectly legitimate for Robert to have and express leadership ambitions,' he said, 'but he went about them the wrong way.'

Puffed up by a rapturous response to his appearance at a UKIP Party Conference in Bristol in October, Kilroy appeared on a David Frost TV programme the next day declaring his intention to stand as leader.

'This was a major miscalculation,' recalls Batten. 'He should have stayed to mingle at the UKIP dinner the night before and to press the flesh with the remaining delegates the following morning. He misjudged the character of the members, and by doing so alienated potential supporters.'

UKIP MEPs tried to keep Kilroy contented by offering him control of several key party committees, but he wanted the leadership or nothing. Believing one of the UKIP MEPs was now briefing against him in the press, he resigned from their Independence and Democracy grouping in the European parliament. He then used the media to make his own attacks on UKIP, calling them 'incompetent.'

'During this time I did my best to try and keep Robert in the party,' says Batten, 'and to build bridges between him and the other MEPs.' But Kilroy was convinced his magnetic personality could do it all by himself. He tried to subvert some of the local branch parties into giving him enough momentum to demand an Emergency General Meeting to make him leader by Christmas, but when the members were canvassed only 13% supported Kilroy. In January 2005, the game was over. Kilroy admitted defeat and left UKIP—after only nine months. He did, however, retain his seat as an independent MEP until 2009.

'Robert's departure from UKIP represents a lost opportunity, perhaps even a tragedy,' says Batten. 'However UKIP is a grass roots party that belongs to its members, not to any one person or clique.'

Shortly after his departure, Kilroy formed his own political party—Veritas. 'While UKIP has turned its back on the British people, I shall not,' he told a press conference. 'I will be standing at the next general election. I shall be leading a vigorous campaign for the causes I believe in. And, unlike the old parties, we shall be honest, open and straight.'

Veritas was Eurosceptic, but its primary concern was to oppose mass immigration into the UK. Kilroys's critics dubbed it 'Vanitas'. 'It's the BNP in an expensive suit,' said one. Several UKIP members resigned to join him, most notably Damian Hockney, one of their two London Assembly members. Kilroy hoped to out perform UKIP in the 2005 general election but its 65 candidates won only 40,481 votes. Kilroy came a poor fourth in Erewash in Derbyshire. In July, following an even worse performance at a by-election by one of their candidates winning only 218 votes, Kilroy resigned from his own party.

'It was clear from the general election result,' said Kilroy, 'that the electors are content with the old parties and that it would be virtually impossible for a new party to make a significant impact given the nature of our electoral system. We tried and failed.'

Since Veritas, Kilroy's electoral appeal was tested only one more time, when he appeared on the TV show I'm a Celebrity... Get Me Out of Here! The audience obliged and Kilroy was the first contestant to be voted off the programme.

The 2005 general election results had not been great overall for UKIP either. Coming fourth with 618,000 votes, it was way behind the Lib Dems on 5,985,454 votes. The Greens got just over a third of the number of UKIP's vote. The Lib Dems gained 11 seats and was the main recipient of protest votes from Labour voters angry at the country's involvement in the Iraq War. They won the most seats for any third party since 1923 with a total of 62 MPs. Their success squeezed the protests votes available for all the other smaller parties.

Some of those remaining votes went to a new left-wing protest party called *Respect*. Co-founded by Guardian journalist George Monbiot as part of the Stop the War movement that had got so many people out on the streets in 2003, the party was supposed to form an electoral alliance with the Greens, but the Greens rejected this and Monbiot soon after left the party. Respect won 87,533 votes in the 2004 London Assembly elections but no seats, and an impressive quarter of a million votes in the 2004 European elections but again no seats, many of the votes coming from Muslim Labour supporters who objected to Blair's War.

A largely socialist party, Respect's most high profile member was Glasgow Labour MP George Galloway. A highly controversial figure who regretted the passing of the Soviet Union and had earlier endorsed Saddam Hussein, he was a vociferous critic of Blair's intervention in Iraq. He became vice-chairman of the Stop the War Coalition in 2001 and repeatedly condemned Blair for lying to the British nation about the war. His comments were deemed to have brought the Labour Party into disrepute and he was expelled from the party in 2003.

In 2005, Galloway stood as a Respect candidate in east London in Bethnal Green and Bow against the sitting Labour MP. It was an ill-tempered contest and Galloway won the seat by 823 votes. He would be Respect's only MP and, overall, Respect won just 68,094 votes, putting it way behind the BNP on nearly three times as many votes, and just ahead of Veritas.

The shocking revelation of the whole election was that Tony Blair had got back into power for a third time but with only a 35.2% share of the vote, the lowest of any majority government ever. He received four million less votes than he got in 1997. The Tory vote had gone down by nearly a million since 1997. Only the Lib Dem vote was up by 700,000. Nearly half a million votes had shifted to UKIP, but that was still down on the combined Eurosceptic vote in 1997, including the Referendum Party, of nearly a million. Clearly, a large chunk of the electorate had given up voting and stayed at home. Commentators said this reflected an increased level of distrust in politicians and Tony Blair in particular, but it also equally represented a lack of issues that concerned the voter. The economy was performing well off the back of enormous government expenditure and mass immigration was not yet riling large portions of voters.

In May 2006, Nigel Farage contested a by-election in Bromley & Chislehurst, as a result of the death of Eric Forth, a fiercely Eurosceptic Tory who had joined the *Better Off Out* group a month before he died of cancer. The result reiterated the sense of disillusionment and disinterest in the two main parties highlighted by the general election result. The Tory candidate clung onto the supposedly safe seat but with a much reduced majority, eaten away mostly by the Lib Dems, but a good 8.1% chunk taken away by UKIP. Farage knocked the Labour candidate into fourth place. It was only the second time Labour had been relegated to this position at an English by-election since 1945.

In September 2006, Farage was finally elected leader of UKIP with 45% of the members' votes, nearly double the votes of his nearest rival. Roger Knapman, a former Tory MP who had been UKIP leader since 2002, had stepped down voluntarily—the only UKIP leader to serve a full four year term. In 2004, Knapman had become a UKIP MEP.

Farage gave a strong speech at the party conference a month later, setting out what would become his familiar line of attack on the three main parties.

'We've got three social democratic parties in Britain—Labour, Lib Dem and Conservative are virtually indistinguishable from each other on nearly all the main issues,' he said. 'Frankly, you can't put a cigarette paper between them and that is why there are nine million people who don't vote now in general elections that did back in 1992.'

He also pledged to take UKIP beyond being a single-issue Eurosceptic party. He advocated a flat rate tax of 33% and a 'proper selective education policy'. Above all else, he was offering an alternative voice for the British people.

'A lot of people,' he said, 'feel like me that we're not being given a choice, we're being given no opportunity, that there is no real voice of opposition in British politics—that is what UKIP is here to provide.'

So far, his voice had been heard most effectively within the European parliament where he had scored a series of triumphs in that arena. In 2004, he had exposed Jacques Barrot, the European Commissioner nominated by France, as a convicted embezzler of £2m of government funds. A conviction he had failed to disclose to the European parliament. Socialist and Liberal groups joined UKIP in demanding he resign.

Gawain Towler, a former journalist who was working as a researcher with UKIP in the European parliament, remembers the furore it provoked.

'People claimed we'd done all this hard work,' he says. 'We were accused of working with various spy operations. All it was we googled Jacques Barrot and, oh look, he's been busted for corruption. In the first top ten but it was [under French law] illegal to mention it. It was a case of the Emperor's new clothes. The hit on Barrot was the first time [Farage] had broken through—and that was five years in.'

In 2005, Farage drew attention to Jose Manuel Barroso, President of the European Commission, spending his summer hols on the luxury yacht of Greek shipping billionaire Spiro Latsis, just a month before the Commission approved ten million euros of aid to the same gentleman's shipping company. Farage led a vote of no confidence in Barroso with 75 MEPs backing him. The motion was defeated but again it earned him publicity for uncovering the murky side of the EU. It was also Farage's stamina in making himself available to the UK media that helped lift his national profile.

'He would travel from Brussels to London to do two minutes on Newsnight,' says Towler. 'He was prepared to put himself and his family out, and because the media was aware he would go the extra mile for them and when they got him he provided good copy, that in part has built up his reputation.'

*

Late on a Friday night outside Hounslow West London Underground station in August 2004, a young man broke a bottle against a metal gate. With nine other friends, carrying different weapons including a broken snooker cue, they entered the station and went to the platform where they saw their target standing alongside two other young men. The gang pounced and in the fight one of the young men was knocked down and stabbed three times in the chest with a broken snooker cue.

'As I got there the driver of the train had jumped out,' said a witness, 'taken his shirt off and placed it over the victim's wounds to stop the bleeding. Lying beside them was a piece of metal sharpened to form a knife-edge, a broken-off snooker cue and some shattered glass. He was going very pale and screaming in shock and pain. He was gasping for air.'

A local newsagent recognised some of the young men.

'I have had to call the police before after a gang started fighting between themselves outside my house,' he said. 'There were up to 14 of them, all Somalian and aged between 16 and 18. You see them around on Friday and Saturday nights—they are renowned in the area for causing trouble.'

The stabbed young man died on the platform before an ambulance could reach him. It wasn't the first and wouldn't be the last time that Somali gangs were causing trouble in longer, more established immigrant communities.

In September 2002, Piara Khabra, Labour MP for Ealing Southall, told BBC's *Today* radio programme that African refugees in his constituency were fuelling a crime wave. Street robberies and assaults had spiralled in just six months from 24 incidents to 190.

'There's a perception in the community that crime is being committed by the Somalis,' said Khabra, 'those who came to settle in Southall particularly, I have been told, the youngsters.' He said the police were not doing enough to protect the community. 'If they do not,' he warned, 'I think the community has every right to organise to protect themselves.'

Fighting had already broken out between Somali and Asian gangs as they fought to secure their territories.

The MP was roundly condemned for 'stoking the flames of prejudice', and what was clearly a law and order issue for his constituents was turned by the liberal media into a 'race row', with the shadow of Enoch Powell cast over it. To avoid controversy, the MP left the country.

And yet, Somali commentators would later admit that there was something particular about how some young Somalis were drawn to crime.

'Somali kids just don't get any help,' said one. 'They come from a war zone and they have no idea about [Britain] in terms of its culture, religion or even how education works.'

'I am sick and tired about our own community blaming other forces in "society" for not helping us or understanding our culture,' said another who had fled Mogadishu in the 1980s. 'I have concluded that we have to shed off all our backward cultural/societal practices and only retain our positive attributes and move forward. I am infinitely grateful for the golden opportunity that I got from the UK. For the rest of you out there who prefer to whine and protect your lazy khat chewing lifestyle my only message is don't bring Somalia to the UK.'

But some of those Somali young men, bringing the extreme violence of their homeland to the streets of Britain, were enjoying the power it gave them over rival gangs.

'Gangs here aren't tough, we're tough,' said a member of the Woolwich Boys street gang, brandishing an assault rifle. 'An AK47 isn't the sort of thing you'll see on the street but it would be used in a hit-job.'

'What you've got to understand is in Somalia life is cheap,' he told an undercover reporter. 'We came here with nothing but now dress in the best trainers, drive nice cars, the lot. And there's f**k all the government do about it.'

'These youths come from a violent place where many have seen killings,' said a Metropolitan Police spokesman in 2002, 'so if someone here is trying to take advantage, they are capable of fighting back.'

The arrival of large numbers of African asylum seekers in the late 1990s and early 2000s disrupted many settled communities in the poorer parts of Britain's major cities. It triggered an arms race as youth gangs armed themselves against violent incomers. Knives and attack dogs became part of their armoury as West Indian, white and Asian gangs competed with the newcomers to dominate local crime fiefdoms. Largely ignored by the authorities, it only really started to cause concern among the Westminster elite when 'knife crime' ballooned and it became a major topic of concern in the mid-2000s. Several high profile murders of young people resulted in a government report published in June 2009.

'The high levels of knife violence since 2006 appear to be the result of an increase in street violence between groups of young people who are sometimes referred to as "gangs",' said the report, finally catching up with reality on the council estates. The careful use of the word 'appear' was mirrored by reference to 'perception' in the findings of *The Street Weapons Commission* established by Channel 4 in 2008 and chaired by Cherie Booth, barrister wife of the former

Prime Minister, Tony Blair.

'In the first six months of 2008,' said their report, '17 teenagers were killed in London alone. This has led to the description of the country as facing a knife-crime "epidemic", being plunged into a knife-crime "crisis" or being in the grip of a knife-crime "culture" that is out of control. The public and media's perception of the problem of street weapons is at variance with the official figures which suggest that although violent crime has increased in the last decade, it is now in decline.'

So there you go, the 'knife crisis' was actually over, but the problem for politicians and the well-meaning was that headlining descriptions of tragic incidents of young people stabbed to death kept on coming—and no one in charge wanted to blame it on immigrants for fear of being called 'racist'. Many people living in areas of high immigrant settlement felt increasingly unsafe and saw it largely as a 'black on black' crime epidemic between 'new' and 'old' immigrant elements.

This was not always true as many violent incidents were committed by 'white' immigrant gangster factions—among them Turks, Kurds and Albanians—as well as Asian and native-born criminals. But the racial dimension of the street conflict proved immensely appealing to the British National Party, which exploited the imagery of out of control street crime caused by immigrant gangs and suddenly pitched itself into the national consciousness at the ballot box.

12

WHITE RIOT

In 1999, the British National Party (BNP) stood on the edge of disintegration. Its founder, John Tyndall had been in prison for inciting racial hatred and the party had performed poorly in several East End elections. Its membership was falling and when Nick Griffin stood as party chairman, he ousted Tyndall from the leadership. The 40-year-old father of four had been a member of the National Front (NF) from the age of 14 and was a committed hard-right activist. Although his party's appeal was to the disenfranchised working class, he was a smart upwardly mobile figure. The son of a Conservative councillor and farmer, he'd won a sixth-form scholarship to an independent school and then progressed to Downing College, Cambridge, where he studied history, then switched to law. He was a successful college boxer, after taking up the sport following a street fight.

'I had a scuffle with a very aggressive member of the Socialist Workers Party,' he remembered. 'Part of a little group that beat up my father quite badly. I gave a reasonable account of myself but thought I'll learn to do it better.'

Griffin got to know the neo-Nazi skinhead band *Skrewdriver*. For three years running, he helped organise a summer music festival on his parents' farm—a kind of extreme right-wing Glastonbury. 'We had 500 or so skinheads bouncing around in our yard in the middle of nowhere.'

An electoral candidate for the NF during the 1980s, his increasingly eccentric views on forging political alliances with Libya and Iran saw him split from the party in 1989. A year later he lost an eye in a shotgun accident and his business life went into meltdown.

Supported by his parents financially, he joined the BNP in 1995 and became a key figure for them, editing two magazines for its founder.

When the BNP got their first councillor elected in Millwall, Griffin described their appeal as being 'a strong, disciplined organisation with the ability to back up its slogan "Defend Rights for Whites" with well-directed boots and fists.' But when Griffin became leader of the BNP, he took the party away from its neo-Nazi image and started to engage with an electorate who he knew had changed over the past decade. He kept Tyndall's shift away from compulsory to voluntary repatriation for non-white immigrants and also dropped its old-fashioned anti-Semitism, allowing Jews to join the party. His inspiration was continental Far Right parties such as the French National Front, which were enjoying considerable election success across the Channel. He also realised that 'colour' was not so much the issue now as 'culture'. White kids identified with black West Indians as they shared the same admiration of hip-hop music. It was now more about alien Asian cultures—especially Islam—in northern English towns.

Oldham is an old industrial town in the north of England near Manchester. Commonwealth immigration was encouraged in the 1960s and 1970s to fill factory places but by 2001 most of those jobs had long gone. In a census for that year over a quarter of its residents identified themselves as Asian. Inter-cultural community relations were poor and many spoke of no-go areas for both whites and Asians. In January of that year, the *Oldham Evening Chronicle* reported that the head of the local police force said there had been 572 racial incidents over the previous year and over 60 per cent of them involved white victims. 'There is evidence that they [Asians] are trying to create exclusive areas for themselves,' said the chief superintendent. 'Anyone seems to be a target if they are white.'

Graphic descriptions of young white men being stabbed or attacked by dogs belonging to Asian gangs further inflamed the local community. This attracted the attention of the BNP and they set up a branch in the town, handing out leaflets to the local white residents. On 21 April 2001, a 76-year-old D-Day-veteran was viciously attacked by a group of Asian youths as he walked home, one of them telling him he was 'not allowed in this part of town'.

This assault made national headlines with photographs of his badly battered face, but MPs of all parties steered well clear of commenting on it. On St George's Day, 23 April, English national flags were flown from Oldham lamp posts but were quickly taken down by a nervous council who argued they were wrongly attached and proved a health and safety issue—distracting passing drivers.

Timing is everything in politics and Nick Griffin chose his moment perfectly, announcing his intention to stand as a candidate for Oldham West and Royton in the upcoming general election.

'That was important for us,' said Griffin. 'It broke the media blackout on covering nationalist parties. The media bit on that and that produced a huge amount of publicity.'

When the National Front applied to march through Oldham, they were banned, but Combat 18—a violent neo-Nazi group—turned up, looking for trouble.

'We were told there was a group of white lads being harassed by the police at a pub,' recalled Griffin. 'I went down as the candidate to get the police under control—try to—but in fact it was Combat 18 who had a long standing policy of wanting to stab me on sight. So we had a bit of an argument with them. We then left. They were part of the tension that caused Oldham to go up in flames.'

The precise incident that sparked a night of rioting on Saturday 26 May 2001 happened outside a chip shop in the Glodwick area of Oldham.

'Some white people came home in a taxi and three white lads went down to the chippy,' said a local. 'Three Asian lads started calling them white bastards and hitting them. The white lads came back home and the Asian lads came up and started kicking at the door. Then it all kicked off and people had to go in and lock their doors.'

'It was mad,' said another. 'Bricks and petrol bombs were flying all over the place. The white lads had gone and the Asian lads were fighting the police. They just wanted some people to fight against. I didn't join in.'

Cars were overturned and set alight, barricades quickly assembled, as the police came under sustained attack from hundreds of local residents, with 90 police officers injured by the end of the night. The fighting only came to an end as rain fell just before dawn. This was the worst of the rioting, but over the next few days, more violent incidents occurred across Oldham with the offices of the *Evening Chronicle* being firebombed, along with the house of the Deputy Mayor. It was later dubbed the 'worst racially motivated riots in the UK for fifteen years.' TV news coverage made it look like a bad night in Belfast.

National outcry at the rioting tended to blame far-right parties for stirring up trouble, while Prime Minister Tony Blair was quoted as pointing the finger at the 'bad and regressive motive of white extremists.' But many Oldham voters didn't care about that and registered their anger at having their problems with immigration brushed aside by voting for exactly those extremists. Just under a fortnight after the riots came the general election. The BNP stood two candidates in Oldham—a solid Labour area. Nick Griffin in Oldham West and Royton won 6,552 votes and came a narrow third just behind the Conservatives, gaining 16% of the vote. In Oldham East, the BNP candidate came fourth with 5,091 votes. It was their best ever electoral results.

In the meantime work began on an official report on the rioting in Oldham. Its conclusions revealed a New Labour government that did not like talking about failures in immigration and was still committed to a multicultural society in Britain. Although it could hardly blame the *Oldham Evening Chronicle* for reporting a rise in Asian assaults on white residents, it said that newspaper editors 'should adopt as a high priority the projection of positive images of multi-cultural Oldham and good role models for people of different ethnic backgrounds.'

Equally, while avoiding criticism of the local chief superintendent, it did 'recommend that release of such statistics should always be part of a wider communications strategy and accompanied by extensive prior consultation with communities through the Racist Incident Panel which we propose.' Next time, it implied, the chief bobby should not tell the papers that whites were being overwhelmingly targeted by Asians. It did, however, admit that 'The key failure has been not facing up to the stark reality of ethnic division within the town, which has been clear, and widely commented upon, since at least the 1970s.'

The report blamed the BNP and NF for exploiting the situation, but said that mainstream political parties should wake up to their growing support. 'BNP success is in one sense to be seen as a symptom of problems in the town,' it said, 'since they would have no more chance of success in Oldham than (say) Guildford unless there was fertile soil for them to sow their seeds.' It noted also that their campaigning language had changed. 'Clearly the BNP have been using the term "Muslims" as code for Pakistanis and Bangladeshis, as a means to avoid anti-racism legislation,' said the report. 'We have found in the context of Oldham for example that there is a strong case for outlawing use of a religious descriptor, such as Muslim, when it is intended to signify people of a particular racial group.'

Aside from recommending the expenditure of millions of pounds of taxpayers' money on improving the quality of public services in Oldham, the report ended on a positive note saying 'Oldham has always been a town of immigrants' and 'the town should value and celebrate its diversity'. A few days after the Oldham riots came disturbances in Harehills in Leeds and a race riot in Bradford in July when cars were burned and businesses attacked by mobs of white and Asian youths.

*

Then came the shocking events of 9/11, when American aircraft hijacked by Islamist terrorists were crashed into the World Trade Center in New York and the Pentagon in Washington DC in September 2001, killing almost 3000 people. In the days and weeks after this, the taboo on discussing foreign immigrants was lifted as the news focus was on Muslim immigrant communities. It subtly shifted the race taboo away from complaints about immigration nationalities towards religion and culture. Most importantly, talking about immigration was no longer tantamount to racism and this made it easier for the BNP to discuss its anti-immigrant agenda and appeal to supporters from beyond its usual working-class roots. In 2002-03, it won a few council seats in the north of England in

Burnley, Blackburn and Calderdale.

When Islamist terrorism hit home territory with the 7/7 bombings in London in 2005, Nick Griffin felt confident enough to release political leaflets across the capital blaming New Labour for the recent outrages, thanks to its war in Iraq and open-door immigration. The flyers said 'maybe now it's time to start listening to the BNP'. The message chimed with an electorate weary of Muslim extremists and escalating knife crime on London streets and by 2006 the BNP were reaching 7% in polls. This translated into gains in local elections, with the BNP winning twice as many councillors and becoming the party of opposition to Labour on Barking and Dagenham council in East London.

The broadening appeal of the BNP across the country was characterised by Simone Clarke, a Prima Ballerina with the English National Ballet Company. An undercover investigation by *The Guardian* revealed that she was a member of the BNP in 2006. A profile of her in *The Mail on Sunday* explained why this Far-Right group was now suddenly pulling in middle class members. 'The BNP is certainly repellent,' said the article, but the ballerina's reasoned justification could not be 'simply brushed aside as a foolish error, let alone ignored.'

'I didn't really know anything about the BNP but they had come up in conversation a few times because they had just won some local council seats,' Clarke told *The Mail on Sunday*. After getting annoyed at a TV news story, she was told by her boyfriend to do something about it and she searched for the BNP on her computer. She read the manifesto on their website.

'I'm not too proud to say that a lot of it went over my head but some of the things they mentioned were the things I think about all the time,' she said, 'mainly mass immigration, crime and increased taxes. Those three issues were enough to make me join so I paid my £25 there and then.'

Access to the internet had certainly made it easier to get politically involved and their authenticity appealed to her as well.

'I think the BNP are honest. They're not trying to dress up what they want, which is change on these issues.'

Her membership was a great coup for the BNP, shifting its image instantly away from working-class skinheads to middle class dancers. Suddenly, they were becoming just that little bit more respectable...

'I have been labelled a racist and a fascist because I have a view on immigration—and I mean mass immigration,' said Simone Clarke, not afraid to tackle head on the monolith unleashed by New Labour, 'but isn't that something that a lot of people worry about?'

She was not racist, she confirmed. He partner at the time was her co-dancer, a Cuban-Chinese immigrant. She had no problem with foreigners coming to Britain, working hard and paying their taxes. It was the rate of immigration that was wrong and the feeling that the government—and the other mainstream parties—were doing nothing about it. 'It's not about removing foreigners,' she insisted. 'It's about border controls.'

A key turning point for her was the case of an illegal immigrant who had run over a little girl and killed her but was jailed for just four months. On his release he could not be deported because the European Convention on Human Rights, enshrined in British law under the Human Rights Act 1998, gave him a right to 'family life'.

'Her story has wider implications,' said the *Mail on Sunday* to its two million readers. 'When one of the country's principal ballerinas, a 36-year-old woman who spent much of her recent working life as the Sugar Plum Fairy, decides to join the British neo-fascists, there is an argument that something has gone badly wrong with democratic British politics.'

Aware that she would forever be known as the BNP ballerina, Clarke did not regret her decision. She retired from professional dancing in 2007 and opened a ballet school in her home-town of Leeds.

'People must stop seeing us as ogres,' said a BNP member to the *Guardian* journalist who had first exposed Clarke's membership. The dancer's firm defence of her beliefs certainly helped pitch the fringe party into the mainstream.

'Membership rocketed,' said Griffin. 'People realised it wasn't just a party of skinheads up north or some such nonsense. It had a big effect in getting ordinary people to join, which was surprising. Because of the leak and lack of security, the intuitive thing would be that people would be scared to join after that, which was obviously what was intended, but it didn't.'

It was, in fact, a bit of an own-goal for the left-wing media in its battle against the BNP.

Unused to this level of publicity and electoral success, however, the BNP was tearing itself apart. Uncomfortable with the balancing act of becoming a more professional, apparently more reasonable outfit and yet still harbouring outspoken racist members, dissension within its ranks led to councillors resigning and some members setting up a splinter group—the Real BNP. Nick Griffin's leadership came under pressure from rivals, but externally, their position as the principal party of opposition to mass immigration and Islamic extremism continued to chime with the general population. And many of these new supporters were fed-up with the media's characterisation of them as neo-Nazi nuts.

At a BNP rally in 2007, a highly articulate working-class woman was caught on film and later posted on the BNP website.

'We are not bloody interested in Nazi Germany,' she said. 'No matter what you read in the national newspapers it's absolute tosh... We are not left-wing. We are not right-wing. We're not middle of anything. We are British. We are nationalists. The majority of our policies if you bother to read them veer towards socialism. In fact we probably are the old Labour party in essence. We care about the working-class people.'

'We do hark back to Bob Blatchford and the very early Labour party,' confirms Griffin. 'We maintain that council houses should be controlled by local government and not self-privatised. We believe that the railways, like the post office, are natural monopolies, which should be controlled by the government and not by foreign or British big business. In a number of ways we are the Labour party before it sold out to the corporates.'

Blatchford was a socialist campaigner who did not regard himself as a Marxist. 'English Socialism is not Marxian; it is humanitarian,' he said in 1907. 'It does not depend upon any theory of "economic justice" but upon humanity and common sense.'

'We represent the working class who feel left behind and completely ignored,' says Griffin. 'Until we came on the scene, the Labour Party's position, which came out very clearly in the leak from

[Andrew] Neather, that the Labour Party decided they could no longer count on the votes of the white working class, because they were going to privatise everything in sight and become a globalist party, so as a consequence they decided to import a new voting bloc.' Griffin believes it was those 'left behind' working-class voters who turned to the BNP.

In 2008, Richard Barnbrook, who was already the BNP leader on Barking and Dagenham council, won a seat on the London Assembly, gaining 69,710 votes from Londoners, over 5% of the total.

'I promise to every single Londoner out there,' he bellowed at City Hall, 'regardless of creed, colour or identity the nonsense of political correctness will be swept aside!'

'This is Britain, it is for the British people,' he said, 'it is not for people to enter into this land dictating what will or will not happen to the people that created it and built it over generations.'

It was an increasingly broad definition of what the BNP stood for. When asked on a radio show whether ethnic minorities should be concerned about his victory, Barnbrook replied: 'Do not be nervous. As long as you abide by our identity and laws of this land, come to me and I will see where we can help.'

One could not imagine this queue being very long, but it was BNP as defender not aggressor. They called for an end to mass immigration, the deportation of all illegal immigrants and offered 'voluntary re-settlement' for any immigrants who wished to return home. Suddenly, this wasn't sounding that extreme at all...

This momentum continued into 2009 with European elections. Anti-European and anti-immigration sentiment expressed itself effectively through proportional representation by propelling two BNP candidates into the European parliament. Nick Griffin won a seat in the North West region with 8% of the vote, while Andrew Brons gained a seat in the Yorkshire and Humber region with 9.8%. A victorious Griffin proclaimed his creed to reporters in Manchester.

'For the last 50 years, more and more of the people of Britain have watched with concern and growing dismay and sometimes anger as an out of touch political elite has transformed our country before our very eyes,' he told them. 'It is not just a matter of mass immigration—although that is the most obvious symptom of it—it's handing us over to rule by unelected bureaucrats in Brussels, it's turning the commonwealth of this country, our public services into private profit centres for giant corporations, it's banning St George's day festivals while encouraging everyone else to celebrate their festivals, usually with taxpayers' money. In so many ways the liberal elite have transformed this country.'

David Cameron didn't get it at all.

'It brings shame on us that these fascist, racist thugs have been elected to the European Parliament,' he said, brandishing his liberal credentials.

Lib Dem leader Nick Clegg, however, could see the value of the protest vote.

'We should not dismiss the reasons why people have voted for the BNP,' he said, 'the anger, the frustration, the sense of alienation, the sense of powerlessness. We must listen to that and must react to that, that much is obvious.'

When later asked by the BBC if his party was still racist, Griffin turned it around by saying: 'There's a huge amount of racism in this country, overwhelmingly it is directed towards the indigenous British majority, which is one reason we've done so well in these elections.'

BNP as defender not aggressor—it was winning them bucket-loads of votes.

In an article for the left-wing *New Statesman*, academic Matthew Goodwin concluded that the BNP—a supposedly right-wing racist nationalist party—was in fact positioning itself to the left of the Labour Party. He said it was attracting support from 'older, less educated, white working-class men—voters from Labour's historical base who feel they have benefited little from the past decade of Labour government, and whose resentments the BNP has succeeded in articulating.'

'They gained little from the Blair boom and will be the first to suffer in the Brown bust,' said Goodwin. 'Their growing cynicism, distrust and detachment from politics have not been taken seriously by Labour, perhaps because the party's strategists believed they have nowhere else to go.'

They certainly had somewhere to go now and in local elections held on the same day as those for the European Parliament, the BNP gained its first three county council seats. By the end of the year, their membership had peaked at 12,632 and their party coffers had swollen to almost £2 million. As a prize for their electoral breakthrough, Nick Griffin was invited to appear on BBC TV's flagship political-discussion show Question Time. It caused a media scandal but the BBC Director-General argued that the BNP's level of support entitled them to occasional representation on such a programme.

Griffin's appearance on 22 October 2009 alongside New Labour's Secretary of State for Justice Jack Straw, Conservative Shadow Minister for Community Cohesion, Baroness Warsi, Lib Dem Home Affairs spokesperson Chris Huhne and African-American writer Bonnie Greer, proved a ratings winner with over eight million viewers switching on—more than double any previous audience for the show. It certainly had a gladiatorial quality about it, for which Griffin said he was prepared.

'I will, no doubt, be interrupted, shouted down, slandered, put on the spot, and subjected to a scrutiny that would be a thousand times more intense than anything directed at other panellists,' he said on the BNP website the morning of the broadcast. 'It will, in other words, be political blood sport. But I am relishing this opportunity.'

New Labour had previously pledged not to appear on any platform beside the BNP but now had to modify this stance. Prime Minister Gordon Brown thought it would be a good opportunity to expose their 'racist and bigoted views'. Conservative leader David Cameron said the appearance made him feel 'uneasy—I don't think the BBC should have done it.'

Coaches brought in some 800 anti-Fascist protestors who crowded around the entrances to Television Centre in west London hours before the programme was recorded. Letting off orange smoke flares, a few broke through the police cordon to enter the building but were quickly expelled. Griffin made his way into the studio on foot, unnoticed, by a rear entrance.

Wearing a smart dark suit and a poppy, Griffin sat between Greer and programme chairman David Dimbleby. The first question from the audience criticised the BNP for using images of war-leader Winston Churchill in their campaign material. This gave Straw the perfect opportunity to compare the BNP to the Nazis, saying they defined themselves by their views on race and that this distinguished them from other parties in Britain. He also explained that many soldiers from other races—from the British Empire—had come to help defend Britain in both the first and second world wars and that laid the basis for a multi-racial society. He had read their names on gravestones in a French military cemetery that held many dead soldiers from his own Lancashire constituency. It was an impressive speech and won an enthusiastic round of applause from the studio audience.

Nick Griffin sounded hoarse and nervous in his reply. He claimed that Churchill was opposed to mass immigration in its early years and that British efforts in both world wars were aimed at securing a national freedom that Straw and New Labour were giving away to the European Union.

'My father was in the RAF during the Second World War,' he gibed, 'while Mr Straw's father was in prison for refusing to fight Adolf Hitler.'

This got a smattering of applause and many boos from the audience.

'What's that got to do with the issue?' said Dimbleby.

'Mr Straw was attacking me. I've been relentlessly attacked and demonised in the last few days. The fact is my father was in the RAF during the Second World War. I am not a Nazi. I never have been.'

Moments later, however, Dimbleby asked whether Griffin was a holocaust denier.

'I do not have a conviction for holocaust denial,' he said shakily, then half smiled.

'Why are you smiling?' said Dimbleby. 'It is not a particularly amusing issue.'

His party's past and continuing infatuation, among some of its members, with Nazi racial views, was hard to escape. Dimbleby then quoted Griffin as saying that his more moderate recent stance on immigration was merely a front for more extreme views.

'Perhaps one day the British people might change their minds,' Dimbleby quoted Griffin saying in a video, 'but if you put that, ie getting rid of all coloured people from Britain, as your sole aim to start with you're going to get absolutely nowhere, so instead of talking about racial purity, we talk about identity. We use saleable words, freedom, security, identity, democracy, nobody can come and attack you on those ideas'. Having come to the end of that devastating quote, Dimbleby concluded that 'The truth is what you are saying there was that's just the start of the story and when we've won public support, then we can go to our proper agenda.'

It got worse for Griffin as he explained he was sharing a stand with David Duke, the leader of a 'non-violent' faction of the Ku Klux Klan, and that he was trying to win him over to his more moderate views. This drew laughs from the audience. When he made a feeble joke about Duke being in disguise wearing a 'hood' he looked desperate. Bonnie Greer turned her back on him

'Why should anybody trust what you say?' insisted Dimbleby. 'Why should anyone think it is any more than a façade?'

'Why should anybody trust any politician?' said Griffin lamely. 'All of us. Simple as that.'

It was looking like a televised car crash for Griffin with more derision heaped on him as he tried to explain his previous doubts about the full horror of the holocaust. Then, a gentleman in the audience asked a very interesting question.

'Can the recent success of the BNP be explained by the misguided immigration policy of the government?'

It was directed at Jack Straw.

'I don't think it can,' he said straight away, then went into a rambling reference to Enoch Powell, his rivers of blood speech and the recruitment of African-Caribbean people in to the National Heath Service.

'You've been in power for nearly 12 years now,' interrupted Dimbleby, 'let's deal with the present. Is the rise of the BNP, which has happened very recently, is that because of your government's policies?'

More history followed from Straw about extremist parties in the

UK. This was the classic New Labour narrative they wanted to get out—that objections to immigration were essentially racist, and very old fashioned. But Dimbleby wasn't having any of it.

'Are you saying there is no worry about the scale of immigration in this country? Is that the point you are making? I can't get out what you are saying?'

'Of course there is a worry,' Straw said, then quoted figures saying immigration was going down and the government was actively seeking to control it. 'But on the issue of can we pull up the drawbridge and stop people coming to this country,' he argued. 'Certainly not. Because one of the great strengths of this country is its diversity. And for the future. Although of course I understand this very acutely in my own constituency where now 30% of the population are of M... [he was going to say Muslim, than changed his mind] Asian origin that it can be very disturbing to people when they see change in front of their eyes...'

'Sorry, can I just try one more time,' broke in Dimbleby, pointing his pen at Griffin. Was the reason for his appearance on the panel that night due to 'failings by your government over the last 12 years to reassure people about the scale of immigration or not?'

'I don't believe it is,' said Straw. 'If you want to know why the BNP won in the North West and Yorkshire... it was a lot to do with discontent with all the political parties, particularly over the issue of expenses.' He was referring to the major scandal that year about MPs abusing their expense claims

At this point, Baroness Warsi intervened.

'I think, Jack, there are certain things that mainstream political parties have to be honest about and I think that answer is not an honest answer.'

The audience erupted in applause.

Warsi had campaigned in Dewsbury, West Yorkshire, where at the previous election they had the largest BNP vote in the country. She had met many of those people who voted for the BNP and immigration was most definitely an issue for them.

'There are many people who feel that the pace of change in their community has been too fast—and that the government has not properly resourced those particular areas to respond to that change.'

'This not a race debate,' Warsi said, to which Griffin frantically nodded. 'There are many people out there who vote for the British National Party who are not racist.' It was up to the main political parties to listen to their concerns and do something about them. The audience were with her, except when one of them pointed out Conservative failings in immigration policy as well.

Lib Dem Chris Huhne saw his opportunity and poured scorn on New Labour's wild underestimation of the rate of eastern European immigration.

'The government projected it would be 56,000 people would come here,' he said. 'It ended up being 766,000. That is probably one of the worst government forecasts on record.'

Squabbling then broke out between the three main party representatives as they pointed fingers at each other for allowing unrestricted EU immigration across their borders. This allowed Nick Griffin to condemn them all.

'It's the fault of the entire political elite, which has imposed an enormous multi-cultural programme, experiment on the British people without so much as a by your leave. All we've got out of it is tax bills. It's transformed our country.'

Then he referred to indigenous people and the entire panel pounced on him, saying he was bringing race back into the debate. Bizarrely, he referred to tours of the Lake District being cancelled because only English people were going on them. The pressure was starting to show. He stood by his statement that mass immigration was an act of genocide against the British people.

'You'll be surprised,' said a member of the audience, 'how many people will have a whip round to buy you a ticket and your supporters to go the South Pole—that's a colourless landscape that will suit you fine.'

Griffin just had to grin and bear it. The evidence was out there before eight million British people. Yes, he articulated frustration at mass immigration, but he and his core party just couldn't escape their weird language of race.

'It was hard going,' he told a reporter straight afterwards. 'It was a bit like a boxing match.' He felt he had landed 'a few punches of my own' but in truth, it didn't do him or the party any favours. He later felt he had been ambushed by a 'lynch-mob' of the panel and audience, who he felt, being a typically multicultural London group, were not his natural constituency. But even his supporters were not happy with the performance.

'It's almost like Nick went on expecting a normal episode of Question Time,' said one, 'it was always going to be a hatchet job and he should have been fully prepared for questions relating to his past.'

'I'm starting to think this appealing to the mainstream approach is the wrong direction,' said another, putting his finger on it. The BNP, with its heritage of racism and fascism, was never going to appeal beyond the fringe. Polls taken immediately after the broadcast were more encouraging, however, with YouGov saying that 22% of the electorate would now consider voting for the BNP and their website claimed to have received 9,000 serious enquiries for membership.

'I don't regret doing it,' says Griffin now. 'It was positive from an external point of view. Having said that, internally, people thought I should have done better. Various factions, who were trying to get rid of me made quite a big thing of it—he's washed up.'

The BNP entered the general election in 2010 with a record 338 candidates, but it won no seats. Griffin, standing in Barking, came third with 16.4% of the vote. The party received over half a million votes, 1.2% of the whole cast, more than ever before, but in local elections held at the same time, the BNP lost all its 12 councillors in Barking and lost more councillors elsewhere, halving their seats from their high point of 55 the year before. Overall, it was a disappointing performance and led to more infighting within the BNP.

In 2011, Griffin was challenged for the leadership by Andrew Brons MEP. Griffin just secured victory, but BNP membership was collapsing and it would never again cause a stir in national politics. Its time had come and gone. In his Question Time appearance, the biggest TV political broadcast he would ever have, he came over as untruthful and evasive about his past. Was he authentic or was he just giving a more moderate line to hide his more extreme views?

This doubt would never leave him.

Ironically, the decline of the BNP occurred at just the time that mass immigration was finally being discussed as a key campaign issue—but they would not be the beneficiaries of this debate. It was another party that would prove more effective at articulating anger at mass immigration—and that was led by Nigel Farage.

'Our people are not voting UKIP because it's not a nationalist party,' argues Griffin, 'it's very different to us in many ways, it's not the old Labour party, it's the most right wing bit of the old Conservative party. But a lot of our people feel well, how can we get anywhere when UKIP is being pushed by the BBC and the Mail?'

'It's well known in UKIP circles that Farage had a meeting with senior people in the BBC,' alleges Griffin, 'and they arranged they would plug UKIP as a way of blocking us. He was happy with that. The BBC and the Labour party then realised that promoting UKIP was a splendid way of damaging the Tories. The right-wing print media have a totally different agenda and they've been using UKIP to push Cameron on Europe and other issues to the right. So everyone from the hard-left through the Labour party through to the traditional right way, they all, for different reasons, have decided to promote UKIP. UKIP is tame and safe.'

Griffin was keen to contest the 2014 European Elections. Despite being declared personally bankrupt in January 2014, he warned, 'We've got a very big war chest.' Adding 'It's a hoax that UKIP is anti-immigration. They're against east European immigration, as we are. But their policy is actually one in, one out. So, a quarter of a million of us leave and a quarter of a million Somalis and Pakistanis in, plus 50,000 with work permits. From a working-class point of view, that's 50,000 people with a right to take your job.'

He does admire Farage but with a few barbs. 'He's a very shrewd politician,' he says. 'He's done his deal with the BBC and so on, which guarantees him the coverage he needs. However, he does undoubtedly watch for rivals and gets rid of them. He's actually quite divisive within the party... how he handles people, how he handles money. So, he's flawed in that regard, but he's played a blinder with the way he comes across in the media. He's slimy, but he is good.'

If events don't go as planned for Griffin, he knows what he's going to do in retirement.

'We've got a couple of acres in the Welsh hills. I gave up keeping pigs when I got elected [as MEP]. When I do retire I'd like to keep Gloucester Old Spots.'

13

BORIS-MANIA

Whenever he enters a room, everyone starts smiling. Whenever he opens his mouth, people start laughing. Boris Johnson is the nearest David Cameron's Conservative Party has to a populist politician—and unlike their leader, he wins elections. The most obvious candidate to succeed Cameron as leader of the party, his tousled appearance, his edge-of-the seat proximity to gaffes, his rococo use of language, his distinctive view of the world—all this suggests he is the maverick leader that the Tories have been waiting for—the man to unite all the party behind him, even the awkward squad of rebels. But it is just those backbenchers that have been so critical of their party leadership's lack of faith in their grassroots beliefs that most see through Johnson's carapace of wit and charm. Would they vote for him?

'I wouldn't vote for him,' says Philip Davies MP. 'The public see him as a likeable buffoon. Whereas that's fine for the Mayor of London, I'm not entirely sure they want their Prime Minister to be a likeable buffoon.'

So is Boris, in fact, a fake maverick?

In 2008, he was the most effective weapon in the Tory arsenal and they directed him at the campaign for the London mayoralty. It was to be a key step in their fight back to power. His task was to take down a truly daunting populist maverick, Ken Livingstone.

The sitting mayor for two terms, Livingstone had won his seat by cleverly setting himself up against his own party and being openly critical of New Labour. Known as 'Red Ken' from his days as Leader of the Greater London Council until Margaret Thatcher abolished it, he was one of the great battling anti-Thatcher figures of the 1980s and compounded this with his unashamedly hard-left views. When his socialism seemed old fashioned, he updated it by embracing the new creed of environmentalism—for him, green really was the new red. Voters would close their eyes to his more extreme views because they liked his authenticity—he spoke his mind, you knew where you stood with him and Londoners definitely thought he'd have the balls to be on their side against central government—he would be no stooge of Blair.

Indeed, Blair didn't even want Livingstone as his party's candidate. A less controversial figure was selected, but Livingstone felt the party vote had been rigged and put himself forward as an independent candidate, leading to automatic expulsion from New Labour. Free of party allegiances, he won a decisive victory, thrashing the official Labour party candidate into third place and comfortably defeating the Tory contender. Once in power, he introduced the popular Oyster Card system of payment for London transport and the less popular congestion charge. By the time he stood again in 2004, he'd been re-admitted into the Labour Party and, despite that, won comfortably for the second time. In 2008, he would be a hard act to shift and the Tories knew it would be a tremendous dent in the power of the Labour government if they did.

The previous year, the Conservatives had struck a significant blow at New Labour at their autumn party conference. Tony Blair had stepped down as Prime Minister in June 2007 to be succeeded by his Chancellor Gordon Brown. Because of Blair's unpopular association with the war in Iraq, Brown enjoyed a bounce in the polls and for a tantalising moment he considered calling a snap election to make the most of it, but he fumbled the decision and it would be a costly error for him as his party began to slide in the polls following a brilliant but unusual piece of populist politics from Cameron's party.

In order to detoxify the Tory brand, Cameron and his followers had done everything they could to disassociate themselves from the supposedly bad old tax-cutting days of Thatcher—and they had openly declared their desire to match Gordon Brown's spending plans—but then George Osborne, the Shadow Chancellor stood up at the party conference in October 2007 and confounded everyone's expectations by pledging major tax cuts!

'I believe lower, simpler taxes are vital for Britain to compete,' he told the serried rows of Tories. 'And I give you this personal promise. I will approach each Budget seeking ways, consistent with sound public finances and economic stability, to reduce taxes on businesses and families striving for a better life. That's the real difference between this Chancellor and the next one. He is always looking for ways to put taxes up. I will always be looking for ways to bring taxes down.'

In actual fact it was still very much a moderniser's speech. Osborne paid full tribute to Cameron for changing the party, making it more relevant to modern Britain, defending the National Health Service and comprehensive education. He even flagged up a shift in taxation 'from income to pollution' with an array of new green taxes. But that was all forgotten when he moved on to announcing two actual tax cuts. First was abolishing stamp duty for first time buyers purchasing a home for under £250,000—but then came the promise that everyone would take away from the conference with a smile on their face.

'When inheritance tax was first introduced it was designed to hit the very rich,' said Osborne. 'But the very rich hire expensive advisers to make sure they don't pay it. Instead, thanks to Gordon Brown, this unfair tax falls increasingly on the aspirations of ordinary people. So now well over a third of homeowners in Britain have the threat of inheritance tax hanging over them. These are people who have worked all their lives. People who have saved money all their lives. People who have already paid taxes once on their income.

'People whose only crime in the eyes of the taxman is that instead of spending their savings on themselves, they want to pass something on to their families. People who feel the most basic human instinct of all: they aspire to a better life for their children and their grandchildren. Our Government will be on their side. The next Conservative Government will raise the Inheritance Tax threshold to £1 million.'

With this one stroke, Osborne set the Tory party back on the path to power. It was not so much the choice of the tax, it was the attitude it represented. Inheritance tax frequently topped the list of most resented taxes simply because it was taxing earnings twice. Homeownership had been at the heart of Thatcher's revolution and the fact that the wealth locked in those homes would be taxed by a greedy government didn't sit well with the aspiring classes—those grassroots Tories. At last, after all the talk about hugging hoodies and huskies, the Conservative party was back on their side and, as result, their poll ratings immediately started to climb upwards.

Straight afterwards at the conference the BBC's Andrew Neil wondered if this was a shot across the bows of the 'uber-modernisers' in the party, but Osborne easily side-stepped that, content in the knowledge that he'd delivered a mortal blow to Gordon Brown's premiership while still waving the modernising flag. 'The shadow chancellor's last conference speech set the course for a dramatic Tory revival and turned him into a "big beast",' acclaimed *Prospect Magazine*. 'His conference speech made the political weather—it changed British politics and that is quite an achievement,' said the novelist Robert Harris, a close associate of New Labour.' The really bold stroke was the £1m round number on inheritance tax and the way in which it contrasted with Brown's fiddling with tax bands.'

Boris Johnson seemed an unlikely candidate to follow up on this triumph, but his sheer amiability was at the heart of his appeal. A journalist with the *Telegraph* and then editor of the *Spectator*, he was a very effective popular writer and this was compounded by amusing appearances on television, most notably the satirical BBC TV show Have I Got News For You? He managed to combine a bumbling caricature of a toff with a witty turn of phrase and most, importantly, a good dose of self-deprecation, which made him both likeable and accessible to many voters who would not normally give any kind of Tory the time of day. He reached parts of the electorate no other Tory could—and still does. The position of Mayor of London, thanks to Ken Livingstone, was judged by the Tories to rely more on character and recognition than on ability and so Johnson was deemed perfect for it. Indeed, by the time of the 2008 mayoral election, Boris and Ken would have appeared on exactly the same number of episodes of Have I Got News for You—seven each!

Johnson had become an MP in 2001, succeeding Michael Heseltine in Henley and progressed to Shadow Minister for Arts in 2004. This came to a rapid end when he was sacked from this post for lying to Tory leader Michael Howard about his extramarital affair with a *Spectator* journalist. David Cameron picked him again when he became leader in 2005 and appointed him as Shadow Minister for Higher Education. When Johnson was shortly after accused of another affair with a journalist, Cameron did not consider it a sacking offence, no doubt valuing his ability to detoxify the Tory brand beyond that of his sexual incontinence. Johnson thrived on the patronage of the Tory modernisers and this culminated in their choice of him as their mayoral candidate in 2008.

Australian political strategist Lynton Crosby was hired to oversee Johnson's campaign, despite having failed to advise the Tories to an election victory in 2005. Crosby told Johnson to get his hair cut and tell fewer jokes in order to appear more serious but also, playing to his strengths, guided him towards lighter television and radio appearances which suited his personality better than more probing news interviews.

Cameron helped accentuate the 'maverick' character of Johnson when he launched his campaign by saying 'I don't always agree with him, but I respect the fact that he's absolutely his own man.' Thus, turning him into a blue Ken Livingstone. Cameron then followed this up by saying 'He's a proper Conservative—practical, open-minded and keen to get things done.' This again, apparently, put distance between Johnson and the modernisers and his mayoral campaign led with a hard-Tory promise to crack down on the knife crime and the youth murders that were blighting the city's streets.

'Proper' conservatives were less than impressed.

'Mr Johnson is not a politician. He is an act,' wrote political commentator Simon Heffer at the time. 'He is serving a very useful purpose for his party. It was decided, presumably by one of the advertising men who now control the Conservatives, that the only way to beat an act was with another, even better one. They certainly went to the right man.'

Johnson is no buffoon, continued Heffer, and uses his act

brilliantly for political advancement. 'Mr Johnson is the most ambitious person I have ever met.'

Beyond deploying Johnson's personality, some hard strategic work helped win over voters by concentrating on the outer ring of London, home to more Tory supporters and usually ignored by Livingstone's electoral machine. It was them bothering to turn out that helped amass 1,168,738 votes for Johnson on the polling day, against Livingstone's 1,028,966. It was a notable victory and helped make the Tories look strong contenders for the 2010 general election.

Once in power, Johnson has proved anything but the maverick Tory and has helped push their modernising agenda. Unsurprisingly, he appointed Nicholas Boles, the third co-founder of Policy Exchange—along with Michael Gove and Francis Maude—as his first chief of staff. His first decision was a distinctly non-libertarian ban of drinking alcohol on London Transport. He broke public office protocol by openly endorsing the US Democrat candidate Barack Obama for President. His keen support of cycling transport measures and the introduction of the 'Boris bike' helped secure Cameron's green credentials.

On the occasions Johnson has clashed with Cameron, it is because he has veered even further to the left, both helpfully reinforcing his image as 'his own man' and connecting with a broader audience—usually just in time to win a chunk of votes. In April 2012, just before his second mayoral election contest, he criticised the government's housing benefit reforms.

'On the housing benefit problem,' he told an ITV news reporter, 'I think it's also common ground you have to reform housing benefit but what I was able to do if you may remember when the reform was first proposed, I said I wouldn't have the Kosovo-style social cleansing because of it and we will not have that.'

The over-the-top reference to Balkan ethnic cleansing infuriated Cameron but delighted *Guardian* readers. He even agreed with Red Ken. 'Where Ken is right, what we need to do is accelerate our programme of house building of new homes for Londoners.'

Though sometimes irritated by his language, the Tory modernisers could not fail to be delighted with such a high profile

Tory who spoke the language of the urban liberal elite and was a star among them. He won his second term with a slightly increased percentage of votes.

When it comes to immigration, Johnson is again to the left of his modernising government and their stated attempts to limit it, although realising it is a leading concern for traditional Conservative voters, he does put out a mixed message—no doubt intentionally. Portraying himself as a 'descendant of immigrants' he is keen to identify with the largely immigrant population of London.

'I'm probably about the only politician I know of who is actually willing to stand up and say that he's pro-immigration,' he said in 2013. He then blamed the Labour government for giving mass immigration a bad name. 'Frankly it was, if I may say so, the active decision of the Labour government to turn a complete blind eye that undermined immigration in the eyes of many people in this country.' So, this was a sin of presentation, and yet in the next sentence he says 'And you should think about that because it did serious social damage.' What? Mass immigration and its negative impact on social services or badly communicating its virtues?

Confusingly, he then condemned illegal immigration saying 'you've got to be very, very tough in dealing with people who break the law. They are undermining the credentials and the hard work of everybody else.' And yet previously he had declared himself in favour of a 'one-off amnesty for illegal immigrants.'

So what is his stance on immigration? It is typically, amusingly contrarian but with caveats that appeal to both those who are for it *and* those who are against it. A brilliant Boris statement that makes you smile and leaves you none the wiser.

In November 2013, Johnson was invited by the Centre for Policy Studies to give their Margaret Thatcher lecture. He began by praising her Churchillian pluck in the Falklands War and her battles against the unions, transforming Britain from a wasteland of bleached dog turds to a groovy, thrusting nation that every foreigner wants to come to. But then he wonders what would Maggie do now with the problems faced by the UK? She would back his government's unpopular HS2 train project, apparently. Implausibly, regarding the EU, he says that she would in fact support his patron's renegotiating stance.

'As it happens,' he said, 'I don't think she would pull out of the single market that she helped to create; not like that, not if she was now the tenant of Number Ten. I think she would recognise that there is a chance to get a better deal'—just like his patron Cameron.

As for immigration. 'It's time to sort out the immigration system so that we end the madness,' he blusters, but then paragraphs later celebrates 'a vast mongrel energy' in our immigrant-stuffed cities making the UK the largest populated country in Europe by the middle of the century. Indeed, if New Labour's purpose was to use immigration to create a new low wages economy and destroy the unions, then the Tories are happy to see continued high immigration turn Britain into a new Germany.

'By 2060,' he says, 'we will have more people than Germany. And yes, I can see you gulp, and no, I don't know exactly where they will all go either; though when I drive through the cities of the north I see plenty of depopulated space.' Has anyone bothered to ask them their views on that vision of the future?

So Boris wraps himself in the cloak of the great maverick Maggie and then says she would have agreed with everything David Cameron is doing. Another Johnson job well done!

'He's got an urban liberal constituency in London and he has to suck up to them in order to keep in with his electorate,' says Heffer, five years after he first criticised his mayoral posturing. 'I don't know whether he would change his mind if he got back into parliament. Boris doesn't strike me as having many principles at all, whether in one direction or another. His principles are available to the highest bidder. Boris will always do what furthers his own ambitions. He always has and always will.'

Freedom Association Chief Executive Simon Richards compares Johnson with Victorian Prime Minister Benjamin Disraeli. 'Both shifty characters but they had style,' he says, and he feels he can be trusted on Europe. 'The thing about Boris is he's shrewd, he wants to be popular, he knows the public doesn't like the EU.'

Safely in his second term as London Mayor, so close to a general election in 2015 and with the economy appearing to be growing again, Johnson has been careful to say little that would rile his modernising patrons in the Conservative Party. If he keeps his head down, he sees himself sailing into the leadership on a wave of personality and a not incompetent record as mayor.

As for George Osborne's tax-cutting pledge that got the Tories off to a poll ascending start in 2007, Heffer is equally unimpressed by that. 'It was made at a time when they thought there might be a general election coming up. That was the only reason that speech happened.'

It took exactly two years for that promise to come to an end. In the year before the actual general election, with the polls swinging in their favour, Osborne thought it would be better to take on a more responsible mantle. Fearing that a cut in inheritance tax was now inappropriate following the financial melt-down of 2008— and worse it might be criticised by Labour as a tax cut for the rich—he ditched his flagship policy, which had done so much to raise the party's standing in the polls, saying his 'first priority is dealing with the debt'. Not that he'd do much about that either.

Those aspiring Tory voters who liked the attitude represented by Osborne's speech now had little to cheer for. Or as Simon Heffer puts it, 'The problem is you can only tell lies to people so often and if you've gone out on a limb on inheritance tax and done nothing about it, you can't play that card again.' The fact that the Conservative Party is now embarrassed by this speech was underlined when they erased all access to it on their website, along with other pre-2010 speeches, in November 2013.

*

If the first decade of the 21st century was one in which UK voters became increasingly disconnected from their main political parties, then this gap would widen at the end of the decade when a major new scandal broke. This time it was the result of dogged research by Heather Brooke, an American journalist who had come to live in Britain. She used the Freedom of Information (FoI) Act introduced by New Labour in 2000, but only coming into force in 2005, to investigate the expenses claimed by MPs of all parties.

Most of these requests were blocked by the Speaker of the House of Commons, Michael Martin. She then appealed to the Information Commissioner who agreed to release some of this material, but this was blocked by MPs who then voted in favour of an exemption for them from the FoI Act. The House of Lords failed to support this exemption. Finally, an Information Tribunal ordered the release of information on 14 MPs, including the leaders of the two main parties. The Speaker again tried to block this but the High Court of Justice ruled in favour of its release.

Finally, the full details of MPs claimed expenses were revealed in May 2009, thanks to the *Daily Telegraph* publishing a leaked, unedited version of the details and weeks of revelations entertained and dismayed the British public. Readers were introduced to the concept of 'flipping' in which MPs re-designated their second homes in order to claim taxpayers' money for buying and decorating both their homes. Sometimes MPs claimed for second homes that were in fact being rented out, sometimes these were in fact third homes if they lived in 'grace and favour' residences in Westminster. Claims for other expenses were frequently rounded up or claimed for just below the figure of £250 for which no receipts were needed at all.

Some specific claims were immensely embarrassing and just plain funny. The husband of Labour Home Secretary Jacqui Smith put two pornographic movies on her expenses. Conservative MP Peter Viggers claimed £1600 for an ornamental duck house in the pond of his garden. These became the iconic stories of the affair, but many more MPs were exposed for being profligate with taxpayers' money. Several ministers resigned and other MPs agreed to step down at the next election. Many MPs paid back the money they had over claimed, while those who had been criminally fraudulent faced prosecution and imprisonment.

Prime Minister Gordon Brown paid back expenses claimed for gardening, as did Lib Dem leader Nick Clegg. Cameron repaid a small sum for excessive mortgage claims. The Speaker of the House of Commons who had done so much to obstruct the investigation was forced to resign. It was a shameful period for parliamentary democracy and it soured even further the public's appetite for conventional politics. Heather Brooke was rightly recognised for her important role initiating this saga and she is now Professor of Journalism at City University London.

The *Telegraph's* publication of the MPs' expenses scandal came just a month before the 2009 European elections. Lord Tebbit, a prominent Thatcherite and Eurosceptic, urged voters to show their disgust with politicians by boycotting the major parties.

'What I am advising people is to show our major parties it is the electors who are the masters,' he said on the BBC *Today* radio show, 'and that the electors are extremely upset with their employees in the House of Commons. I have said don't vote for the major parties.'

When later asked exactly who they should vote for, he replied: 'I wouldn't seek to give advice on that. But if there was an enormous fall in the vote for the major parties the message might get through. People could vote Green, they could vote for all sorts of wider people, or they could choose not to vote at all. That's the only message these people understand – when voters refuse to vote for them.'

He drew the line at the BNP, however, calling them 'Labour with racism'. He did not say vote UKIP, but hinted as much. To have done so openly would have invited immediate expulsion from his party. But one major Tory donor had no such fears. Sir Stuart Wheeler had made a fortune in the City founding the spread betting firm IG Index. He had given the Conservative Party £5m in 2001, the largest ever political donation. But he did not like the path pursued by the Tory modernisers and backed David Davis as leader against Cameron. Increasingly annoyed by Cameron's stance over the Lisbon treaty, the 74-year-old Wheeler gave £100,000 to UKIP in March 2009. The next day, he was thrown out of the party.

'It was perfectly reasonable for them to have done that,' recalls Wheeler. 'It was done by Eric Pickles by email.' Pickles, who was then the Tory chairman, later claimed he'd had a long discussion with Wheeler about it. 'I've never spoken to him in my life,' says Wheeler. 'It was very odd that.'

Wheeler has long enjoyed gambling and still regularly visits Las Vegas for the poker championships. In the 1960s he used to play a blackjack system in Vegas and did very well until, after one successful hand of cards, he smiled—at which point the pit boss asked him to leave. Moving in London gambling circles, he knew Sir James Goldsmith.

'I had a funny arrangement with Jimmy,' says Wheeler. 'When we used to meet, he would toss a coin and if I got it wrong I would pay him a thousand pounds, but if I got it right he'd pay me £1100. It suited me because I got the right odds and it suited him because he knew it mattered like hell to me.'

One evening, Wheeler was in Aspinall's with his girlfriend when Sir James challenged him to a coin toss again. Wheeler lost twice in a row and stopped at that point, but an Iranian gambler came up to him and said 'Never mind Stuart, you've really won £100.' 'Of course he was right because if you carried on doing it for the rest of your life you would actually average £100 profit.' Wheeler's girlfriend was mystified, but it can't have bothered her much because she ended up marrying him. Wheeler did not later get involved with the Referendum Party because politics didn't interest him at the time. That all changed with New Labour's victory in 1997.

Wheeler would eventually become Treasurer for UKIP in 2011, although he feels he isn't best suited to it—'I don't really like asking people for money,' he says modestly. He is very well connected. His youngest daughter works for Tory strategist Lynton Crosby. 'My duty is to spy on her, her duty is to spy on me.'

In the June 2009 European elections, UKIP came a strong second after the Tories with 2,498,226 votes, knocking Labour into third. It was the first time they'd come second in a major election with 16.6% of the vote. The Lib Dems were just behind Labour and both the Greens and BNP came in with a strong polling, the Greens on 1,223,303 and the BNP on 943,598, both of which entitled them to two MEPs each.

With results like that behind him, a nation outraged by the behaviour of their MPs and Stuart Wheeler placing a sizeable bet on UKIP, Nigel Farage felt that at last the political climate was with him. With a general election coming in 2010, now was the time for the big political gesture that would focus public opinion on his party. Like Wheeler, he is a gambling man and this time he would take on the establishment directly. In September 2009, he announced he would stand as an MP against John Bercow—the new Speaker of the House of Commons—in his Buckingham seat.

Although Bercow was apparently a Conservative, he was generally loathed by his own party and became Speaker thanks to the votes of Labour MPs who delighted in winding up the Tories. A keen claimant of parliamentary expenses and a home flipper, he seemed to epitomise all that was wrong with the old politics. Parliamentary convention dictated that none of the three main parties should oppose the Speaker in his own constituency—so Farage thought he would.

To focus more attention on the campaign, Farage stepped down as leader of UKIP. A party leadership election followed, which Lord Pearson, a former Tory peer, won, but Gerard Batten, who came second, feels Malcolm Pearson won only thanks to Farage's endorsement.

'When I stood against Pearson,' he says, 'I'm convinced I won the activists. Every hustings meeting I went to, I won. You could just tell. Pearson got nowhere. But he won because Nigel said the others are rubbish, vote Pearson, and the armchair voters went for him.' It was, on reflection, a mistake, as Lord Pearson proved a poor performer on camera, making many gaffes that confirmed their opponents' view of them as a party of bumblers. Or perhaps, it was a clever bit of politicking by Farage to make sure he'd be welcomed back with open arms as leader. It didn't play well with voters.

As Farage started to campaign in Bercow's seat by drinking a pint in every constituency pub, he discovered that the loathed Westminster figure was in fact a very good local MP. 'I have never been anywhere and met a more popular local MP,' he told Bercow's biographer. 'He worked very hard in a way that most MPs wouldn't. You can paint it in a positive or a negative light. But you can't deny it exists. I came face to face with it and was very surprised.'

Farage had also hoped the Tory knives would be out for Bercow and although there was an initial suggestion of a deal in which Tories would back Farage in Buckingham if UKIP laid off some of their marginal seats, this came to nothing, and in a startling display of tribal loyalty, David Cameron overcame his distaste for the Speaker and endorsed him in February 2010. His irritation with Bercow was overwhelmed by his fear of UKIP.

In the same month that Cameron backed Bercow, Farage got nationwide publicity with his performance in the European Parliament. He stood up among the MEPs and unleashed a ferocious tirade on Herman Van Rompuy, the newly selected President of the EU.

'We were told that when we had a president,' said Farage, 'we'd see a giant global political figure, a man who would be the political leader for 500 million people, the man that would represent all of us on the world stage, the man whose job was so important that of course you're paid more than President Obama.'

'Well, I'm afraid what we got was you,' continued Farage, to the groans of MEPs around him. 'I don't want to be rude but, really, you have the charisma of a damp rag and the appearance of a low-grade bank clerk and the question I want to ask is: "Who are you?" I'd never heard of you. Nobody in Europe had ever heard of you… I can speak on behalf of the majority of British people in saying that we don't know you, we don't want you, and the sooner you are put out to grass, the better.'

'It was a positive decision,' argues UKIP former head of press Gawain Towler. After tens years of campaigning relentlessly and relatively politely against the EU monolith and getting little attention, UKIP had wanted to shake things up a bit in the European Parliament.

'These people are dangerous, what they are proposing is dangerous,' recalls Towler. 'It is time we step up the attack. What was astonishing was the international response. It, sadly, shows the way the media operates. It doesn't matter how serious and sensible you are, you're not going to get any coverage. As soon as you stand up and be rude about someone "ooh there you are".'

Unfortunately for Farage, the speech might have served to amuse his grassroots supporters but for the majority of UK viewers, watching the clip on TV, he came across not so much as righteously angry, but rudely bombastic, bullying the poor bespectacled Eurocrat.

It did not help matters at home either when Europhile ex-MEP John Stevens joined the electoral contest as the candidate for the Buckingham Campaign for Democracy, focusing on Bercow's sleaze factor by having a man dressed in a Flipper dolphin costume follow him around to remind voters of his home flipping. It confused and split voters further.

As the day of the election came close, Farage decided on one final publicity stunt to win votes. He hired a light aircraft with a UKIP banner fixed to its tail that would stream across the sky above Buckingham. Although Farage has a fear of flying, he took a deep breath and climbed into the cockpit beside the pilot. An aircraft cannot take off with a banner attached to it, so on that day the pilot had to swoop five times before he hooked it up—and five times Farage had to endure the stomach-churning of a shallow dive. Finally, the aircraft picked up the banner and shot across the Buckingham landscape but moments later came the dreaded realisation from the pilot that the banner was wrapped round the rudder on the tail. They would have to make an emergency landing and it wasn't going to be smooth. Farage's last words before impact were 'Oh, f**k.'

The banner hit the ground and made the aircraft crunch into the earth nose-first. Farage endured a flurry of blows to his body that left him breathless. Opening his eyes, he was amazed to still be alive, but then he smelt aircraft fuel and a sudden fear gripped him of being burned to death. He pawed at his safety harness but couldn't open the buckle. It was only when his aide sprinted to the crash site and reached in to release the buckle that Farage could scramble out of the wreck. A journalist was on hand—there to film the banner—and photographed the battered and dazed UKIP candidate caked in blood. The pilot was alive too and cut out of the smashed plane.

Taken to hospital in an ambulance, Farage had a punctured lung, fractured sternum and several broken ribs. It is not surprising he found it difficult to breathe. He had two chipped vertebrae, which still bother him now, preventing him from playing his beloved golf. Although he recovered from his breaks and bruises, the psychological impact of the crash is still with him.

'Now, whatever goes wrong,' says Farage, 'I think of being stuck in the wreckage of that aeroplane thinking I was going to burn to death. There is no day when I don't think about that, when it doesn't come into my thinking, it probably comes into my thinking 20 or 30 times. *That* is a very strong bit of my life. When I get out of bed in the morning I think about it because the back isn't as good as it ought to be. I've been so bloody lucky.'

Surviving the crash helps him keep a perspective on all the problems he has faced since then in his political career. The photograph of him dripping blood as he stumbled out of the aircraft made all the news, but it certainly did not win him any significant sympathy votes.

Bercow won his parliamentary seat convincingly and John Stevens came second. Farage came third with 17.4% of the vote and 8,410 votes. Even putting the second and third party votes together would not have unseated Bercow. It was very disappointing for Farage. For little effect, it had cost him a lot physically and mentally. Across the nation, UKIP came fourth but they did not perform as well as he had hoped, winning just 3.1% of the vote from just 919,471 voters. The problem for Farage was that most of those protest votes that he had quite rightly expected to flow away from the two main parties had in fact gone to the most successful protest vote party of the campaign—the Lib Dems led by Nick Clegg. In fact, it had gone so well for them that they ended up in government!

14

SHATTERING THE MOULD

The 2010 general election was shaping up to be an old-fashioned contest between a fading Labour Party and a rising Conservative Party, until Prime Minister Gordon Brown and Tory leader David Cameron agreed to a series of television debates in the run-up to the election. Oh dear! They were the first such live political debates to be broadcast on British TV and they would change the whole dynamic of the election campaign. It was David Cameron's idea, supported eagerly by Nick Clegg, leader of the third party—the Lib Dems. Traditionally, Prime Ministers have rejected the request, quite rightly feeling they have nothing to gain from putting wannabe leaders on an equal pedestal as themselves, but Gordon Brown surprisingly agreed to it—leaving Cameron to be the one who would regret it.

The leaders' three debates took place over three weeks in April—the topics were domestic, international and economic affairs. The first debate was hosted by ITV and took place on the evening of 15 April. From his very first words, the 43-year-old Nick Clegg was quick to assert that he and his party were different from the old mainstream parties.

'I believe the way things are is not the way things have to be,' said Clegg. 'You're going to be told tonight by these two that the only choice you can make is between two old parties who've been running things for years. I'm here to persuade you that there is an alternative.'

After 13 years of New Labour and with an electorate not quite ready to trust the Tories, this was very appealing—and so was Clegg—a good-looking, vigorous young man, he'd have done well if he'd been singing on X Factor.

'So don't let anyone tell you that the only choice is old politics,' continued Clegg. 'We can do something new. We can do something different this time. That's what I'm about. That's what the Liberal Democrats offer.'

Gordon Brown banged on about times being tough and the importance of a strong economy—yes, the one he'd managed to utterly cock-up. Cameron led with his weak chin, bringing up the scandal of MPs expenses and saying he was very sorry for it.

'Your politicians, frankly all of us, let you down.' This was true as much of the Lib Dems as Labour and the Conservatives, but the problem was that Labour and the Tories had been in power—the Lib Dems had not, so they were not as tainted with the corruption of the old politics as the two main parties.

Cameron then went very detoxifying Tory, pushing his modernising agenda.

'Now, not everything Labour has done in the last 13 years has been wrong. They've done some good things and I would keep those, but we need change, and it's that change I want to help to lead.'

Praising your opponent is a high-risk strategy but he believed this was how New Labour got in, by promising to stick to the previous government's spending plans. He wanted to reassure the electorate in the same way. Nothing would change too much under him—and in many ways he would be proved right.

Interestingly, the first question from the audience put its finger on the most contentious issues of the election campaign—mass immigration. Gordon Brown answered it by saying: 'You know, I've heard the concerns around the country. I've been listening to people.' This was 13 days before he would notoriously berate Mrs Duffy for daring to bring up her concerns about mass immigration.

Cameron gave a figure to the mass migration of two million over a decade and shared the nation's angst by saying: 'It's been too high these last few years, and I would dearly love to get it down to the levels it was in the past so it is no longer an issue in our politics as it wasn't in the past.'

Clegg answered the question by reiterating that his party would be different from the rest. 'You have had lots and lots of tough talking about immigration from both Conservative and Labour governments, and complete chaos in the actual administration of the system.' What he recommended was actually quite minor tinkering with the system, but that didn't matter. The two main parties had tried and failed—so why not give the Lib Dems a chance?

The three leaders were then allowed to criticise each other's approach. Cameron took the risk of referring to a Royal Navy rating as a 'black man', which seemed suddenly terribly old-fashioned for a moderniser. Shouldn't he be calling the gentleman an African-Briton or Caribbean-Briton or just not mention colour at all?

As Brown argued with Cameron over disarray in the immigration system, Clegg could stand back and observe the 'Punch and Judy' politics he so frequently derided.

'I think this is partly what's been going wrong for so long,' he said. 'We have had both major parties running governments over the last 20 years talking tough about immigration and delivering complete chaos in the way in which it's run.'

Brown then made the dreadful error of saying 'I agree with Nick'. Then in a question about MPs' expenses, he said it again 'I agree with Nick.'

The Lib Dems leapt on this after the debate, wearing hastily printed 'I agree with Nick' t-shirts for the rests of the campaign.

Further into the debate, when the two main leaders clashed over education, Clegg could again take the position of amused observer, looking straight into the camera, addressing the home audience directly: 'I'm not sure if you're like me, but the more they attack each other, the more they sound exactly the same.'

He further distanced himself from them by calling them 'These two…'

After an exhausting 90 minutes, the three leaders were allowed to have a concluding statement and Clegg returned to his overriding argument.

'Don't let them tell you that the only choice is between two old parties who have been playing pass the parcel with your government for 65 years now,' he said. 'Making the same promises, breaking the same promises. Making the same old mistakes over and over again…'

On cue, the two main party leaders attacked each other. Gordon Brown doubted whether Cameron could keep to Labour's funding plans for education and the NHS. Cameron retorted with his detoxifying line. 'One of the things I've heard during this debate is just repeated attempts to try and frighten you about a Conservative government. And I would say, choose hope over fear.'

That night it was clear that the television audience of nearly ten million had chosen Clegg over the other two. Instant opinion polls showed Clegg had been the decisive winner with Cameron a distant second and Brown a poor third. The *Sun/You Gov* poll had Clegg on 51%, Cameron on 29% and Brown on 19%. Both Cameron and Brown had to agree that Clegg had had a good first debate. The party's poll ratings soared to 24% and five days later this went up to 28%. It was heady stuff and maybe finally promised that elusive Lib Dem breakthrough.

The second debate was held on 22 April in Bristol and was hosted by Sky News. The subject was international affairs and this time Cameron performed more effectively. Polls varied putting either Cameron or Clegg just nudging into the lead over each other. But viewing figures had more than halved so far less people had seen Cameron's improved show. The third debate about economics, held in Birmingham by the BBC, took place in the shadow of Brown's insult of Mrs Duffy the day before. The Prime Minister confronted it straight away in his opening statement.

'There's a lot to this job, and as you saw yesterday, I don't get all of it right, but I do know how to run the economy in good times and in bad.'

He might have hoped that would be the end of it, but a member of the audience brought them back to the topic by asking 'Are the politicians aware that they have become removed from the concerns of the real people, especially on immigration, and why don't you remember that you are there to serve us, not ignore us?'

The BBC host turned to Brown.

'The only reason I came into politics was because I saw what was happening in my local community,' said Brown unconvincingly.

Cameron was more assertive and managed to deliver a few good blows on other topics too, not least making the point that if it had been up to the Lib Dems, the UK would have joined the disastrous eurozone.

'This is really getting desperate,' responded Clegg. 'No, I'm not advocating entry into the euro, I'd only advocate it, by the way, if ever, if the economic conditions were right...' Parroting Blair's views on this, he looking decidedly old party.

Cameron came over better and was generally judged by the polls to have won the last debate, but Clegg was a close second. Overall, the Lib Dems were the undoubted winners of the TV debates. Given an equal platform to Labour and the Conservatives, they looked a real alternative to them, their ratings soared and they hoped to carry on this momentum to election day. It didn't quite work out that way as voters began to have their doubts about the newcomer to the show in the final week of the campaign, but it was a high point for them as a protest-vote party.

The Liberal Democrats have traditionally attracted a combination of anti-Westminster protest votes and regional rural tribal support. They came out of the marriage of the Liberal Party and the Social Democratic Party (SDP) in 1988. Before that the two parties had been joined in an SDP-Liberal Alliance for seven years. The Liberal Party had evolved out of the Whig Party in 1859 and been a big force in the late 19th and early 20th centuries, providing three notable Prime Ministers. Its progressive, reforming appeal suffered a blow it never recovered from with the rise of the Labour Party and its democratic socialist agenda in the 1920s, leaving the Liberals to slump to third place in the polls for the rest of the century. The SDP had only existed since 1981 when it split from the Labour Party.

Their first leader Paddy Ashdown did a good job of keeping the Lib Dems alive in the late 1980s, especially from the threat of the Greens. In their first general election in 1992, they won 20 seats in parliament with 5,999,384 votes and 17.8% of the vote. In 1997, they doubled their representation, with 46 MPs, but with less votes—5,242,947—and a slightly smaller percentage of 16.8%. This had been achieved through the clever use of tactical voting and concentrating their limited resources in achievable seats. It was a brilliant model that continues to inspire other protest vote parties, especially UKIP. The Lib Dems have proved particularly efficient at getting their members elected as councillors and then these Lib Dem-dominated councils have provided excellent springboards for getting their MPs into Westminster.

The Lib Dems continued to add to their seats in the first decade of the 21st century under the leadership of Charles Kennedy, culminating in 2005 with 62 seats and 22% of the vote. For the Lib Dems, however, this had been disappointing as they had hoped for a breakthrough at this point, ending the two-party dominance, but the first-past-the-post electoral system does not favour them and they have always strongly argued for a change to proportional representation. The 2005 results were more bad news for the Tories as the Lib Dems had replaced them as the chief opposition to Labour in some British cities. Kennedy stepped down as leader in 2006 due to his alcoholism and was replaced briefly by the elderly Menzies Campbell. Nick Clegg became leader in 2007, beating his closest rival Chris Huhne by a margin of only 1.2% (lucky for them, given the fact that Huhne would later be gaoled for perverting the course of justice).

On 6 May 2010, the Lib Dems won 57 seats in parliament and 23% of the electorate with 6,836,248 votes. Again, it was disappointing for the Lib Dems, to be down five seats on the previous election and all this despite Clegg's brilliant TV performances. But it had not been a great night for the Conservatives either. With only 306 seats and 36.1% of the vote, they had failed to win an overall majority in parliament and could not form a government. It was a profound rebuff for David Cameron and his Tory modernisers. Despite being up against the electively unattractive Brown and with 13 years of New Labour culminating in a catastrophic recession, they could still not win a decisive victory. So much for being the 'nice' Tories.

For the first time since the Second World War, there was talk of forming a Coalition government. At first, the generally left-of-centre Lib Dems might be expected to form a pact with Labour but Clegg and his team decided it would be wrong to form a government with the losing Labour Party. The British people wanted an end to Brown—but they didn't quite want Cameron either. It made more electoral sense to form a Coalition with the winning Conservatives, as it would more truly represent the consensus for change. Remarkably, considering the visceral dislike held by many Tories and Lib Dems for each other, a joint government was formed—and, ironically, this may indeed be the greatest achievement of Cameron's detoxifying campaign in that it made his party look less unattractive to Clegg than to the rest of the electorate.

With this agreement made, Brown resigned as Prime Minister and Labour leader. Cameron moved into No 10 Downing Street and Clegg was appointed Deputy Prime Minister. It was an amazing achievement for a protest vote party leader and represented the pinnacle of Lib Dem electoral progress.

It was all looking so good, then came a stroll in a rose garden. To introduce this new team to the public, Cameron and Clegg took a press conference on 12 May among the roses in the garden of No 10 Downing Street. They strode out into the sunlight looking like two handsome brothers overly pleased with themselves. And that was the problem… To paraphrase George Orwell in his novel *Animal Farm*—'The creatures outside looked from Tory to Lib Dem, and from Lib Dem to Tory, and from Tory to Lib Dem again; but already it was impossible to say which was which.'

*

Another surprise of the 2010 general election was that the Green Party got their first ever MP, Caroline Lucas. After years of declining votes, it looked set to be another disappointing turn out for them as the Lib Dems and UKIP made the most of the voters' discontent. Getting just 265,243 votes nationally, less than a third of UKIP's total, less than 1% of the electorate, how did they still manage to get an MP into Westminster?

The answer lay partly in the character of the 49-year-old Lucas herself.

'Caroline Lucas is the most brilliant person,' says former leading

Green Sara Parkin, 'and the Green Party is extraordinarily lucky that she has stuck with it. She has been an MEP but realised that it is not about doing European politics over there, it's actually doing national politics. That's what helped her to get elected. As well as being a really good constituency MP, she's carefully picked the things she does. The previous Green candidate in Brighton had got a lot of votes. She went in with a higher profile and really put everything into it.'

Dr Caroline Lucas had been with the Green Party since their heady days of 1989 with Sara Parkin. Coming from a middle class background in Malvern, she studied English Literature at the University of Exeter where she gained her PhD. As a student she got muddy at nuclear disarmament protests at Greenham Common in the 1980s. She joined the Green Party in 1986 and was quickly recognised for her organisational and communication skills, becoming their press officer and spokesperson. She won the Green Party's second council seat in the UK in Oxford in 1993 and then became one of their first two MEPs in 1999, being re-elected twice more. In the European Parliament, Lucas has been a diligent MEP and served on many committees, but as Sara Parkin says, she has used that, much like UKIP has, to maintain a high profile in British politics.

In the 2005 general election, the highest Green Party vote was won in Brighton Pavilion by Keith Taylor with 22% of the vote. As the most promising constituency in the whole country, it attracted Lucas' interest, but this posed a problem as Taylor had done all the hard work and didn't exactly want to be elbowed out of the way by the party's big beast. Councillor Taylor had served his constituents well for ten years, having helped to quadruple the number of Green councillors on the city council. With this local party infrastructure established, he was well placed to win the seat. Both of them had been Principal Speakers, the Green Party's version of shared leadership. The stage was set for an epic example of Green Party bitching and back-stabbing. Lucas took the classic line of any ambitious leader that she had been *invited* by others to stand.

'The reality is that, over the past few months,' she confessed to members, 'I have been encouraged to consider standing for selection in Brighton Pavilion. A number of local party members have asked me to do so, along with others whose views I value and respect.'

But it was not easy for her—it had to be seen to be a struggle.

'I have therefore spent some weeks agonising over what has honestly been the most difficult decision of my life,' she said. 'Not only are there personal and family commitments to consider but also, of course, my loyalty and commitment to Keith Taylor, who is a person and a politician for whom I have great admiration and respect. I also know how much contesting this seat means to him.'

When it came to the vote in July 2007, the local party was sharply divided, but by 55% to 45% it chose Lucas as their PPC. It was a remarkable triumph over party in-fighting and showed that Lucas really had the ability to surmount what for many years had been the fatal flaw of the Greens. Even more amazingly, in the following year, the Green Party ditched its attachment to its eccentric form of shared leadership and appointed a proper single leader to the party and, of course, that was Caroline Lucas with 92% of the vote (although on a turnout of just 38%). As the national figurehead of the party, this gave her even greater heft when it came to campaigning in Brighton Pavilion and in 2010 she won 16,238 votes, 31.3% of the total, putting her ahead of the Labour candidate on 14,986 and the Conservatives on 12,275. In a general election that produced a hung parliament, she had decisively won protest votes from both main parties. It is a recipe that UKIP is keen to follow. Keith Taylor got his reward when Lucas immediately gave up her seat as an MEP and passed it on to him.

In order to concentrate on her constituency work, Lucas stepped down in 2012 as leader of the Green Party and was succeeded by Natalie Bennett, an Australian journalist. Bennett had stood as a parliamentary candidate in 2010 in Holborn and St Pancras and celebrated her colleague's great achievement by 'going to bed'. The party's strategy for Brighton in 2010 signalled an end to their previous approach of racking up the proportion of votes across the country without wanting to win any specific seats—the approach that had finally persuaded Sara Parkin to leave the party. It was Parkin's plan for power that was now back on the Green agenda.

'As a party we focused on three seats,' recalls Bennett. 'There was Brighton, Lewisham Deptford [Greens got 2,722 votes and came 4th] and Norwich South [Greens got 7,095 votes and came 4th]. The one that was our top target and the one that paid off was Brighton Pavilion. We focused our money much more in 2010 than we ever had previously. It is a question of focussing resources in places that you can win. Under the first-past-the-post electoral system the total number of votes you get is absolutely meaningless.'

In May 2013, the Green Party won 22 council seats in the local elections, up by five. It was not a great figure compared to UKIP's 147 seats—a gain of 139—but Bennett is optimistic about it.

'We got our first county councillors in Cornwall, Essex, Surrey, Kent, in various parts of the West Midlands,' she says. 'That reflects very much a spreading out. That helps towards the European elections where we're looking to hopefully trebling our MEPs. That would only take a 1.6% swing. That takes us into 2015 with a lot more people having a Green on their local council and Green parliamentarians, albeit in Brussels. We are now a [British] parliamentarian party, so you can't now say that a Green vote is a wasted vote.'

Ironically, at the Green Party conference in September 2013, Bennett said that the Greens could learn something from UKIP's appeal to voters fed-up with the main parties. 'Obviously our politics are very different,' she said. 'But people are looking for new answers and we're going to see big shifts in British politics in the next few years.' The party that had to some extent inspired Nigel Farage was now wanting to learn from him.

But experience of life under a Green council and a Green MP in Brighton and Hove has not been altogether utopian. Bitter infighting within the Greens grew worse than usual over a strike by local refuse-collectors in 2013 that saw rubbish piling up in the streets. Caroline Lucas supported the strikers; the Green council leader had to bring in pay-cuts for them. Locals began to have their doubts over whether the Greens could run the administration and balance its budget, while Labour sensed it might be able to claim back the council and the parliamentary seat.

'I don't think you can hold an MP answerable for decisions they had no control over,' says Lucas, distancing herself from the failures of the Green council. 'People like to have an independent Green voice in parliament, and irrespective of their views about the local council, I think many people would be very sorry to lose that voice, sticking up for Brighton.'

*

In March 2011, at his party's spring conference, Deputy Prime Minister Nick Clegg tried to define what it was to be a Lib Dem by setting them apart from the core beliefs of Labour and the Conservatives.

'For the left, an obsession with the state,' he said. 'For the right, a worship of the market. But as liberals, we place our faith in people. People with power and opportunity in their hands. Our opponents try to divide us with their outdated labels of left and right. But we are not on the left and we are not on the right. We have our own label: Liberal. We are liberals and we own the freehold to the centre ground of British politics. Our politics is the politics of the radical centre.'

It was a brave effort, but once in government, both parties, on the whole, worked together too well for the tastes of some of the electorate—especially those who had voted for the Lib Dems in the first place. Part of this was a matter of personalities. Clegg just looked too much like Cameron.

'Cameron had long been intrigued by what he saw as a "mini-me",' noted Lib Dem speechwriter and political journalist Jasper Gerard. 'As the photos are re-shown [of the rose garden press conference] the couple seem, in retrospect, a little too close, a little too similar, a little too at home in their lovely new house.' Former Tory leadership candidate David Davis had wickedly dubbed it the '*Brokeback Mountain* moment', referencing a 2005 romantic film about homosexual cowboys.

Like Cameron, Clegg came from a highly privileged background. The son of a bank chairman, he went to Westminster School, one of the top five private schools in the country, and proceeded to Cambridge University to study anthropology. After university, he travelled across the US with his school-friends Louis and Marcel

Theroux. At the University of Minnesota he wrote a thesis on the Deep Green movement and worked as an intern for the left-wing Christopher Hitchens at the *Nation* magazine. Back in the UK in 1990, he took a second masters degree at the College of Europe in Bruges, founded by the EU to educate the continent's elite in its ideals. There, he met his wife, Miriam, a Spanish lawyer and daughter of a senator.

Clegg's first job came when he worked in the European Commission, working on aid programmes for Central Asia, but he got this thanks in part to family neighbour Lord Carrington writing a letter of recommendation to EU Trade Commissioner Lord Brittan. Brittan then picked him to work in his office as an adviser and speech writer.

It is little wonder Clegg is so supportive of the EU. It gave him his start in his political career. Brittan was keen for him to be a Tory but his political mentor was Paddy Ashdown who saw great promise in the articulate and good-looking young man. In 1999, Clegg became a Lib Dem MEP for the East Midlands, but he was not enamoured with all EU institutions and co-founded a campaign to reform its parliamentary expenses and accountability. At the same time, he wrote a regular column for *The Guardian* on EU affairs.

In the end, Clegg wanted to contribute more to politics at home and stepped down as MEP in 2004. Within the year, he was selected as PPC for the Lib Dems in Sheffield Hallam and kept the seat for the party in 2005. In 2007, he became Lib Dem leader. It had been an extraordinarily rapid advance within the party. Indeed, within five years of becoming an MP he would be Deputy PM at the age of just 43.

While undoubtedly a talented and impressive young man, the ease and privilege of this brief career laced with a good deal of high-end education, puts him on a par with the leaders of both the Conservative and Labour parties. So, looking from Clegg to Cameron to Miliband, we see representatives of the urban liberal elite at the head of each party—each holding similar values and views on keys matters such as Green energy policy and Britain's relationship with the EU. For a brief moment in those TV election debates, Clegg managed to persuade the British electorate he was 'different' from the rest, but in reality he is not at all—he is the same kind of political creature that seems more and more out of touch with grassroots' concerns.

But this was not the principal disappointment of the voters who had put Clegg into government. That was the matter of a massive U-turn on policies dear to Lib Dem voters. During the election campaign, the Lib Dems had been strongly opposed to a proposed rise in student tuition fees. Clegg had signed the National Union of Students' pledge against this and student voters flocked to his party.

'I pledge to vote against any increase in fees in the next parliament and to pressure the government to introduce a fairer alternative,' Clegg clearly stated.

Once in power, Clegg and his party supported the increases. During Prime Ministers' question time, Labour deputy leader Harriet Harman seized on this blatant *volte face*.

'During the election [Clegg] hawked himself around university campuses pledging to vote against tuition fees,' she said. 'By the time Freshers' week was over, he had broken his promise. Every single Liberal Democrat MP signed the pledge not to put up tuition fees; every single one of them is about to break that promise.'

Clegg and his party were now hate figures to the thousands of students who protested against the increases in November 2010.

'You need to be careful. I should have been more careful perhaps in signing that pledge at the time. At the time I thought we could do it,' he said lamely. 'This is an extraordinarily difficult issue and I have been entirely open about the fact that we have not been able to deliver the policy that we held in opposition.'

Such compromises and changes are all part of being in government, but it had definitely underlined the fact that Nick Clegg and his Lib Dems could no longer claim to be a protest- vote party. Whereas the Lib Dems had been able to break the electoral mould by benefiting from the growing belief among the electorate that Labour and Tory politicians could not be trusted with government, they had now tarred themselves with the same brush. At the first hurdle, the Lib Dems had proved themselves to be indistinguishable from the Tories both in presentation and actual government decisions.

'Clegg thought it was absolutely essential that he "owned" the Coalition,' says Jasper Gerard. 'That he was seen to be a good team player and not run against the government of which he was deputy prime minister. I think the first year he was in office he took a big electoral hit for that.'

Now that Clegg was part of the system that protest voters wanted to change, what was the point of the Lib Dems? Support for the party ebbed away and, by 2013, the Lib Dems were regularly polling around 8%, putting them consistently at fourth place behind UKIP on around 13%.

'I think a lot of the protest voters are gone to be honest. I can't see huge numbers of them coming back,' admits Gerard. 'The fluffy bunny protest voters that thought the Lib Dems would be nicer people than the other parties. For those people, it has tarnished their view of the Lib Dems. I hope—and there are signs of this—that conversely other voters are thinking rather then being a protest party than they can actually be trusted with important decisions.'

Gerard hopes so as he is standing as a prospective parliamentary candidate for the Lib Dems in Maidstone and Weald. There, he believes the Tories are being squeezed on the right by UKIP and if Cameron moves to the right to shore up those votes, it will leave the middle ground to the Lib Dems. In his speech at the Lib Dem conference in Glasgow in September 2013, Nick Clegg addressed his party's identity crisis.

'Here we were, this anti-establishment liberal party, which hadn't been in power for 70 years, smack bang in the middle of Her Majesty's Government,' he told the audience. 'I know how hard it has been getting here—facing down all the vitriol from our opponents… But the big question mark that has always hung over the Liberal Democrats—could we handle Government, and handle it when the going got tough? That question mark is now gone. This recovery wouldn't be happening without us.'

It was a big claim that could be laughable but then he moved on to the one high profile and genuinely populist achievement of the Lib Dems in Coalition—which the Tories would loved to have claimed for themselves—and he mentioned it in the context of his triumphant TV election debates.

'But do you remember the TV debates?' he said. 'David Cameron turned to me, in front of the whole country, and said: "I would love to take everyone out of their first £10,000 of income tax Nick, but we cannot afford it". Well, we can afford it. And we did it. A stronger economy and a fairer society too.'

He then used this as the bridge to his big new concept for the Lib Dems, not as a party of protest—because clearly that was shot—but as one of moderation in government.

'We're not trying to get back into Government to fold into one of the other parties,' he argued. 'We want to be there to anchor them to the liberal centre ground, right in the centre, bang in the middle. We're not here to prop up the two-party system: we're here to bring it down.'

It was this new concept that Clegg came back to in the concluding lines of his speech. 'In the past the Liberal Democrats would eke out an existence on the margins of British politics,' he said. 'Now we hold the liberal centre while our opponents head left and right. I have spent my entire life watching the other two mess it up… Our mission is anchoring Britain to the centre ground. Our place is in Government again.'

It was a curious and pretentious message, but clever too at making the best of a bad situation. Clegg and his team no longer want to be a protest vote party. They liked being in government and wanted to carry on being in government. So who was now left to represent those voters fed-up with every leading politician looking and sounding the same? If the Lib Dems had ruled themselves out—having been the most successful of all recent protest vote parties—that left the stage clear for the one party that had soared to a new electoral high in 2013.

BLOOM GLOOM

It was midday on Friday 20 September 2013 and Nigel Farage was coming to the end of his key speech at UKIP's autumn conference. The cavernous space of the Methodist Central Hall in Westminster, London, was packed with rows upon rows of supporters, many more standing at the back, all to see their leader deliver a triumphant speech, topping off a dynamic year for the party. Face glistening with sweat, standing at the purple podium, Farage revealed his plan for the European Parliamentary elections in 2014.

'Given all these broken promises, what I suggest we do is we turn the European elections on May 22nd into the referendum we never had, so that we can express our opinion on the European Union...'

Applause rippled along the rows of seats.

'... and on open borders.'

The applause swelled.

'Let's use it as an opportunity to send an earthquake through Westminster politics and let's stand up as a nation and say "We want our country back!"'

The audience stood up and roared their approval, whistling and cheering. It was just what they wanted to hear from their confident and defiant leader, but, of course, the most important person in the hall at that moment was not Nigel Farage or the hundreds of UKIP supporters. The most important person in the hall was the 55-year-old Channel Four News journalist Michael Crick, because it was he who would define how the message of that day's conference would be received in the rest of the UK.

Sidling into the hall towards the end of Farage's speech, Crick wasn't interested in listening to it. He played with his mobile phone and pulled funny faces as Farage spoke, then when it was finished he sprinted forward to join the journalists and photographers surging around Farage as he left the hall. His skilful *modus operandi* is to pursue politicians on the hoof, microphone in hand, and goad them into some ill-advised comment. Farage simply ignored this familiar technique, refusing to talk to him, so a frustrated Crick went in search of a more compliant prey.

Godfrey Bloom was a 64-year-old UKIP MEP and their party's spokesman on defence. He had already caused a media storm earlier in the year when he criticised the British government for giving aid to 'Bongo Bongo Land.' He had been reprimanded by the party leadership, but had got away with the comment because the public was used to him being the 'colourful' face of UKIP. Indeed, as UKIP moved towards becoming a more professional party with tighter control over its utterances, it could be argued that Bloom served to reassure its hardcore supporters that it had not gone too PC—he was the maverick of the maverick party.

On that first day of the autumn conference, Bloom attended a lunchtime fringe meeting about women in politics. He was a member of the European Parliament's Women's Rights and Gender Equality Committee, despite having earlier joked that women don't 'clean behind the fridge enough.' It was all part of his sense of humour, he claimed, provoking the media with his sexist comments to get their attention so he could then put over a more complex argument. Two UKIP women members bantered with him, saying they didn't clean behind their fridges and he responded by saying 'oh well, you're all sluts'. In the meeting everyone laughed, perceiving it as a typical Bloom joke, but outside the Methodist Central Hall, Sky News picked it up as an offensive use of the word 'sluts' and questioned Bloom about it. He managed to brush it off by putting it in its comic context in the meeting, but then Channel 4's Michael Crick saw his opportunity and pounced. Shouting over the TV journalists and waving a copy of the conference brochure, Crick asked 'Why are there no black faces on it?'

This is where Bloom made an appalling decision to go on the offensive—a decision that would overshadow the entire day's conference. Thinking he was being clever by turning the argument back on to the journalist, he said 'What a racist comment is that! How dare you? That's an appalling thing to say. You're picking people out for the colour of their skin. You disgust me!'

Bloom then pushed his way through the journalists. Crick, seeing he had rattled Bloom, pursued him along the street. Bloom continue to call Crick a racist, then grabbed the brochure from his hand and hit the journalist over the head with it. Crick had got exactly what he wanted, more than earning his wage for CH4. He had created a story and the rest of the grateful press hoard followed Bloom.

As Bloom returned to the hall to give his speech on defence, photographers crowded round him. As he left the hall, journalists blocked his way as he tried to step into a taxi. A few yards away a grim faced Farage was explaining to the cameras what UKIP was going do about the incident. That clip was now the only UKIP story the media was interested in and would dominate the weekend's coverage. All the effort gone into organising the conference and its speakers had come to nought.

'I was really angry on Friday,' said Farage shortly afterwards. 'I felt it was selfish, boorish, unnecessary. He'd been warned and warned and warned. I'd listened to the one o'clock news on the car radio and it was to die for. Item number one: Farage wants to turn the European election into a referendum that we've never had. Item number two: UKIP energy spokesman Roger Helmer proposes the setting up of a sovereign wealth fund. I thought we've really pressed all the buttons here. By four o'clock it was all a catastrophe.'

Three days later, on Monday afternoon at 3.30 p.m. sitting in his headquarters in Mayfair, Farage still didn't know how the affair was going to play out.

'Point number one, under our constitution,' he told a *Sun* newspaper reporter on the telephone, 'I have no direct legal say on disciplinary issues at all. All the press reports saying I've removed the whip [from Bloom], no I haven't. Am I looking for an amicable solution to somebody who has been a great supporter and friend of ours over many years? Of course. But at the moment the ball is a bit more in his court than ours. And we're waiting to see what he has to say to us. I don't know how this is all going to finish up. Am I inclined to try and sort this thing out in a civilised way? Yes. He's like the curate's egg.'

The next morning, Bloom quit from his high profile role in UKIP.

'I have felt for some time now that the "New UKIP" is not really right for me anymore perhaps than New Labour was right for the Dennis "The beast of Bolsover" Skinner,' he said in his statement. 'However our message is clear. Self government. Our wonderful and loyal membership will win through with their dedication and hard work.'

Bloom was no longer a spokesman for UKIP and would sit as an independent MEP in the European Parliament, but he would remain a member of the party and help their campaigning. Though the incident has been a terrible 'distraction', as Farage called it, it was a good move for the party to be seen to disassociate itself from a growing liability. As Bloom himself recognised, the party was growing up and he no longer fitted into the more professional outfit.

It was a great pity for UKIP that the Bloom incident had drowned out its conference as it was putting a more considered face forward, widening its policies and presenting some impressive figures—making it more than just the Nigel Farage show. Among the most interesting speeches was one made by the shaven headed Paul Nuttall, a 36-year-old former university history lecturer from the North West and now a UKIP MEP and deputy leader of the party.

Nuttall was brought up in Bootle in Merseyside, one of the poorest constituencies in the country, hit hard by the closure of its docks. It is one of Labour's safest seats in the country, but Nuttall knows these people and thinks they are no longer well represented by their party.

'I genuinely believe that Labour voters are easy picking for UKIP,' he told the conference. 'Labour voters are instinctively anti-European Union, Labour voters are the people most effected by uncontrolled, mass immigration.'

This had been demonstrated in 2009 in the European Elections when UKIP won in Hartlepool, Sunderland, Dudley, Hull, Grimsby, and Plymouth—'all Labour heartlands.' In recent by-elections, they have finished second in Barnsley, Rotherham, Middlesborough and South Shields, with voter shares of over 20%. In polls in the north of England, UKIP regularly runs second to Labour. 'It is clear now that UKIP is the real opposition, the only opposition to Labour in the north of England.'

'The Labour Party has abandoned its working-class roots,' Nuttall explained. 'Opinion polls show that between 1997 and 2010, the majority of Labour votes lost were in working-class areas. These people are either looking elsewhere to other political parties: many of them voted Liberal Democrat—they won't be doing that again. One or two will vote Conservative. Some, unfortunately, will hold their nose and vote for the BNP. But most have not voted at all. They've given up. Why? It's because Labour MPs don't represent them anymore.'

'In the day of Clement Attlee,' said Nuttall, 'Labour MPs came from the mills, the mines and the factories. Labour MPs today follow the same routes as the Conservatives and the Liberal Democrats. They go to private schools, they go to Oxbridge, they get a job in an MP's office and they become an MP. None of them would know a working men's club, none of them would know a council estate if it fell on them from the sky... It is no surprise the working classes have abandoned the Labour Party. At UKIP, I believe we have the policies to attract Labour voters: our policies are not right, they're not left; they're not Conservative, they're not Labour; they're not middle class, they're not upper class—they're just common sense.'

It is a persuasive argument that still continues to be ignored by the media, who prefer to stick with their characterisation of UKIP as grumpy old Tories. Nigel Farage agrees it is a largely untold story.

'[Nuttall] is working class and there aren't many working-class people in British politics. UKIP started off as very middle class, aged, all World War Two veterans, all just disgusted by Maastricht. I remember looking at the membership list for Salisbury. There was virtually no one below the rank of squadron leader. DFCs, MCs were two a penny in 1994/95. Hence disgusted of Tunbridge Wells. That's the way it was.'

But as UKIP has spread across the country, its appeal is going beyond the southern suburbs and reaching into cities and estates in the Midlands and the North. Worcester in the West Midlands is a marginal seat that has been identified as an emblematic electoral battleground swinging between Labour and the Conservatives depending on which party best expresses their concerns. 'Worcester Woman' is typified as a working-class mother worrying about quality of life issues, shifting from Thatcher to Blair. Cameron got her back in 2010, but she may well be looking elsewhere in future elections.

'The only national journalist that's got close to recognising it is Fraser Nelson [Editor of the *Spectator*],' says Farage. 'He came to a meeting I did in Worcester Guildhall. It was the first time, since Churchill, that there had been too many people to be allowed in the hall. Blair went there, Thatcher went there, but we filled it. We did two meetings. Fraser Nelson said after that meeting that UKIP are increasingly the working-class party. He got it. He saw it.'

'Worcester Guildhall felt like the Tory party conference in the days when grassroots members actually turned up,' wrote Fraser Nelson in the *Daily Telegraph*. 'There were young couples, families and a chap in his thirties who said he'd come because it would be "better than watching EastEnders".' Nelson argued that general elections can be won by just a four per cent swing in marginal seats like this and that Farage is effectively speaking to those voters about topics that matter to them.

'This creates a gap which UKIP is now trying to fill,' he contends. 'It's considering changing its name, and ditching its pound sign logo to reflect its widening into what would, in effect, be a working-class party with two aims: small government and individual liberty. And if he is laughed at for crude language and basic arguments, then he'd argue he's in good company: so was Mrs Thatcher, whose directness was appreciated by blue-collar workers. A recent audit of UKIP's support showed its supporters were more likely to be working class than those of any Westminster party.'

The only problem for UKIP is reaching those disconnected voters.

'Postal votes in the north of England are tucked up already [by Labour],' says Farage, but he feels with more funds, more advertising and grassroots campaigning they will get to them. 'There is a raw appeal of UKIP to working-class people.'

*

Having had his 2013 autumn conference messed up by Godfrey Bloom, Nigel Farage was in the mood for sabotaging the Tory conference ten days later. In Manchester on Monday 30 September, he blitzed three fringe conference meetings in one day. At a Bruges Group debate at Manchester Town Hall in Albert Square, he skewered veteran Eurosceptic MP Bill Cash when Cash asked UKIP not to fight Tories in marginal seats.

'I have to say Bill,' said Farage, 'but listening to you this afternoon, I've realised that you are a hopelessly out of date tribal politician who has not recognised that British politics has fundamentally changed. To ask me, to support a party led by Mr Cameron, in order we can get back our national independence. I'm sorry, you've got to do rather better than that.'

Then came the personal attack that had the audience in uproar.

'You voted 47 times against the Maastricht Treaty,' Farage said to Cash, 'but there's one thing you forgot to tell this audience, you voted [on the 48th time] for the Maastricht Treaty by supporting John Major in the motion of confidence debate. When it came to the ultimate test, you failed the test, you put your party before this country.'

From there, Farage moved on to the Freedom Zone in the Bridgewater Hall, just a few hundred yards from the Conservative conference itself. Organised by Simon Richards of the Freedom Association, it hosted a number of fringe meetings that pulled prominent UKIPers and Tories together for a series of public discussions. Farage entered the hall to a rock star reception. Richards had hoped to have a more intimate Q&A session with the UKIP leader, but Farage wasn't having any of that. He bounded up to the podium and immediately started to taunt the Tories. As he spoke, Richards quietly slid his prepared notes to one side.

'Although lobbyists and politicians of all hues are allowed inside the secure zone [of the Conservative conference hall],' he said, 'I am banned, and my name is not to appear in any of the conference programmes advertising fringe events. I've just been for a meeting with Alastair Campbell [Tony Blair's former Director of Communications]. Alastair Campbell is welcome inside the Tory party conference, despite the fact that he spent years trying to destroy the Conservative party. And me, who has been as helpful as he possibly could to David Cameron at all opportunities, is not allowed in!'

Farage described how the Tory party was dying in northern cities, just as it had done in Scotland and that there was little chance it was going to win a majority in 2015—and so Cameron's pledge for a referendum on EU membership in 2017 was worthless.

'This referendum pledge is only there because of the strength of UKIP.'

He wanted the referendum a month before the next general election. As for doing electoral deals with the Tories, he could see some value in alliances being struck on a local level between UKIP and outspoken Eurosceptic Tory MPs, but not on the national level.

'Tory high command view UKIP frankly as being lower orders, not really of sufficient class to be treated seriously,' he said. 'They must be appalled that as the deputy leader of UKIP we've got a working-class boy from the docks of Mersey. That isn't good enough for the modern day Conservative party. They view us with contempt.'

He re-emphasised the point he'd made to Bill Cash that Tory rebels will always put their party before their country.

'UKIP was set up after the ultimate failure of the Maastricht rebels to stop that treaty going through,' said Farage. 'Yes, they tried damned hard. But in the end, when it came to a motion of confidence—and that was the method that Major used to get the treaty through—apart from Rupert Allason [MP]—all the rest of them traipsed through the lobby and supported the Major government... Twenty years on, UKIP has created its own political space.'

The battle lines between the two parties had been drawn.

In a later political debate at the Freedom Zone in Manchester, entitled 'Why I left the Tories versus Why I'm staying', Mark Wallace, Editor of ConservativeHome, made an eloquent speech of regret and sorrow that stalwart Tories had left his party for UKIP, but that was not the whole story.

'UKIP are telling the truth when they say that a minority of UKIP voters are ex-Conservatives,' said Wallace. 'The Conservative Party makes a great mistake when it patronises UKIPers, saying "come home", when actually the majority of them have not been in the Conservative Party to start with... There are voters who haven't voted for anyone in 20 years that UKIP are appealing to instead.'

In reply, Lewes UKIP Councillor Donna Edmunds explained why she had quit the Tories.

'I did love the Conservative Party,' she said. 'It has done amazing things. It has a long, rich history of bringing freedom to this country. I'm very much a Thatcherite. That's because of my own family experience. My mother is an immigrant, my father working class. They bought their first home at the age of 19, thanks to Thatcher's policies. I went to public school on an assisted place, thanks to Thatcher's policies. So I can understand the emotional attachment to the Conservative Party, I share it. The problem that we have is we need to find a new word for Thatcherism because what the Conservative Party stands for now is not what I would consider Thatcherism.'

Remarkably, in the year in which Margaret Thatcher had died and 23 years after she had left power, her populist attitude and her appeal to a broad range of voters from different backgrounds, working class and middle class, was still a template for a new generation of politicians seeking to make politics work better for voters.

*

Just when Nigel Farage might have sat back with a pint of bitter and thought the great political story of 2013 was the rise of UKIP to third place in British politics and the subsequent panic among the Tories, then the most unlikely candidate made an appeal to fed-up protest voters.

After three years of looking too much like his fellow party leaders, Ed Miliband, stood up at Labour's autumn conference in

Brighton and delivered a speech that would add pace to the race to the general election in 2015. After a dismal summer in which Labour was losing its lead in the polls thanks to an increasing tide of good news about a recovering economy, the 44-year-old geek with a dented nose struck back with a dazzling display of populist politics.

'If we win the election 2015,' he promised, 'the next Labour government will freeze gas and electricity prices until the start of 2017. Your bills will not rise. It will benefit millions of families and millions of businesses. That's what I mean by a government that fights for you. That's what I mean when I say Britain can do better than this.'

How can you possibly do this, wondered his opponents? It's a ridiculous state intervention in the market that would put off investors, disrupt the energy sector, result in blackouts and three-days weeks and Slade would be number one in the charts again! The Tory press dubbed him Red Ed, but this, amazingly, was the first time for some while that a major political leader had connected directly with the concerns of his electorate. For once the intellectual platitudes and vague statements were abandoned and here was an offer of direct action to cap the rising cost of living—it was his George Osborne Inheritance Tax moment. The public loved it and Labour support surged back to a ten-point lead over the Tories. Just as UKIP success had shifted Cameron on his referendum pledge on the EU, so Miliband got the Tories focused on what really matters to the voter.

For the 2013 Autumn Statement, Cameron allegedly told his team to cut the 'green crap' and remove the environmental energy taxes from fuel bills to give families a real reduction in their home energy costs. The modernising Tories who had once said 'vote blue, go green', appeared to have dumped that, with one anonymous senior Tory source claiming 'It's vote blue, get real.' A Downing Street official denied the wording, but the Chancellor confirmed a cut in energy charges in his Autumn Statement. The full impact of this was muted, however, partly because Osborne didn't trumpet the cuts, maybe afraid of highlighting the U-turn, but largely because the budget coverage was upstaged by the death of Nelson Mandela, with one political journalist comparing him to Jesus Christ. Politics halted for a few days as all party leaders flew to South Africa to attend the memorial service.

Despite this, the Conservative party had already put itself on a war footing by hiring full-time the Australian election campaign guru Lynton Crosby. It was also doing its best to use the levers of government to stimulate an economic recovery in time for the next general election by increasing expenditure on capital projects and, through schemes such as Help to Buy, using taxpayers' money to guarantee mortgages for first-time buyers and thus inflating the housing market—as though historically low interests rates weren't doing enough for that. Osborne's 2014 Budget played well to voters with good news for savers and pensioners.

Suddenly the conventional parties were fighting back and proving they could play populist politics as well as the protest vote parties. The only good news for Farage was that a previous multi-millionaire donor said that he would come back to support UKIP in the 2014 European elections.

'There is only one political party at present that says it wants to be out of the EU, and there is only one political party that would deliver it – and that is UKIP,' said Yorkshire businessman Paul Sykes. 'It is the only game in town. I am certainly not wasting my time, energy and money on any of the others.'

Although officially delighted, a source close to Farage said 'I'll believe it when I see it'. But there was more good news in a poll carried out in one of the seaside constituencies that Farage thought best suited UKIP's appeal—indeed where he might finally win the vote to become an MP.

The poll was commissioned by a UKIP donor in the Tory-held marginal of Thanet and asked over 500 locals their voting intentions. Labour came in first place with 35% (up 5% from 2010), UKIP was a close second on 30% (up 24%), beating the Tories on 28% (down 20%) with the Lib Dems a very poor fourth on 5% (down 10%). The poll was especially interesting for Farage because the sitting modernising Tory MP had just declared her intention to stand down at the next election, leaving the door open for him.

UKIP donor Alan Bown thought his poll contradicted the polling narrative put out by the Conservative Lord Ashcroft who saw UKIP primarily as a threat to the Conservatives and a vote for them risked putting Labour into power.

'I did not share this view,' said Bown, 'and was sure that UKIP's increasing popularity and support meant that the picture was much more complicated. I believed that we were taking significant numbers of votes from Labour and the Liberal Democrats as well as the Tories.' Further polls, he said, revealed the 'relationship between UKIP and Labour and whether in some northern areas, where the Conservative brand is badly damaged, UKIP might have actually established itself as the official opposition to Labour.'

A good test for this came in February 2014 with a by-election hastily called in Wythenshawe and Sale East, in Greater Manchester, following the sudden death of its Labour MP. Considered a safe Labour seat, Nigel Farage wanted to come a strong second there and UKIP activists from across the country rallied to help him achieve that. Julian Deverell came from Bath in Somerset to help out and was pleasantly surprised by the welcome from some of the traditional Labour voters.

'An elderly couple invited me in for a drink and loo break and both pledged their support for UKIP and promised their vote,' noted Deverell. 'I was only the second political canvasser to visit them in the 11 years they had lived there and they wanted to talk to someone!' These were the ignored voters UKIP wanted to reconnect with. 'The local working men's club served us instant coffee and welcomed us in out of the rain. We kept our rosettes on and displayed leaflets on the table. We held court there with some retired men drinking ale, all were extremely friendly, two pledged their votes, another had already voted UKIP in the postal ballot.'

Convincing younger voters was more of a challenge, especially where Labour campaigners had been busy. 'Many told us they simply refused to vote because politicians were "all the same",' said Deverell. 'Many were public sector workers who were scared of voting anything other than Labour in case they lost their job. We actually heard that in some estates Labour activists had been telling benefit claimants that if they didn't vote Labour they would lose their homes… a pathetic scare tactic.'

In the event, the Labour MP secured a safe win with 55% of the

vote, but UKIP did come second, with 18% of the vote, pushing the
Tories into third place. It was not enough to rock the establishment
as Eastleigh had done, but it did continue UKIP's narrative that they
are the party of opposition in northern working class constituencies.
The problem was that UKIP had very little local political infrastructure—no councillors—to build on.

'It represents really good solid, steady progress, not an easy
constituency for us, we have got no history here,' said Nigel Farage.
'When you start from a base of nothing and your level of public
recognition is very low then to do what we have done in a very short
space of time – delighted. Anything over 15% was what I was
hoping for and had it been over 20%, it would have been a terrific
result for us so 18%, I'm very pleased.'

On 26 March 2014, Deputy Prime Minister and Lib Dem
leader Nick Clegg initiated the first of two TV debates with Nigel
Farage on the EU and immigration. Significantly, while most
Westminster media commentators felt it had been a 'score draw', the
public in a YouGov poll gave the victory resoundingly to Farage by
57% to 36%. Yet again, the establishment doesn't quite get the
appeal of UKIP.

So, will Nigel Farage ever win power in Westminster? The
progress of protest vote parties seems to be changing. While it is not
easy for protest parties to win MPs, recent history has shown some
ground-breaking successes—the elevation of the Lib Dems to a
position in government being the most extraordinary one. What
might have been inconceivable a decade ago seems now entirely
possible. Though the success of UKIP has depended on many
factors, there is no longer a ceiling to what may be achieved.

Many people will say Farage already has won power at the heart
of government. In October 2013, he was nominated the second
most influential right-winger in the UK, after David Cameron, by
the *Daily Telegraph* and a panel of political commentators.

'What a year it has been for UKIP leader Nigel Farage,' wrote
Iain Dale. 'His media profile is bigger than ever and UKIP is now
consistently polling as the third most popular party in the UK. They
were launched into the stratosphere this year with a phenomenal
performance in the local elections scoring a quarter of the votes and

gaining more seats than Labour. That game-changing result means it is going to be hard for any party to stop UKIP topping the polls in the 2014 European Elections.'

That was the expectation. Anything less would suggest the British public did not have a strong enough appetite for the UKIP agenda to give them seats in parliament in 2015. But regardless of whether they pursue the electoral strategies of the Lib Dems and the Greens, UKIP has already demonstrated enormous stamina and resilience as probably the most important protest vote party in Britain in the early 21st century.

The worry for Farage's supporters is that their success depends very much on their leader's energy. Senior UKIP figure Mick McGough praises his 'fantastic work rate'. 'I don't know how much sleep he gets,' says McGough, 'but it can't be much. Just as Maggie Thatcher survived on very little sleep, so does he.' 'I think he is pushing himself too hard,' says another. 'He's got to give himself a break every now and then.'

'I get up at 5 o'clock in the morning,' says Farage. 'By one o'clock I fancy a cleansing pint of London Pride. All to the good. I probably shouldn't smoke as much as I do. That is bad.'

UKIP is a 24-hour-a-day, seven-days-a-week commitment for Farage and he admits he can't turn off from it. In the middle of the night he'll be worrying about the next step in his party's progress. 'Pacing the house, drinking cups of tea, chain-smoking,' he says. 'This is an all-devouring monster. There is no escape from this. It's been at times in the last 15 years totally fanatical. My utter determination to prove everybody wrong.' He bursts out laughing. 'There's been some very black periods, but I think I have kept my sense of humour. There are a lot of people I have worked with over the years whose company I have enjoyed. UKIP is still fun.'

SOURCES

Major interviews
Nigel Farage, UKIP MEP and leader
Stuart Wheeler, treasurer UKIP
Gawain Towler, former head of press UKIP
Gerard Batten, UKIP MEP
Roger Helmer, UKIP MEP
Mick McGough, UKIP
Tim Congdon, UKIP
Alan Sked, founder of UKIP
Douglas Carswell MP, Conservative
Philip Hollobone MP, Conservative
Philip Davies MP, Conservative
David Nuttall MP, Conservative
Jasper Gerard, Lib Dem PPC
Simon Richards, Chief Executive of The Freedom Association
Robin Birley, former Referendum Party, stepson of Sir James Goldsmith
Matthew Elliott, founder TaxPayers' Alliance
Jonathan Isaby, Chief Executive TPA and former ConservativeHome
John Edmonds, former General Secretary of GMB Union
John Monks, former General Secretary of the Trades Union Congress
Natalie Bennett, leader Green Party
Sara Parkin, former spokesperson Green Party
Ann Mallalieu, President of Countryside Alliance
Dr Simon Heffer, political journalist
Nick Griffin, BNP MEP and leader

Preface
'Parking protest party launched' *Islington Tribune*, 24 September 2004.
'Now we have a vote against traffic wardens' by Peter Oborne, *Evening Standard*, 4 October 2004.
'Parking: the new poll tax' by Sir David Bell, *Evening Standard*, 11 October 2004.
'Veteran councillor joins parking protest party' *Islington Tribune*, 29 October 2004.
'Growing support for Local Freedom' *High & I*, 28 January 2005.
'Anti-parking party gets cash boost' *Islington Gazette*, 3 February 2005.
'Zero tolerance—we hate it when we get it' by Nick Cohen, *Evening Standard*, 17 February 2005.
'Polls test for anti-parking campaigner' *Islington Tribune*, 1 April 2005.
'Put your money where your mouth is…' *Islington Gazette*, 7 April 2005
'Voters relegate Lib Dems to third' *High & I*, 13 May 2005.
'Cutting the cost of parking' *High & I*, 20 May 2005.
'Decision to end clamping was too little, too late' *Islington Tribune*, 1 July 2005.
'Traders delight over parking zone victory' *Islington Gazette*, 30 March 2006.

1
Interviews with Simon Richards, Nigel Farage MEP, and Jennifer Salisbury-Jones.
BBC Blog by Ben Cooper, Controller, BBC Radio 1, 12 April 2013.

246246erort>246

Estimates of crowd at Thatcher funeral: 100,000 *Daily Telegraph*, 250,000 *Daily Mail*.

Quotes from people in crowd at Thatcher funeral: 'Final Journey into History' *Evening Standard*, 17 April 2013; 'London halts for ceremonial funeral' BBC News, 17 April 2013.

'Margaret Thatcher funeral BBC TV coverage attracts 4.4 million viewers' the *Guardian*, 18 April 2013.

Ipsos Mori poll conducted between April 13-15 2013, asking 'which if any, of the following prime ministers do you think would do the best job of getting Britain out of the economic crisis?' Thatcher got 31%, above Blair on 21% and Cameron on 12%.

Cameron's *Today* comments reported in 'Thatcher funeral: Cameron says "we are all Thatcherites now"' The *Guardian*, 17 April 2013

'Baroness Thatcher would have joined us, says UKIP leader Nigel Farage' The *Telegraph*, 23 April 2013

'Nigel Farage: I'm the only politician keeping the flame of Thatcherism alive' *Sun,* 14 April 2013

'Looks who's grabbed the baton of conviction politics' Adam Boulton, *Sunday Times*, 14 April 2013

'The hapless Tories were doomed from the start' Andrew Pierce, *MailOnline*, 4 March 2013

'Seven reasons why UKIP should back Maria Hutchings in Eastleigh' Daniel Hannan, The *Telegraph*, 12 February 2013.

'Farage suggests Conservative pact at secret dinner with Murdoch' The *Telegraph*, 7 March 2013.

'UKIPpered' by Jack Grimston and Isabel Oakeshott, the *Sunday Times*, 3 March 2013.

'Equality laws should aid the working class' the *Telegraph*, 13 December 2013.

'End of the party - how British political leaders ran out of followers' by Ross Clark, the *Spectator*, 14 September 2013.

2

Interviews with Ray Finch, Nigel Farage MEP and Mick McGough.

Transcript of speech by Cllr Roger Arthur, 22 April 2013.

'Ken Clarke Brands UKIP Politicians "Clowns"' Sky News, 28 April 2013.

'Wind your (polo) neck in, Kenneth' the *Sun*, 29 April 2013.

'Local election 2013: Ken Clarke brands UKIP "clowns"' BBC News, 28 April 2013.

'Ramsey nominates first UKIP mayor in country', *Hunts Post*, 19 May 2011.

Independence—the official magazine of the UK Independence Party, May issue, 2013.

'UKIP: We would do deal with Boris' and 'The Rise and Fall of the Political Class' *Sunday Times*, 5 May 2013.

Transcripts of Gillian Duffy and Gordon Brown 'bigot' incident, BBC News, 28 April 2010.

Oborne, P, *The Triumph of the Political Class*, London: Simon & Schuster, 2007.

3

Interviews with Nigel Farage MEP, Philip Hollobone MP, Alan Sked, Gerard Batten MEP, and Gawain Towler.

Farage, N, *Flying Free*, London: Biteback Publishing, 2011.

'Academics form group to oppose a unified Europe' *The Times*, 9 February 1989.

'Bruges boy fights back' by Laurie Weston, *The Times*, 9 February 1989.

'Thatcher loyal to Major' *The Times*, 12 April 1991.

'Debate for Maastricht', letter in *The Times*, by Dr Alan Sked, 12 October 1991.

'The ERM: my part in its downfall' by Dan Hannan, *Telegraph*, 12 September 2012.

4

Interviews with Robin Birley, Alan Sked, Gerard Batten MEP, and Mick McGough.
Thatcher, M, *The Downing Street Years*, London: Harper Collins, 1993.
Thatcher, M, *The Path to Power*, London: Harper Collins, 1995.
Fallon, I, *Billionaire: Life and Times of Sir James Goldsmith*, London: Hutchinson, 1991.
Clark, A, *The Last Diaries*, London: Weidenfeld & Nicolson, 2002.
Wansell, G, *Tycoon: Life of James Goldsmith*, London: Grafton, 1988.
'Sir James Goldsmith' Obituary, *Telegraph*, 21 July 1997.
'King of the beasts' by Michael Gove, *The Times*, 19 October 1996
'Desperate Lucan dreamt of fascist coup' *Guardian*, 9 January 2005.
Goldsmith, J, *The Trap*, Lonmdon: Macmillan, 1994.
'A big Little Englander', *Independent*, 26 April 1996.
'Why we need a referendum' by Sir James Goldsmith, *The Times*, 27 January 1995.
'Tories in turmoil over Goldsmith' *The Times*, 6 March 1996.
'Goldsmith offers £20m for anti-European fight' *The Times*, 23 October 1995.
Referendum Party advert, 25 October 1995.
'Goldsmith to fight 600 seats' *The Times*, 15 April 1996.
'Worried Tories press for talks with Goldsmith party' *The Times*, 17 April 1996.
'Rival party threatens Goldsmith' *The Times*, 27 June 1996.
BBC1 TV interview with Dr Alan Sked for *On the Record*, 26 January 1997.
'McAlpine faces loss of the whip for backing Goldsmith' *The Times*, 8 October 1996.
'Santer rebuffs Sir James over call for debate' *The Times*, 19 October 19 1996.
'Mohammad goes to Brighton' by Ian Buruma, *Prospect*, 20 December 1996.
The Referendum Party—Speeches from the Brighton Conference, London: The Referendum Party, 1996.

5

Interviews with Robin Birley, Alan Sked, Gerard Batten MEP, and Nigel Farage MEP.
Gardiner, G, *A Bastard's Tale*, London: Aurum Press, 1999.
'Europe, Goldsmith and the Referendum Party' by Neil Carter, Mark Evans, Keith Alderman and Simon Gorham, published in Ridley, FF, & Jordan, G (editors), *Protest Politics: Cause Groups and Campaigns*, Hansard Society Series in Politics and Government, Oxford: Oxford University Press, 1998.
'Goldsmith organiser quits "party of nothing"' *The Times*, 1 January 1997
'Time to pack up, Sir James' by Michael Gove, *The Times*, 10 February 1997.
'Mellor gets in training for his toughest match' *The Times*, 11 April 1997.
'Genial don gives Britain a lecture on lone survival' *The Times*, 8 April 1997.
'Principle Not Party' *The Times*, 29 April 1997.
'Goldsmith vows to fight on for a referendum' by Ben Macintyre, *The Times*, 30 April 1997.
'General election results, 1 May 1997', House of Commons Research Paper 01/38, 29 March 2001.
'I owe it to Jimmy to keep his dream alive' by Rachel Sylvester, *Telegraph*, 13 January 2001.

6

Interview with Sara Parkin.
'Teddy Goldsmith—Obituary', *Telegraph*, 25 August 2009.
Goldsmith, E, and editors of the *Ecologist, Blueprint for Survival*, Boston: Houghton Mifflin, 1972.
Don't let your world turn grey, Green Party European Election Manifesto, London, 1989.
'Wooing of the Greens' by Jonathon Porritt, *The Times*, 20 June 1989.
'From Iron Lady to earth mother' by Robin Oakley, *The Times*, 18 September 1989.

'The protector of planet Earth' by Bryan Appleyard, *The Times*, 22 June 1989.

'How Green Was My Party?' by John Morrissey, *Synthesis/Regeneration* 13 (Spring 1997).

'Another Green World', blog interview with Derek Wall, March 2005.

Wall, D, *Weaving a Bower Against Endless Night: An Illustrated History of the Green Party*, Dyfed: Green Party, 1994.

Parkin, S, *Green Parties*, London: Heretic, 1989.

Porrit, J, *Seeing Green*, Oxford: Basil Blackwell, 1984.

7

Interviews with John Edmonds, John Monks, Alan Sked, Gerard Batten MEP, Tim Congdon and Nigel Farage MEP.

Jacques Delors' Speech to Trades Union Congress, Bournemouth, 8 September 1988, published in *The Pro-European Reader*, Palgrave editions, 2002.

'How the Trades Union Congress learned to love the European Union and how the affair turned out: the "coup" of 1988' *History & Policy Trade Union Forum* 27, November 2010.

Booker, C, & North, R, *The Great Deception: The Secret History of the European Union,* London: Continuum, 2003.

'BNP link allegation hits Euro party' *The Times*, 5 June 1999.

'I would advise people voting on Thursday to help the Tory revival' by Alan Sked, *The Times*, 8 June 1999.

'Make the break, Ken' by John Stevens, *Guardian*, 13 June 2001.

'Former UKIP leader quits party' BBC news report, 21 March, 2000.

'Far-right' fear splits UKIP as 200 leave party' *The Times*, 29 April 2000.

8

Interviews with John Edmonds and John Monks

'Labour made a "spectacular mistake" on immigration, admits Jack Straw' *Telegraph*, 13 November 2013.

'The *New Statesman* Interview—Barbara Roche' by Jackie Ashley, *New Statesman*, 23 October 2000.

Migration: an economic and social analysis by Stephen Glover, Ceri Gott, Anais Loizillon, Jonathan Portes, Richard Price, Sarah Spencer, Vasanthia Srinivasan and Carole Willis, RDS Occasional Paper No 67, 2001.

Preliminary Report on Migration, 11 July 2000, by PIU and Home Office, 'Restricted - Policy' but published following FoI request.

UK Migration in a global economy, speech given by Barbara Roche MP, Immigration Minister to IPPR, 11 September 2000.

'Don't listen to the whingers - London needs immigrants' by Andrew Neather, *Evening Standard*, 23 October 2009.

'After the flood', *Economist*, 7 September 2000.

'Call for immigration rethink', BBC News, 12 September 2000.

'Labour wanted mass immigration to make UK more multicultural, says former adviser', *Telegraph*, 23 October 2009.

'How I became the story and why the Right is wrong' by Andrew Neather, *Evening Standard*, 26 October 2009.

'Labour censored links between immigration and crime in report' *Daily Mail*, 28 October 2009.

'One in 10 of population born abroad', the *Telegraph*, 9 December 2009.

'Hideously Diverse Britain: The immigration "conspiracy"', *Guardian*, 2 March 2011.

Heffer, S, *Like the Roman: The life of Enoch Powell*, London: Weidenfeld and Nicolson, 1998.

Billig, M, *Fascists: A social psychological view of the National Front*, London: Academic Press, 1978.
Walker, Martin, *The National Front*, London: Fontana, 1978.
Transcript of ITV *World in Action* interview with Margaret Thatcher, January 1978, held at the Margaret Thatcher Foundation.

9

Interviews with Ann Mallalieu, Nigel Farage MEP, Matthew Elliott, Jonathan Isaby, Andrew Allison, John Monks and Douglas Carswell MP.
'Tally ho! I'm off, says Ann', *Daily Mail*, 7 December 2006.
Transcript of Baroness Mallalieu's speech, Hyde Park Rally, 10 July 1997.
'Liberty & Livelihood—reflection on the March which galvanised a nation' by James Stanford, Countryside Alliance website, July 2012.
Straw, J, *Last Man Standing*, London: Pan, 2013.
'Labour taking anti-hunt group's cash for policies' *Telegraph*, 4 May 2001.
'Tony Blair accidentally supported fox hunting ban', *Telegraph*, 24 September 2012.
'Celebrities rally to the call of the alliance's hunting horn' *The Times,* 23 September 2002.
'Money matters but freedom brought us here,' *The Times*, 23 September 2002;
'Who is behind the Taxpayers' Alliance?' by Robert Booth, *Guardian*, 9 October 2009.
'Allister Heath: Youth is just what the founders of City AM were looking for' by Ian Burrell, *Independent*, 21 April 2008.
'Taxpayer Funded Lobbying and Political Campaigning' by Matthew Sinclair, London: TPA, August 2009.
'Placards? They're so last year—make way for the mighty mouse' by Rod Liddle, *Sunday Times Magazine*, 10 March 2013.
Hay, C, *Why we hate politics*, Cambridge: Polity Press, 2007.
Carswell, D, & Hannan, D, *The Plan: Twelve Months to Renew Britain*, self-published, 2008.
Carswell, D, *The End of Politics and the Birth of iDemocracy*, London: Biteback Publishing, 2012.
'iDemocracy and a new model party' by Douglas Carswell, *Spectator*, 15 July 2013.
'Make the Conservative Party like Spotify' by Douglas Carswell, *Mail on Sunday*, 4 March 2013.

10

Interviews with Douglas Carswell MP, Robin Birley, Simon Richards, Roger Helmer MEP, Philip Davies MP, David Nuttall MP and Jonathan Isaby.
'I can't fight my feelings any more: I love Tony' by Michael Gove, *The Times*, 25 February 2003.
'Clever move' by Oliver Burkeman, *Guardian*, 31 January 2005.
'Francis Maude: My brother's Aids death transformed my views on gay marriage' by Patrick Sawer, *Telegraph*, 17 March 2012.
'A Phoenix, Not A Dodo' by Francis Maude, *Spectator*, 23 March, 2002.
Transcript of Conservative Party chairwoman Theresa May's speech at Tory party conference in Bournemouth, October 2002.
Harris, R, *The Conservatives—A History*, London: Bantam Press, 2011.
Scholefield, A, & Frost, G, *Too 'nice' to be Tories?* London: The Social Affairs Unit, 2011.

11

Interviews with Nigel Farage MEP, Gerard Batten MEP and Gawain Towler.
Farage, N, *Flying Free*, London: Biteback Publishing, 2011.
'Howard rages at UKIP gadflies' *Telegraph*, 31 May 2004.

'Robert Kilroy-Silk; the self-styled saviour of Britain' by Paul Vallely, *Independent*, 5 June 2004

'Kilroy—the inside story' by Gerard Batten, *Freedom Today*, March/April 2005.

'Murder on the Tube' *Evening Standard*, 13 August 2004.

'MP in race row over crime' *BBC News*, 3 September 2002.

'Somalis' struggle in the UK' *BBC News*, 30 May 2006.

'Jail won't stop Somali criminals coming to the UK…' *Sun*, 30 March 2010.

Knife Crime, House of Commons Home Affairs Committee report, June 2009.

The Street Weapon Commission Report, Channel 4, London, 2008.

12

Interview with Nick Griffin MEP.

Eatwell, R, & Mudde, C, *Western Democracies and the New Extreme Right Challenge*, London: Routledge, 2009.

'Huge Rise in Race Attacks on White Men' *Oldham Chronicle*, 31 January 2001.

'Race Attacks: Three More in a Day' *Oldham Chronicle*, 1 February 2001.

'No-go Asians attack veteran' *Telegraph*, 24 April 2001.

'This has been building up for years' *Guardian*, 28 May 2001.

Oldham Independent Review, Panel Report (also known as the 'Ritchie Report' after its chairman David Ritchie), 11 December 2001.

'The BNP Ballerina' by Elizabeth Sanderson, *Mail on Sunday*, 30 December 2006.

'Exclusive: inside the secret and sinister world of the BNP' by Ian Cobain, *Guardian*, 21 December 2006.

'BNP wins seat in London Assembly' BBC News, 3 May 2008.

'BNP secures two European seats' BBC News, 8 June 2009.

'The BNP's Breakthrough' by Matthew Goodwin, *New Statesman*, 16 April 2009.

Goodwin, M, *New British Fascism: Rise of the British National Party,* Oxford: Routledge, 2011.

'Nick Griffin: Question Time will be a political blood sport' *Independent*, 22 October 2009.

Transcript of Question Time BBC1, broadcast on 22 October 2009

'Anti-fascist protesters breach security at BBC' *Associated Press*, 22 October 2009.

'Nick Griffin attacked by his own BNP supporters over Question Time' *Observer*, 25 October 2009.

13

Interviews with Philip Davies MP, Simon Heffer, Nigel Farage MEP, Gerard Batten MEP and Gawain Towler.

'George Osborne' by Jonathan Ford, *Prospect Magazine*, 26 July 2008.

Transcript of George Osborne 'inheritance tax' speech, Conservative Party Conference, October 2007.

'Why treat the London election as a joke?' by Simon Heffer, *Telegraph*, 29 April 2008.

Gimson, A, *Boris: the Rise of Boris Johnson*, London: Simon & Schuster, 2012.

Purnell, S, *Just Boris: A Tale of Blond Ambition*, London: Aurum Press, 2012.

Edwards, G, & Isaby, J, *Boris v Ken: How Boris Johnson Won London*, London: Politico's Publishing, 2008.

'Boris Johnson vows to block Kosovo-style cleansing of the poor' *Guardian*, 25 April 2012.

'Why Boris Johnson is missing Westminster' by James Pickford and George Parker, FT Weekend Magazine, 28 September 2013.

'Boris: I am the only British politician who will admit to being pro-immigration' *Telegraph*, 25 October 2013.

Transcript of Boris Johnson's Margaret Thatcher lecture for Centre for Policy Studies, 27 November 2013.

'Conservatives wipe all pre-election pledges from their website' *Telegraph*, 13 November 2013.

Brooke, H, *Your Right to Know: A Citizen's Guide to the Freedom of Informaiton Act*, London: Pluto Press, 2006.

Brooke, H, *The Silent State: Secrets, Surveillance and the Myth of British Democracy*, London: Windmill Books, 2011.

Winnett, R, & Rayner, G, *No Expenses Spared*, London: Bantam Press, 2009.

'MPs' expenses: Lord Tebbit says do not vote Conservative at European elections' *Telegraph*, 12 May 2009.

Friedman, B, *Bercow: Rowdy Living in the Tory Party*, London: Gibson Square, 2011.

14

Interviews with Sara Parkin, Natalie Bennett and Jasper Gerard.

Transcript of first prime ministerial debate, 15 April 2010.

'Greens battle to be the first MP' *Brighton Argus*, 14 June 2007.

'Natalie Bennett says Greens are only alternative' *BBC News*, 13 September 2013.

'Have the Greens blown it in Brighton?' by John Harris, *Guardian*, 15 December 2013.

Gerard, J, *The Clegg Coup—Britain's First Coalition Government since Lloyd George*, London: Gibson Square, 2011.

Transcript of Nick Clegg's speech to the Liberal Democrat conference, 17 September 2013.

15

Interviews with Nigel Farage MEP, Simon Richards, Mick McGough and Julian Deverell.

'Godfrey Bloom: UKIP MEP Calls Women Sluts' Sky News, 20 September 2013.

'Eight pints for me and a flogging for wrong 'uns' profile of Godfrey Bloom by Cosmo Landesman, *Sunday Times*, 11 August 2013.

'Margaret Thatcher listened to voters – now it's Nigel Farage who hears their despair' by Fraser Nelson, *Telegraph*, 11 April 2013.

Transcript of UKIP autumn conference speech by Paul Nuttall, 20 September 2013.

Transcript of Ed Miliband's 2013 conference speech, 27 September 2013.

'Miliband's midsummer meltdown' *Sunday Times*, 28 July 2013

'Stayin' Alive' *Sunday Times*, 29 September 2013

'Cut the green crap! Cameron reveals his private view of energy taxation and orders ministers to dump the eco-charges adding £110-a-year to bills' *Daily Mail*, 21 November 2013.

'Top 100 most influential Right-wingers' by Iain Dale, *Telegraph*, 2 October 2013.

'Paul Sykes: 'I want to set Britain free from the EU' *Telegraph*, 17 November 2013.

'Farage's party beats Conservatives into third place in survey of constituency where Tory MP is quitting' *Guardian*, 26 November 2013.

'Turning right: Europe's populist insurgents' *Economist*, 4 January 2014.

'Labour targeting UKIP as Nigel Farage's party aims to become main threat to Ed Miliband in North' *Mirror*, 10 February 2014.

'UKIP has done more than any other party to destroy the racist BNP' by Nigel Farage, *Independent*, 2 February 2014.

'Blow for David Cameron as UKIP finish second in Wythenshawe' *Daily Telegraph*, 14 February 2014.

Ford, R, & Goodwin, MJ, *Revolt on the Right: Explaining Support for the Radical Right in Britain*, London: Routledge, 2014.

ACKNOWLEDGMENTS

Many people have helped me with my research and writing, but I would especially like to thank the following: Nigel Farage, Kirsten Farage, Stuart Wheeler, Gawain Towler, Gerard Batten, Roger Helmer, Mick McGough, Tim Congdon, Ray Finch, Alan Sked, Douglas Carswell, Philip Hollobone, Philip Davies, David Nuttall, Jasper Gerard, Robin Birley, Matthew Elliott, Andrew Allison, Jennifer Salisbury-Jones, John Edmonds, John Monks, Natalie Bennett, Sara Parkin, Ann Mallalieu, Nick Griffin, Simon Heffer, Andrew Roberts, Ollie and Peter Newark, Chris Newark, Lucy Wildman, my agent Andrew Lownie, and Jonathan Isaby, for pointing out errors. Big thanks go to Simon Richards, who has been such a jolly and generous guide to me throughout the research for this book, and, of course, Martin Rynja, my publisher.

INDEX

22/09/15
Newport Community
Learning & Libraries